# AT HOME IN THE ANTHROPOCENE

Amy D. Propen

THE OHIO STATE UNIVERSITY PRESS
COLUMBUS

Copyright © 2022 by The Ohio State University.
All rights reserved.

Library of Congress Cataloging-in-Publication Data
Names: Propen, Amy D., author.
Title: At home in the Anthropocene / Amy D. Propen.
Description: Columbus : The Ohio State University Press, [2022] | Includes bibliographical
  references and index. | Summary: "Applies the tenets of posthumanism, compassionate
  conservation, and entangled empathy to a set of wildlife stories to demonstrate how
  humans can best coexist with their nonhuman kin during the age of climate change and
  crises"—Provided by publisher.
Identifiers: LCCN 2022019417 | ISBN 9780814215258 (cloth) | ISBN 0814215254 (cloth) | ISBN
  9780814282380 (ebook) | ISBN 0814282385 (ebook)
Subjects: LCSH: Human-animal relationships. | Animals—Climatic factors. | Wildlife
  conservation. | Posthumanism.
Classification: LCC QL85 .P758 2022 | DDC 590—dc23/eng/20220624
LC record available at https://lccn.loc.gov/2022019417
Other identifiers: ISBN 9780814258477 (paper) | ISBN 0814258476 (paper)

Cover design by Alexa Love
Text composition by Stuart Rodriguez
Type set in Minion Pro

♾ The paper used in this publication meets the minimum requirements of the American
National Standard for Information Sciences—Permanence of Paper for Printed Library
Materials. ANSI Z39.48-1992.

*For my sweet boy Milo, who sat on my lap throughout the writing of most of this book. I will always be grateful for the gift of your loving companionship.*

# CONTENTS

*Acknowledgments*                                                                                    ix

INTRODUCTION                                                                                          1

CHAPTER 1     What Counts as Home in the Anthropocene?                                               27

CHAPTER 2     Fire-Lost and Trying to Cross                                                          47

INTERLUDE I   From Climate Anxiety Emerges the Gift of a Whisper Song                                75

CHAPTER 3     Storied Places and Species in Flux: Connectivity as
              Reciprocity                                                                            86

INTERLUDE II  Fostering a Culture of Reciprocity during the
              Anthropause                                                                            111

CHAPTER 4     At Home with Big Kin                                                                   120

CHAPTER 5     Gratitude for the Trail and the Gift of Roadside Geology                               147

*Notes*                                                                                              161

*Bibliography*                                                                                       181

*Index*                                                                                              193

# ACKNOWLEDGMENTS

This book emerged over the course of several years and neared completion in the midst of the ongoing pandemic. I am grateful to be able to share this work with readers now.

My thinking about this book really started when writing the conclusion for *Visualizing Posthuman Conservation* (2018). When I was completing that project, I realized there were more stories that I wanted to tell, and I knew that I wanted to further explore and integrate narrative and place-based writing in my subsequent work. Around the time that I was starting work on this project, and as I was considering how storytelling and ideas about home and place would function within it, I received an invitation that would ultimately help shape the direction that this book would take.

In the fall of 2018, when *Visualizing* first came out, I received an invitation from my colleague in environmental rhetoric, Associate Professor Tim Jensen, to speak at Oregon State University's "Critical Questions" lecture series. After some correspondence, we worked out a visit date in April 2019. To this day, I remain grateful for the wonderful and engaging conservations that this visit allowed for, beginning even with our discussions of what I would actually talk about during my lecture. That is, I knew that I wanted to talk about the idea of wildlife, specifically mountain lions, venturing closer to areas of significant human habitation due largely to the habitat loss incurred by wildfires, as well as the work of wildlife corridors to help mitigate the kinds of habitat degradation wrought largely by practices of human development. In early spring of 2019, Tim and I chatted to work out some ideas for the talk. I knew that I needed a good title for the lecture—one that could appeal both to a scholarly and a broader audience, for this talk would also be open to the public. As I also worked on what is now chapter 2 of this book, I'd been thinking a lot about the recent news story of a mountain lion who had wandered into an Oregon resident's home (this seemed an especially apt topic to engage my audience at Oregon State), and how such encounters are becoming more common as wildfires and natural disasters more frequently inform our experiences of place and home. What, then, counted as home, I wondered, as I considered not only that case of a tired, displaced mountain lion seeking refuge in human-built spaces but also the wildlife rehabilitation work that I do, which is in many ways connected with how species are impacted by human development and climate crisis.

As my colleague at Oregon State and I chatted about possible title ideas for the lecture, we considered that these questions about what counts as home seemed especially accessible and engaging, and so emerged the title for that lecture, "What Counts as Home in the Anthropocene?," which later became the title of chapter 1 in this book. It was also during this lecture that I first presented some of the material that would eventually become chapters 2 and 3 of this book. The concept of "home" also made its way into the title of the book itself, for I soon realized the many ways that I wanted to engage the question of "what counted as home," not only for vulnerable species who often make their way to wildlife rehabilitation facilities through no efforts of their own but also for those who wind up fire-lost or displaced due to other events related to climate change and the projects of human development. In sum, I recount some of this timeline here because I wish to express my gratitude to Tim Jensen and my colleagues at Oregon State University's School of Writing, Literature, and Film, for all the conversations during that trip that helped shape some of my earlier thinking about this project.

What ultimately distinguishes this book from *Visualizing Posthuman Conservation* is that this book goes even further in considering the everyday practices and places that shape, constitute, and refashion ideas about what counts as "home," and how to coexist empathetically with our more-than-human kin. Put differently, whereas *Visualizing Posthuman Conservation* focused largely on the role of photos, maps, and public discourse in prompting a decentering of the human perspective in order to promote a more posthuman version of conservation, this book goes further, to consider such decentering *in action,* with a focus on the shared places where multiple forms of habitation occur, such as forested areas and wildlife corridors, trails, and wildlife rehabilitation centers, and the actions and lively habits that take place in such settings. In this book, then, what I think of at times as "posthuman nature writing" is, in essence, a narrative approach that incorporates travel and nature writing to complicate our relationships with and perceived responsibilities to our more-than-human kin and the worlds in which we reside together in an age of climate crisis.

Finally, I also liked the concept of "home" for the title of the book because I wanted to work with an idea and framework that had some recuperative power. In this work, I endeavor to tell stories from a vantage point that engages ideas and questions about home and belonging, but in generative ways that attempt to open up rather than close off possibilities for sustainable futures in which we may productively coexist with our more-than-human kin. It is my hope that this book has come close to reaching this mark.

Throughout the book, I draw on research from various departments of fish and wildlife and related organizations and agencies, and I have been lucky enough to speak with several professionals who work with these or other such organizations. I will note, though, that all views, narratives, and interpretations expressed in this work are my own and do not represent or express the views of any other person or organization. If I have directly quoted someone in the context of a personal interview, I have obtained their permission to do so. I am grateful to everyone who has been willing to return my email inquiries or chat with me about my research, especially during a cultural moment that sometimes made communication more challenging to arrange.

Thank you to Steve Biddle at the City of Santa Barbara, Parks and Recreation, as well as John Johnson, Owen Duncan, and Terri Sheridan at the Santa Barbara Museum of Natural History for responding to my questions about the history of Franceschi Park.

I would like to thank Vicky Monroe at the California Department of Fish and Wildlife for an informative discussion about California's mountain lions, and Jaclyn Comeau at the Vermont Fish and Wildlife Department for a fascinating conversation about the habits of black bears in Vermont.

Thank you to Beth Pratt and Clark Stevens for speaking with me about the Liberty Canyon Wildlife Crossing, which in 2022 became known as the Wallis Annenberg Wildlife Crossing. Thank you also to Alan Salazar for granting me permission to quote from and summarize his telling of the Rainbow Bridge story in chapter 3.

Chapters 2 and 3 are based on my lecture, "What Counts as Home in the Anthropocene?," given at Oregon State University April 2019.

I would like to thank Ariana Katovitch at the Santa Barbara Wildlife Care Network (SBWCN), as well as my wildlife colleagues at the SBWCN, for the opportunities and experience I have had there over the years, all of which have informed not only my writing of chapter 1 but also my own understanding of the different ways that we may participate in a culture of giving back to our wild kin.

Thank you to Tara Cyphers at The Ohio State University Press for her consistent support of and guidance on this project. Thanks also to Rebecca S. Bender for her editing expertise and Alexa Love for the wonderful cover design. And I would very much like to thank both rounds of external reviewers for their feedback and insights at various points during this book's development; all of their input and suggestions have helped inform some of the direction that this work takes.

As always, I would like to thank my friend, colleague, and mentor, Mary Schuster, for her sustained connection and helpful advice on many matters, including those related to the writing of this book. Thank you to my colleagues at the UCSB Writing Program, as well as Beth Britt, Karen Dias, Cristina Hanganu-Bresch, Clancy Ratliff, and Mike Zerbe for your support and friendship over the years. And thank you especially to Laura Zeitz for your kindness, patience, and good conversation related to this project, and for alerting me to new research on the Anthropause as soon as you first read about it. Our adventures have informed this project in unanticipated but fruitful ways.

Finally, I would like to thank my family—especially my parents, Beverly and Michael Propen, who read each chapter as I drafted it. At times when my writing energy was waning, they would always ask me "when the next installment was coming." Thank you to my parents for giving me the motivation to keep writing during these challenging times. I am ever appreciative for the comradery of all my furry companions, Topher, Tuck, and of course, Milo. Thank you also to my siblings and fellow wildlife advocates, David Propen and Mindy Howley Propen, and to my uncle, Allen Schoen, who helped cultivate my love and respect of all creatures at an early age. This book truly would not be possible without the support of my family.

# INTRODUCTION

It is the first of March 2020, and I wend my way up a local side street into the foothills of Santa Barbara—this is the regular walk I do here; rather, it is more of a "walk/hike," as I sometimes call my version of exercise, and I've been traversing this route regularly since I moved here eight years ago. Because I write the first iterations of this chapter in early March, I feel compelled to acknowledge that the novel coronavirus is just beginning to take hold in northern California and areas of the Pacific Northwest.[1] And while even outdoor exercise would eventually become stressful at times during the pandemic, here in central California in early March, we are still relatively sheltered from it—at least for now. But I will admit that I've been reading all the news and setting boundaries for myself around just how much I can take in before my anxiety becomes too much to tamp down with exercise like this. Instead, I try to reset my focus to the beauty of this moment and the gifts that it provides: the shuffle of the spotted towhee, the noisy curiosity of crows, the intoxicating scent of orange blossom and white jasmine. These are "good distractions" from my anxiety, and they provide a grounding effect in this moment. This walk is one of my favorite things about residing in this place, and I am grateful for it now more than ever. Doing this walk at this moment provides clarity and important reminders about the gifts that are all around us, that is, if we are present enough to recognize and respect them.

1

This book is, in part, an effort at such respect and recognition. Throughout it, I explore some of the places that I know and love, from varied, informed perspectives, in order to help reveal new ideas about our roles and responsibilities as humans residing on a troubled planet. Simply put, I suggest that how we communicate about such places can help shape our understandings of and relationships with them.[2] More specifically, I maintain that to be mindful of the multiplicity of languages of our "more-than-human" animal kin— and to become mindful of the places that are hardly just our own—can help shape our accounts and perspectives of the ecosystems that we share and may inform how we approach projects of human development in an age of climate crisis.[3] Following the work of biologist, botanist, and Indigenous studies scholar Robin Wall Kimmerer, when we are attentive to the languages of our more-than-human kin—when we engage in these conversations between humans and other forms of life—we receive a gift from the world. I build upon Kimmerer's work to further consider how, when we see the world as full of gifts, and when we become mindful of the lively languages spoken by a place and all its kin, we may "truly be at home."[4] Moreover, by listening to our kin and by "bestowing our own gifts in kind," we also "celebrate our kinship with the world."[5] This book seeks to celebrate our kinship with the world, and in doing so, asserts that to engage with a multiplicity of more-than-human lives and languages means that we must think critically about what such engagement and communication requires.

I suggest that such engagement requires, in part, what philosopher Lori Gruen refers to as "entangled empathy," and in this book, I show how entangled empathy can help us acknowledge the challenges and tensions that accompany our struggle to share an ecosystem in peril for reasons often due to our own making. I maintain that to grapple with these communicative challenges is a necessary part of understanding the places that we love and call home in an age of climate crisis. To engage with entangled empathy and to understand our world as full of gifts to be received and reciprocated may also provide one productive path forward in reconciling the ongoing projects of human development with the need to account for the lives of our more-than-human kin. I also believe that, and endeavor to illustrate how, sharing stories from the more-than-human world can provide one productive path forward as we grapple with and further explore these communicative challenges. In this moment, however, I am most interested in the communicative practices of the songbirds whose melodies I always look forward to on this walk.

Early spring is nesting and mating season for the birds that reside in this region of central California. As such, everyone has more to say than usual: northern mockingbirds, California thrashers, scrub jays, and black phoebes are all out and about; a male Anna's hummingbird whistles and burbles atop a bougainvillea bush whose bright magenta flowers match the color of this little bird's throat. These are our chatty, feathered kin—our neighbors and our extended family. Each of their songs bears a little gift that provides a welcome reprieve from the anxious cacophony of human discourse right now. I am grateful in this moment for the melodic persistence of songbirds.[6]

It is about 8:00 a.m. on a typically overcast but unusually humid morning. I am up and out early here, but for different reasons than when I would hike in New England, where I am originally from. I do this walk early here, not because rain clouds loom overhead and threaten to put a damper on exercise, as they often do on New England mornings in the spring and summer, but because it will soon be too hot, and the sun too bright to hike here—too much so, at least, for my preference. Right now, the marine layer still buffers the sun, and clouds hang in layered suspension, creating a terraced horizon of peach, gray, and blue hues. This blended pastel skyline sits in relief against the subtle, bassy *koo-koos* of Eurasian collared-doves.

The language of these doves is one that I've come to recognize over time and through my familiarity with this place. It is part of what makes my experience of the world meaningful here and now—it is part of how I have come to see, know, and understand the world. In this way, place "is not just a thing in the world but a way of understanding the world."[7] As geographer Tim Creswell describes: "When we look at the world as a world of places, we see different things. We see attachments and connections between people and place. We see worlds of meaning and experience."[8] At that more personal level, place is part of what gives the world specific meaning for each of us, and the language of these doves is one aspect of what I find meaningful about this place. At the same time, my singular, individual experience of this place is hardly what singularly defines it; rather, there are many ways to know or generate knowledge about a place.

On the one hand, it is the case that I happen to be doing this walk *here*, in this place; on the other hand, there are many different ways of knowing a place, and some critics have in fact questioned the privilege of the knowledge that arises from "the body as knower," contending that our relative closeness or proximity to any one object doesn't necessarily "offer a closer, purer, or less biased view into the truth of that object."[9] Rather, we might consider what kind of knowledge is generated by the more collaborative or joint relationship of *a body in a place*.[10] Such ideas also look at how ethnography, or the study of different cultures, can offer new perspectives on personal narrative.

To this end, my colleagues Casey Boyle and Jenny Rice draw on the work of anthropologist James Clifford to consider how this joint relationship of a body in a place can potentially inform an approach to writing that engages multiple questions about culture, beyond that of just the writer's immediate experience. Such methods for writing about place, and an approach that considers the implications beyond solely an individualized experience of place, can prompt us to be more mindful of the ways that "cultures—in their historical, material, and political contexts—are always interfacing with bodies and language."[11] Again, the meaning I derive from this place, in part through encounters with my more-than-human kin on this morning's walk, is hardly the only thing that makes this moment significant; I am, by extension, also interested in the other important cultural connections and ways of being that are generated and revealed through such "body-place" collaborations of emplacement. Put simply, it is my hope that in writing about some of the places that I know and love, from different informed perspectives, this book can help weave together, tease apart, and generally reveal some new connections and ideas about our roles and responsibilities as humans residing on a troubled planet, and how the ways that we communicate about such places can help shape our understandings of and relationships with them.

Next, while I happen to be writing from *this place now*, there are other places that I describe in this book, which I know equally well, or have written from, but in which I am not currently situated for various reasons. Here, too, I consider how writing about a place may involve *being there*, or *having been there*, or may involve an assemblage of types of narrative accounts and encounters that, when approached with care and sensitivity, can help account for and generate new knowledges and stories about the places and ecosystems that we share.

In this way, for instance, to become familiar with the calls of the specific birds who reside here—American crows, scrub jays, northern mockingbirds, and lesser goldfinches, to name a few—is not only to derive personal meaning from a place, but also it is to learn the language of another and to learn the language of a place, and, when considered with care, to become mindful of the ways that we share these places and coexist with other animals, or our more-than-human kin. To listen to the language of these feathered kin is, working in the positive, to become mindful of the languages of places and ecosystems that are not our own but that we share with our more-than-human kin. Environmental journalist Elizabeth Rush writes that "by listening . . . by tuning our ears to the sounds of beings unlike ourselves, we begin to reenter what Thomas Berry, the Catholic eco-theologian, calls 'the greatest conversation' between humans and other forms of life."[12] Along similar lines, animal studies and communication scholar Emily Plec describes what she calls "internatural communication," which "explores interaction among and between natural communities and social groups that include participants from what we might initially describe as different classifications of nature. Internatural communication includes the exchange of intentional energy between humans and other animals as well as communication among animals and other forms of life."[13] Indeed, when I am more attentive to the plurality of voices that constitute the many species of my feathered kin, and the internatural communication in which they likely engage, I realize there is much more happening in my immediate environment than I am initially aware of. The human-exacerbated pothole that I try not to trip over as I trudge uphill contains bits of dried grass that constitute important nesting material for my mockingbird friend. The white jasmine that I appreciate for its aromatic and aesthetic value provides arguably more critical sustenance for the bees and Anna's hummingbirds who spend far more time communing with this plant than I do. But I wouldn't make any such observations if I didn't slow down for even just a moment. While I speak here of birds and other animals, or our more-than-human animal kin, Kimmerer additionally refers to species like plant life, trees, and other such earthly life forms.

Part of the work of this book is, in fact, to complicate and build on these ideas—to consider, for instance, that we may understand these melodic encounters with our feathered kin as gifts, and that we may then reciprocate these gifts in kind. For, again, as Kimmerer points out, it is only then, when we see the world as full of gifts, and when we listen for the lively languages spoken by a place and all its kin, that we can "truly be at home."[14] Along similar lines, geographer Sarah Wright notes that "belonging is not only created by people in places, or more-than-humans in places, but actively co-constitutes people and things and processes and places."[15] Indeed, at a time when so many of our own inner resources have become especially depleted, we may see "how wealthy we become" when we begin to recognize that "all the world is a gift in motion."[16] Moreover, by listening to our kin and by reciprocating their gifts, we may also begin to engage with what Wright refers to as a "language of animacy," which is one way of becoming more mindful of our engagements with the world around us.

The English language doesn't provide many tools for "incorporating respect for animacy. In English, writes Kimmerer, "you are either a human or a thing."[17] Kimmerer's perspective on a language of animacy and her understanding of the world as full of gifts are likely informed by her own Potawatomi heritage, as she is a member of the Citizen Potawatomi Nation.[18] And for the Potawatomi people of the Great Plains, Kimmerer tells us, for instance, that "rocks are animate, as are mountains and water and fire and places. Beings that are imbued with our spirit, our sacred medicines, our songs, our drums, and even stories, are all animate."[19] She subsequently suggests that a "grammar of animacy" offers a productive alternative to an anthropocentric mindset that privileges humans over other animals and life-forms, and instead "lead[s] us to whole new ways of living in the world, other species a sovereign people, a world with a democracy of species, not a tyranny of one."[20] To imagine a world with a democracy of species helps work against the more engrained Western, anthropocentric paradigm that hierarchically privileges humans over other species.

This is a challenging paradigm to work against, for it is so culturally entrenched, but it is a necessary one to call into question if we are to more fully address our ecosystems in crisis. Kimmerer's more relational vantage point has much to offer when considering a more respectful and holistic approach to understanding our relationships with and ethical obligations to our more-than-human kin and the ecosystems we share; as such, her approach informs—or rather, inspires, much of the theoretical work of this book. In addition, I would add that to understand the world as full of gifts and to become mindful of the lively languages spoken by a place and all its kin is compatible with what Gruen describes as "entangled empathy," or "a type of caring perception focused on attending to another's experience of wellbeing." Entangled empathy is an "experiential process . . . in which we recognize we are in relationships with others and are called upon to be responsive and responsible in these relationships by attending to another's needs, interests, desires, vulnerabilities, hopes, and sensitivities."[21] I build on and extend Kimmerer's and Gruen's ideas in this book to suggest that a "gift mindset" that is grounded in entangled empathy and a language of animacy can have productive implications for how we understand the projects of contemporary human development as well as our relationships with our more-than-human kin and the ecosystems in which we coexist with all species.

I pause mid-hill to catch my breath and get a glimpse of the ocean on the horizon. The vistas on this walk never get old, but I've also learned not to take this version of beauty, or the relative beauty of any thriving environment, for granted. Rather, I feel privileged and lucky to be able to do this walk right now; again, the songs of my feathered kin are gifts that I don't want to take for granted, and that I can work to reciprocate. Part of why I write is to help reciprocate these gifts—it is one small contribution that I feel able to make.

I climb Jimeno Road now, where the dense vegetation combined with the steep incline make this walk feel more like a hike. I'm reminded of my urban environment, however, as an acorn woodpecker hammers on a telephone pole while a northern mockingbird sings perched on the same stretch of power line just a little farther up the road. Here, like in so many of our contemporary favorite places, the world of technology intermingles with what we know as "natural" beauty. I wonder at what point these power lines became invisible to us—just a mundane part of the landscape for both humans and other animals alike—infrastructure as communication modality, infrastructure as perching material. It's easy to forget that these techno-perches have not always been part of our visual landscape—that they did not always merge with our experience of "nature." Moreover, we are hardly the only group, or flock, to ever occupy what is currently this neighborhood; rather, this place is layered with a multitude of experiences and understandings of what constitutes our "natural" world.

As literary scholar Jeffrey Jerome Cohen rightly acknowledges: "'Nature' is a difficult word. It names something at once 'everywhere and nowhere,' leading some critics to argue that we are better off without the term."[22] Because I use the term "nature" frequently throughout this book, I think it merits some unpacking here. To this end, Cohen argues, and I would agree, that in order for our sense of ethical connectedness to the world to become more tangible, we must understand nature in more nuanced ways, which he describes more complexly as "interfactual, transcorporeal, and transmaterial."[23] If we understand nature as interfactual, for instance, then it is always mediated by humans and our technoscientific proclivities. If we view nature as transcorporeal, then it pervades and intersects multiple kinds of corporeal bodies, including humans and other animals and species across ecosystems and places. Finally, if we understand nature as transmaterial, then nature pertains to the many "forces and things that may at times be utterly indifferent to Homo sapiens," but not to other life-forms such as earth, mosses, stones, or plant matter, "with whom a multitude of relationships are composed."[24] In all of these different ways, then, nature also incorporates what we commonly think of as "wildlife."

Traditional understandings of wildlife, much like traditional notions of nature and wilderness, similarly picture animals as "over there," in places separate from humans. But as feminist philosopher Val Plumwood explains, "'Wilderness' is not a place where there is no interaction between self and other, but one where self does not impose itself."[25] Similarly, as the chapters in this book help demonstrate, the Anthropocene, or an age in which human action is having an even more pronounced impact on our environment than ever before, prompts us to rethink the assumption that wildlife exist only in "places defined by human absence."[26] Rather, as geographer Jamie Lorimer describes, wildlife live among us, and include even those "feral plants and animals that inhabit urban ecologies."[27] Thus, when I use terms such as "nature" and "wildlife" throughout this book, I use them with the understanding that they are aligned with these broader, more relational perspectives. That said, when most mainstream media or journalistic articles mention wildlife, they tend to talk about more commonly referenced birds and large mammals, and when I draw upon such media articles throughout the book, I am interpreting their use of "wildlife" more directly in this way, so as not to change meaning. Even so, I understand "wildlife" as able to account more broadly for both our more-than-human animal kin as well as other earthly species, depending on the context of the discussion.

Such understandings of nature and wildlife also then take a more posthuman vantage point, in which we acknowledge the need for more porous or even indiscernible boundaries between humans, other animals and species, and the ecosystems in which we all coexist. Broadly speaking, a posthuman perspective would call into question anthropocentrism, or the more hierarchical perspective that humans are to be privileged over all other forms of life. Posthumanism, as I am describing here in the context of environmental studies, tends to align with a ecological and relational perspective that favors simultaneous coexistence as well as consideration for the plurality of lives and experiences of our more-than-human kin.[28] While it is important to clarify that Kimmerer and Gruen do not call themselves posthumanists exactly, I suggest that their ideas implicitly align with such a perspective in some specific ways.

Posthumanism would, for instance, resist the notion that humans are at the center of any given context and would thus posit that our culture is composed of a web of interwoven, entangled relationships of humans and more-than-humans. Such a perspective requires that we step outside of our sometimes human-centric vantage point to consider a perspective that looks even farther beyond the realm of the human in accounting for our complex and entangled relationships with other animals and species.[29] In this conception, there is no singular category of nonhuman "Animal" as set apart from humans; rather, when we become mindful of the rich plurality of unique animal languages that surround us, we see how much we may learn from our more-than-human kin. As I have described elsewhere, for instance, the philosopher Jacques Derrida helps work against the human tendency to group all nonhuman animals into a single category of "Animal" when, in his essay, "The Animal That Therefore I Am," he famously questions the nature of his relationship with his domesticated cat, and more broadly the relationships between humans and other animals.[30] Here, as Gerald L. Bruns puts it, "Derrida does not want to erase this difference but wants to multiply it in order (among other things) to affirm the absolute alterity or singularity of his cat, which cannot be subsumed by any category (such as *the* animal). His cat is an Other in a way that no human being . . . could ever be."[31] Moreover, as feminist philosopher Donna Haraway notes, in pondering his relationship with his cat, Derrida aptly "identified the key question as being not whether the cat could 'speak' but whether it is possible to know what *respond* means and how to distinguish a response from a reaction, for human beings as well as for anyone else."[32] In doing so, as Haraway suggests, on the one hand, Derrida "did not fall into the trap of making the subaltern speak"; on the other hand, however, "he did not seriously consider an alternative form of engagement either, one that risked knowing something more about cats and *how to look back,* perhaps even scientifically, biologically, and *therefore* also philosophically and intimately."[33] Such curiosity about what our more-than-human kin might be "doing, feeling, thinking," or making available in their communications with us is a key feature of entangled empathy.[34] Such curiosity also helps advance more recuperative or "positive knowledge of and with animals" that is not built on false binaries or groupings that cordon off humans from all other animals and life-forms.[35]

Moreover, as we will see, views of posthumanism that are ecologically informed and grounded in an ethic of entangled empathy for all life-forms are not incompatible with what Kimmerer describes as an "Indigenous worldview" that understands the ecosystems we share as composed of a "a community of sovereign beings, subjects rather than objects."[36] And as Jennifer Clary-Lemon describes, in fact, those who study rhetoric and communication may find that "an emphasis on the non-rational, the embodied, the affective, or the power of things not only resonates with Indigenous knowledge, but it is emerging from it directly" in ways that not only merit such direct acknowledgment, but can also be culturally and ecologically beneficial for humans, more-than-human animals, and other earthly species alike.[37] I would agree, and would also add that these more embodied and ecologically oriented, posthuman relationships not only resonate with an Indigenous worldview, but may also participate in what anthropologist Tim Ingold calls "meshworks," or the highly contextualized "lines of life, growth and movement" in which our in/organic entanglements with the material world take shape.[38] I seek to illuminate some of these resonances and interconnections in part through an interpretive framework that builds on, extends, and merges ideas about entangled empathy, a language of animacy, and posthuman perspectives about compassionate conservation.

Jimeno Road finally levels off at its northern end, and much to my relief, I pick up the flatter, although busier road, Almeda Padre Serra (APS). On APS, sirens punctuate and inform the natural soundscape, at times competing with the multiplicity of bird calls. Truck motors and single-engine Cessnas above mix with the screech of scrub jays and the *pewwww* of lesser goldfinches bouncing in the rosemary that lines the concrete sidewalk of the local middle school that I walk past. What some may think of as ambient or artificial noise merges with the melodies of these songbirds to constitute my experience of nature in this elemental moment.

In this very moment, my specific and complex experience of nature is, again, part of what contributes to my knowledge of this place as meaningful—it contributes to what geographers might refer to as my sense of place. "Sense of place" is one aspect of what makes a place meaningful; it refers to a multifaceted sense of identity, or the various connections to a place that make us feel at home, or immersed in our relationships with specific places. These more immersive and multisensory, and yet sometimes hard-to-describe, ineffable, embodied experiences of being in a place, and the knowledges that arise from such relational experiences, can help us identify with a specific place, or feel a sense of belonging, arguably more so than enactments of boundaries or exclusionary practices.[39] As feminist geographer Doreen Massey describes, "the identities of place are always unfixed, contested, and multiple," as well as linked and interconnected with the places beyond them.[40] And as anthropologist Thom van Dooren similarly notes, place is not an abstract entity but rather "nested and interwoven with layers of attention and meaning" that happen over time, and through our various experiences of and with a place.[41] In these ways, sense of place not only involves the individual "body as knower" but can also have broader implications for the interplay of culture, bodies, and language beyond an individual's immediate experience of a place.

The stretch of road in front of the local middle school is wide enough for good visibility, and the sidewalk here is densely lined with jasmine; for both these reasons, I slow down for a moment before crossing APS and heading up into a small, mixed-use area called Sylvan Park. Here, a series of winding, dry concrete swales meant to channel rainwater traverse this small park, much like a flume ride that lets out into a series of empty catch basins—evidence of California's ongoing drought. In this unassuming urban park, I can feel and hear the crunch of dried oak leaves and chunks of fallen palm fronds under my feet. I am used to this tactile crunch underfoot, but until moving to California, I always attributed this palpable sound to fallen snow mixed with slush and ice.

Eventually, I arrive at a hidden sandstone staircase that leads up into Franceschi Park. This staircase is open to the public and well maintained but challenging to find—it is a little Easter egg for the knowing visitor. To find these steps requires either some advance research or local knowledge—they are built quietly into the landscape along a local side street and shrouded in rosemary on both sides. These steep stairs lead up to the southern or lower portion of Franceschi Park.

Franceschi Park is a fourteen-acre city park that was established in 1931 and is named after the Italian botanist Dr. Francesco Franceschi, who moved from Italy to California in the late nineteenth century. In 1904, he purchased forty acres along Mission Ridge Road in Santa Barbara. On the northern part of the property, he and his wife built a mansion, which they called "Montarioso," or "airy mountain," based on the "Italian villa tradition," but which people now refer to simply as "Franceschi House."[42] In 1927, a few years after Franceschi's passing, a local philanthropist purchased the house and some of the property, and in 1931 donated the land to the city such that it could be converted into a park.[43] In recent years, the house has fallen into disrepair and has become the focus of a periodic but ongoing local debate about whether it should be demolished.[44] Nonetheless, many of the plants that Franceschi originally planted on the property can still be located in sections of the park near the mansion.[45]

In its early years, the mansion was the site of Franceschi's nursery and botanic garden, and was home to myriad plant species that he introduced to the area through a horticultural process called "acclimatizing," which essentially involves introducing plants from one region of the world to a new region with a similar climate, and, "through appropriate culture, mak[ing] them thrive and bear."[46] Specifically, he wanted to test whether plants from around the world could thrive in California's more Mediterranean climate.[47]

Acclimatization efforts were not uncommon in the nineteenth and early twentieth centuries. As environmental historian Harriet Ritvo describes, acclimatization efforts were present even in the earliest agricultural practices, and frequently accompanied domestication efforts, especially when the plants and animals in question were viewed as useful to humans or as having utilitarian value.[48] Acclimatization efforts, however, may also be critiqued for their anthropocentric tendencies, as they are often grounded in the assumption that nature is easily subject to human control.[49] Finally, Ritvo cautions that humans ought to consider the unintended consequences of acclimatization, as this process can open a Pandora's box revealing the limitations of human attempts at the mastery of nature, which may result in the dying out of certain species, or conversely in their ability to take over certain ecosystems.[50] While Franceschi's contributions to American horticulture are well known, especially within California, they raise important questions about the broader ecosystem implications of such anthropocentric efforts to manage or control landscapes.

Indeed, ideas about how to more empathetically conceptualize and approach various projects of human development underpin many of the stories in this book. How, for instance, may we reconcile these seeming efforts to master or control nature with a more relational understanding that considers all the world a gift? Kimmerer, a plant biologist herself, has said that even though she is trained as a scientist, "she cannot hear the phrase 'natural resources' without feeling profoundly uneasy"; rather, "she has an idea for a potential replacement: 'Earthly Gifts.'"[51] How, then, might such a wonderfully inviting, conceptual replacement of "natural resources" with "Earthly gifts" come to shift our mindsets in practice? I raise these questions here because part of the work of this book is, again, to better understand and think through these conflicting and often anthropocentric attitudes about the natural world and the role of humans as "managers" of landscapes and species, in an effort to create more compassionate, livable, and sustainable habitats for ourselves, and other animals and species in an age of anthropogenic climate change. With these ideas in mind, I argue, again, that a "gift mindset" that is grounded in entangled empathy and a language of animacy can productively inform how we understand projects of human development and our relationships with our more-than-human kin and the ecosystems in which we coexist with all species.

The route of my walk does not actually take me past the Franceschi mansion itself but rather through what is known as the "Lower Park"—my favorite part of this area.[52] The Lower Park is a beautiful labyrinth of terraced, concrete pathways lined with sandstone boulders and local plants like rosemary, jade, prickly pear, California sagebrush, tree spurge, and laurel sumac. These winding pathways are built into the steep hillside and eventually wend their way up to the northern section of park. From the Lower Park this morning, I have a hazy view of the Channel Islands and Santa Barbara Harbor, even though the marine layer still conceals a full view of the horizon and the city. This morning is oddly comforting—the humidity comes with a breeze that feels reminiscent of the East Coast, and yet the breeze carries the songs of birds specific to this area, like lesser goldfinches, scrub jays, and Anna's hummingbirds.

I love this place—it has been a source of comfort, rejuvenation, and inspiration since I have lived here. But the history of this park is a source of dissonance for me as well. I seek to reconcile my love of this place with the knowledge of its predominantly, or at least more explicitly celebrated, masculinist history—one that is also arguably anthropocentric given the tenor of its horticultural endeavors. To be sure, my observation here is not intended to create or perpetuate any oversimplified or false binaries about masculinist versus feminist histories of a place, for that is not my aim here or throughout this book; rather, I mention these ideas to complicate and help articulate my dissonance about enjoying a place whose histories also produce cultural tensions.

I discovered this walk soon after I moved to Santa Barbara. At the time, I did not refer to Franceschi Park, proper, as part of my route, because the lower half of the park feels similar to hiking through a neighborhood. It was through a series of accidental observations and purposeful inquiry that I eventually learned more about one of my now-favorite places. And as I started to research this route even more thoroughly, especially over the course of writing this book, I began to realize that I am hiking through a park that is technically, ostensibly, named after a white settler. This fact alone has not deterred me from enjoying the hike, nor is it necessarily reason to cast the fascinating history of Franceschi Park in a wholly negative light, which is not at all my intention. The park's history, however, does cause me some dissonance, especially when juxtaposed with the fact that this same area, like all of Santa Barbara, was originally home to the Chumash people, who resided in southern California and on the Santa Barbara Channel Islands, well before the arrival of Europeans in North America.[53]

I try to reconcile this dissonance in part by learning about and giving voice to the fuller histories of this place, and by reciprocating the fuller world of gifts that this place knows and bestows. Like many of the places that I describe, encounter, and think through in this book, a fuller picture of a place necessarily accounts for the varied and valuable constellations of temporal, artifactual, and embodied knowledges that can help "create sustainable frames" for communicative and discursive practices.[54] In attempting to learn the language of this place, I am also trying to reciprocate the gifts that this place has given me, albeit in the ways that I know how. It is through honoring constellations of knowledges that we are better able to conceptualize and practice a gift mindset and be at home in a place. And when histories of a place seem out of balance, we may try to address some of the imbalance by recasting the light and sharing stories and perspectives that are often less amplified or culturally salient. In this way, knowledge is not necessarily built or codified by specific individuals; rather, as communication scholars Phil Bratta and Malea Powell have described, it is, "instead, accumulated through collective practices" across different communities, ecosystems, and places.[55]

The Chumash people have a long and rich history in Santa Barbara that precedes not only Franceschi's early twentieth-century efforts at horticultural innovation but also that of the Spanish-era missionaries, who colonized the region in the late eighteenth century and subjugated the Chumash peoples of Santa Barbara during the development of some of the city's earliest infrastructure. It bears stating that I am not specifically an Indigenous studies scholar, per se, and I certainly do not want to mispresent my areas of research in any way, but as a Santa Barbara resident, and as the writer of this book, I have become quite interested in learning about the rich histories of this area. In this chapter, I seek to share some of what I've learned, at least insomuch as it pertains to the narrative that I weave here through my walk. Narrative is about learning, after all. And learning, I would argue, requires curiosity, openness, and respect. These are, in essence, the elements that guide much of my inquiry, and much of my interest in sharing knowledge with my readers. Again, places are not discrete or abstract entities but rather interwoven with layers of meaning that happen over time and through various experiences of a place.

The temporal layers of this place intersect and become interwoven, in part, for instance, through the knowledge that Franceschi arranged to "have water from the Spanish-era Mission reservoir pumped to his own reservoir. He located plants based upon how much water would be necessary to sustain them."[56] Much of Santa Barbara's original irrigation system is, in fact, still intact today, including the Mission Dam and Aqueduct, which were built in the early nineteenth century, around 1806 and 1807, by the then-subjugated Chumash people who labored "under the direction of the Franciscan padres."[57] The Lavanderia, or main wash basin at Mission Santa Barbara, was also built between 1808 and 1818 by the enslaved Chumash people.[58]

While local Chumash history in Santa Barbara often focuses on the later period, after the arrival and colonization of Spanish missionaries, it is important to convey that the Chumash people resided and thrived in this region for thousands of years prior to the arrival of Spanish missionaries in the late 1700s. The imposition of Christianity on the Chumash eventually led to the loss of much of their traditional religious and social systems, and within sixty years of the imposition of the mission system on the Chumash people, their "society ceased to exist in its original form."[59] Subsequently, as the Spanish missions expanded, populations of Chumash villages declined, resulting in the eventual dissolution of their religious and social systems.[60] The Chumash did manage to preserve some of their traditional customs and beliefs throughout that period, but after California became a US territory in 1850, the preservation of their culture only became more challenging. Wright's work on belonging helps contextualize this history by describing that "for Indigenous people, terrains of belonging and citizenship are particularly complex and contested. Profound and violent experiences of colonization sit alongside continuing struggles for self-determination and rich cultural attachments to place."[61] As such, Wright says, Indigenous peoples' experiences of belonging are "highly fragile" and fraught with "the legacies and contemporary realities of colonization."[62] The Chumash peoples' legacy of colonization, for instance, endures in part through the ongoing challenges of preserving their rich cultural histories.

The Chumash did not have a written language, but some Chumash leaders conveyed knowledge of customs, crafts, and songs through an oral tradition, and much of this oral history has been documented by the remaining but small Chumash communities in Santa Barbara, and in nearby San Luis Obispo and Ventura Counties, as well as by local anthropologists.[63] It is common local knowledge that all of Santa Barbara was Chumash territory before the European settlers arrived here, but as I delved more deeply into this cultural history, my own interests in archaeology led me to wonder how the Chumash people may have lived in this specific place, even as specific as the area of my own walking route. The Chumash's way of life was very much an expression of their surrounding environment, and as hunters and gatherers, they relied on plants and animals native to the Santa Barbara region as their primary source of sustenance. They likewise relied on local ecosystems as their source of craft materials and tools; from local plants they made homes, beds, and baskets, and from stone they made artifacts such as grinding tools, knives, arrowheads, and cooking pots.[64] These expressions of belonging, these elements of home, are still woven into the fabric of this place today.

In early 2020, the Santa Barbara Museum of Natural History was contacted by a local Santa Barbara resident who, over the course of some excavation work, had come across a large basin metate (pronounced mə-'tä-tē), or millingstone. The metate was made of sandstone—a prevalent and common building material in this area, and had been discovered by the local resident's husband while excavating a swimming pool in the vicinity of Franceschi Park; her husband had brought the artifact home at the time, and the woman later brought it to the natural history museum for their collection.[65] As the curator of anthropology for the museum describes, basin metates "were used to grind wild seeds and perhaps acorns during what archaeologists call the Initial Early Period or Millingstone Horizon, which dates perhaps as early as 9,000 or 10,000 years ago and continued to about 6,500 years ago. By 5,000 years ago, basin metates had been replaced, at least in [the Santa Barbara area], by mortars and pestles as the favored type of milling equipment." Thus, he noted, the presence of a basin metate demonstrates that Indigenous peoples "have used the Franceschi Park area for many millennia."[66]

The story of the found basin metate is more than just an intriguing story of a local archeological discovery. For a local resident to find such an artifact buried in the vicinity of Franceschi Park is arguably a metaphor for the less amplified histories of a subjugated people. It is a metaphor perhaps for how the white settlers of this region sought to bury the history and culture of the Chumash people—one that still resonates, and is still right here with us today, only waiting to be rediscovered. If, however, such a metaphor seems a reach to some, then I will offer instead, or in addition, the notion that this metate is a found "expression of belonging."[67] That is, the Chumash used basin metates to process acorns, piñon or pine nuts, and other small seeds like chia and sunflower, among others.[68] These kinds of bowls and grinding implements were vital for food preparation in Chumash culture.[69] The metate, then, is more than just a ground stone tool—it is an artifact of home, an expression of belonging—a handmade tool that was used to prepare food on a daily basis. The metate helps to provide sustenance, and in doing so, makes use of the gifts of the natural world; as such, it is an artifact that helps tell part of the long story of this place and some of the people who were its earliest inhabitants.

When I hike through this section of Franceschi Park today—a place that carries much personal meaning, I consider that the explicit naming of this park does not necessarily speak to the fuller history of this place. I try to reconcile my own dissonance by allowing room for the multitude of relationships that constitute this place, including but not limited to my own relationship with it. I wonder if I am walking on the same ground upon which a Chumash person once used that basin metate, and I wonder who specifically may have used it. I imagine that person's relationship with this place, and how they may have used that metate each day. I am quite sure that their relationship with the plants and seeds that they relied upon for sustenance bears no resemblance to my own relationship with the plant life of this place. Hiking here in 2020, for instance, I use a plant identification app on my smartphone as I endeavor to learn more about the local flora that were interwoven into the very fabric of Chumash culture.[70] Even so, I like to imagine that there are different ways of appreciating a place and acknowledging and reciprocating its gifts, and that we may each try to appreciate and respect a place and give voice to its rich histories through the different ways that we know how.

As I climb these terraced pathways, rooftop shingles blend with the tops of pines and a vast sheet of rosemary and tree spurge, to form a canvas composed of organic and inorganic textures. Here, local flora blends with inorganic, composite materials like cement and asphalt to create a horizon of earth tones that redefines my more traditional notion of nature. I am surrounded by a natural habitat that, today, also incorporates a contemporary neighborhood; this terraced landscape affords a view of local rooftops and the city, just as it does the Channel Islands and the Pacific Ocean. If I shift my focus, I am also easily in the woods; that is, the Lower Park is built into the urban landscape and surrounded by homes, but it is also so ensconced by trees and plants that it is easy to overlook these more structured surroundings. My experience of nature here is nuanced and complexly comforting.

But the literal presence of homes, or what at times amounts to hiking through a neighborhood, is not necessarily why I feel comfortable here. Rather, as I mentioned earlier, my sense of place and feeling of identification with this area is related to a nuanced combination of factors: a recognition of the arrivals and departures of different species that comes with having done this walk for eight years, and an awareness of how the landscape changes when (or rather, if) it's rained, for instance. My sense of place, then, is informed by a knowledge of species and landscape that comes with a receptiveness to the interfactual, bodily, material, and elemental aspects of knowing a place. In this case, my knowledge of a place is rooted in my residing *here currently*; however, there are other places in New England that I know just as well, which I also write about in this book, but in which I do not currently reside and often miss dearly. In other words, there are many ways of knowing a place, and I believe it is possible to move between those ways of knowing as we honor and engage with the gifts that they provide.

Ideas about "home" that are related more traditionally to "house and family" come from the classical Greek, and those ideas are fairly structured and boundaried. The concept of home, as configured in the English language, is actually rooted in the ancient Greek term *oikos,* which typically refers to a more traditional notion of family, or the house and the household.[71] Subsequently, however, as we complicate ideas about what counts as home and for whom in the Anthropocene—in an age of human-induced climate change, and at a time when landscapes change in sometimes fast or unpredictable ways—it quickly becomes clear that this more structured notion of home starts to feel constraining.

On the one hand, I hesitate to overdefine the idea of "home" at the outset of this book, as the concept is so nuanced and multifaceted. On the other hand, I will note that I understand "home," especially as it pertains to the narratives in this book, as necessarily linked to the impacts of anthropogenic climate change and human development, and thus as inextricably connected to ideas about connectivity or displacement, and as impacting the interwoven lives of humans, other animals, and life-forms. As described in a recent article by the Yale School of the Environment: "Fifty-five animal species in the United Kingdom have been displaced from their natural ranges over the past decade due to rising temperatures. The species have shifted as far as hundreds of miles poleward in search of cooler climes, with some crossing seas to arrive for the first time ever in the U.K."[72] And, in *Rising: Dispatches from the New American Shore,* Rush similarly chronicles how rising sea levels have forced the migrations of species in ways that are calling into question what counts as a sustainable habitat and for whom. In the context of discussing the migration of various bird species to H. J. Andrews Experimental Forest in Oregon, where she was studying at the time, she writes: "I think about the places these birds pass through on their way here. . . . The birds are all nomads, at home in movement. But what happens when points along their paths begin to disappear? What disorientation will settle upon all of us then?"[73] Rush alludes here to the idea of "climate anxiety," which I discuss in more detail later in this book; briefly put, though, climate anxiety refers to the "fear that the current system is pushing the Earth beyond its ecological limits."[74] One way that I respond to the anxiety associated with impending and ongoing climate change is through writing. I understand my encounters with these feathered kin, for instance, as momentary opportunities for gratitude, and I try to reciprocate these moments in the ways that I know how. At a time when human development impacts the lives of other animals and species more than ever before, I argue that we have an ethical responsibility to conceptualize and practice a different kind of interaction with the environment—one that takes a more sensitive and nuanced understanding of the natural world, and as Gruen and Kimmerer help describe, one that understands the natural world as full of earthly gifts that we may reciprocate.

At this moment, thankfully, a seemingly content flock of lesser goldfinches flits around in the rosemary that lines the perimeter of this park. A particularly fancy-looking adult male, green-backed lesser makes himself most prominent. Lesser goldfinches are typically year-round residents of central and southern California; however, they tend to move around a lot and are sometimes referred to as "short-distance migrants," as they relocate "from higher elevations to lower country in winter."[75] Like many local avian species who migrate through here in the winter, these small, melodic, acrobatic birds are drawn to this place because their food source is here; these birds "are all nomads, at home in movement."[76] The scrubby habitat of the rosemary and other plants such as thistle provide stable resources for these finches. Thus, this place is home to these birds for parts of the year, and I am grateful that they continue to find sustenance here enough to thrive in this habitat; however, many vul-

nerable species must now migrate or forage farther to find adequate food supplies, and we cannot make assumptions about their consistent ability to find
food, or the ability of an ecosystem to consistently provide food sources from
one year to the next. This book argues in part that it is our ethical responsibility to help foster sustained and nuanced connectivity among ecosystems; we
may start with a willingness to engage in more relational ideas and practices
about what counts as home and belonging in an age of climate change.

These more traditional ideas about home also feel constraining when we
start to complicate them from a more posthuman, relational, and ecological
perspective, whereby the distinctions between inside and outside, for instance,
become blurred. Or, as I describe throughout the book, when the forces of
climate change and contemporary human development lead to ever-closer
encounters between humans and other animals, and when our more-than-
human kin unwittingly find themselves closer to areas of human habitation.
So, then, while *oikos* is a useful enough starting point, as it helps us understand where some of these ideas come from, it also becomes necessary to
move forward from this point as we begin to think more about more nuanced,
relational, and *ecological* ideas about home, kin, belonging, and place.

Not surprisingly, "ecology" is also derived from the Greek, *oikos,* which
relates to the English prefix, eco-, for "ecology." Thus, ecology deals with all
forms of life, environments, and "places to live." It is here that we may begin to
see some connections between an ecological, relational perspective and ideas
about place. Or, as my colleague Tim Jensen put it during a recent conversation: What is ecology, if not the study of home?[77] An ecological vantage point
is also situated in ideas from human and feminist geography that are related
to "sense of place." In such ways, "home" does not necessarily exclude but
also transcends notions of built structures or literal property markers. Home
relates more complexly to our feelings of connectedness or belonging with a
place, how a place or an ecosystem provides connectivity itself, or conversely,
how connectivity gets disrupted by forces of human development and prevents
or hinders sustained connection with a place. As Wright describes, home is
an important site for understanding ideas about belonging, for it is "neither
strictly a place nor a feeling, but comes about through the interactions of
place and feelings"; moreover, home is also a site "where contradictions must
co-exist and may be partially reconciled."[78] It is often through narrative and
stories that we can more easily describe, engage with, learn from, and perhaps
reconcile multifaceted ideas about home, belonging, and place.

Melody Walker, who is a Vermont-based "educator, activist, artist, and
citizen of the Elnu Abenaki Band of Ndakinna," suggests that "our connection
to place is cemented through . . . stories, old and new."[79] In this book, I con-

sider the work of storytelling and narrative as a means for offering new perspectives about how to more compassionately, productively, and respectfully understand ideas about home, connectivity, and coexistence across a range of places and ecosystems. Walker writes that people often crave a sense of belonging: "To name what is felt but is rarely spoken. 'People' in dominant society refers only to humans. Abenaki stories teach us what belonging means, what it means to be a person, and what it means to walk as if all things mattered. Dominant society is largely devoid of these ideas, and naming a difficult concept without the proper words must come from other viewpoints."[80] In this book, I endeavor to account for such other viewpoints, as I consider more fully what it means to walk as if all things mattered. And in the process, I am learning important lessons myself that I hope to share with readers.

I continue now on the downslope as I start to head out of Lower Franceschi Park. Along one of the winding concrete pathways, I come across some coyote scat filled with berry seeds—what communication scholar Natasha Seegert might refer to as a "coyote text," or one of the many texts that "coyotes themselves produce that are disseminated across the paw-trodden terrain: scat, urine, dens, howls, animal trails in parks . . . as well as their phantom shapes furtively wandering the city."[81] On this morning's walk, I see only evidence of the coyote's recent presence in this area—they must have come through here earlier this morning. I wish I'd seen a little glimpse of them. About a year ago, however, I was doing this walk when a coyote, possibly the same one, trotted shyly and very quickly across my path, maybe about twenty feet ahead of me, just about in this same area. It was a similarly overcast morning around 9:00 a.m. I recall that the little coyote walked with her center of gravity set so low—it appeared as though she did not want to be noticed. Her fur was a muted grayish-beige, and her tail was so full and bushy, such an endearing creature. My most vivid recollection, though, is really how shy she seemed; it was so clear that she did not want to be seen or disturbed. Our encounter was brief and quiet—just two beings crossing paths at the same moment—just a quick moment of peaceful coexistence, and, to my mind, at least, a wonderful gift to see such a beautiful creature thriving in her natural habitat. Just moments later, another woman hiked down one of the terraced pathways in my direction—she had come from farther up the hillside. I said good morning and mentioned that a coyote had just come through here. "Oh yes," the woman said, happily unfazed, "this is a corridor for them."

Yes—this is a corridor for them. This place—this route of my regular walk, this previous site of horticultural, technoscientific endeavor, this home to countless species, is also a relatively safe corridor for our coyote friend. It is a route well-known to her and one that she presumably, hopefully, relies upon for safe passage. This contemporary urban corridor allows the coyote to get to and from her home—perhaps to and from her family. Equally important, this corridor, working in the positive, provides one small means of coexistence for humans and our more-than-human kin. Our coyote kin provides, as Seegert rightly notes, one of many opportunities "to bound into a space of *animal rhetorics*" that challenges dominant paradigms about "which bodies are given standing in discourse and who is capable of producing discourse."[82] And as Beth Pratt of the National Wildlife Federation tells us, connectivity is really about fostering "a new paradigm of conservation, which is coexistence."[83] And one way that humans can reciprocate the gifts of the natural world is to reciprocate with the gift of connectivity—the gift of room to move, which can in turn help maintain biodiversity.

Connectivity also allows for movement to and from home. As some of the stories in this book help illustrate, when species are unable to move between places or return home—when connectivity is threatened or lost—then so potentially is biodiversity, and so potentially is all of our ability to thrive. To think about connectivity as a gift that we may reciprocate is also an opportunity, if carried out with care and critical thought, to engage with compassion and entangled empathy. That is, this coyote is simply trying get from one point to another; when she crosses my path, I don't want my presence to frighten her. I hope she feels safe in traversing this area, and I hope that local residents respect her presence as much as the other hiker and I did. It is humbling to think that many generations of this coyote's kin have thrived in this area for far longer than the eight years I have resided here. People are often scared of these creatures, but coyotes are generally far more scared of us, and for good reason. Part of our ethical responsibility in an age of climate change, then, as this book endeavors to show, is to respect the homes and the place-based needs of our more-than-human kin and to be grateful for any brief encounters along the way. I feel privileged that I can share this place with this coyote, but I know that her context, her experience of this place—her *story*—obviously differs from my own.

We all bring our own contexts to bear on places, or, as Van Dooren says, we all "story" our places uniquely. In this way, "story" becomes not just a noun (as in, to tell a story), but also an adjective and a verb: This is a "storied place"; "to story" a place; we story our places. Moreover, we humans are not the only creatures for whom place is imbued with meaning and history; other species story their places as well—we just need to be more attentive to the ways that their narratives might be different from ours. In using the word "story" as a verb, "to story," van Dooren is not claiming that other species "know and 'do' places in the same way that people do, but simply that their relationships with place might also be productively understood" through a lens that involves narrative or storytelling, and that other animals might also engage in place-making and story their places in "complex and diverse ways."[84] To understand storied places in this way also works against, as Susan McHugh describes, an anthropocentric mindset that views "knowledges of animal life as ends in themselves, insisting instead that concerns about their accumulation, endangerment, and other operations can never be exclusive to any creature."[85] Rather, we are co-constituted beings in relationship, and we story our places uniquely, together.

As I head downhill and out of the park, a salamander runs out in front of me and hides in a crack in the concrete pathway. A chipmunk similarly makes a dash for a cactus stand. I hear the short whistle of a shy California quail foraging in some rosemary. I walk down the last set of stone steps on the way out, and a young man with a full backpack hikes past me, and we exchange perfunctory but friendly greetings. It does not yet occur to me to keep a six-foot distance from him, as cautioned in this time of Covid. Instead, I say hello and am quickly distracted by the call of a red-tailed hawk that soars on the thermals overhead. I watch the hawk for a moment—how effortlessly it glides in easy spiral formations—and I begin my walk home.

It bears noting that this is not a book about the pandemic; however, much of it was written in its shadow, and subsequently this unique cultural moment made its way into this book in ways that I had not anticipated. The pandemic is (hopefully) a specific, discrete point in time, but one that will forever shape our culture, and one from which we can and will continue to learn important lessons about connectivity and coexistence. In many ways, I feel fortunate to be able to write this book at this cultural moment and to share some of what I've learned, and relearned, along the way.

While the pandemic prevented some of my intended travel to certain places that I'd planned to visit while writing this book, I was also able to travel to other places that I had not initially planned on visiting. And really, I remain grateful that travel was even a possibility for me at all during these times; in fact, the pandemic, and the travel that I was able to do, served to further emphasize several of the themes that I had already planned to address in this book, albeit from an unanticipated vantage point. That is, this book builds on and extends ideas from Gruen and Kimmerer, respectively, about engaging empathetically with our more-than-human kin, and understanding the world as full of gifts to be received and reciprocated. More specifically, it considers how we may approach conservation and the projects of contemporary human development differently if we remain open to a language of animacy and more empathetic ways of understanding our relationships with one another. This book also argues for the importance of maintaining ecosystem connectivity, even when doing so becomes increasingly more difficult for reasons that sometimes appear beyond our control, and even when that potentially lost connectivity is, in part, a product of human development. These ideas and concepts build on one another cumulatively from chapter to chapter. Each chapter then draws on different examples, and I use stories and narrative in particular to help complicate ideas about belonging and what counts as home, and to emphasize the value of understanding these broader concepts from multiple, nuanced perspectives.

As mentioned earlier, while I happen to be writing from this place now, there are other places that I describe in this book, which I know equally well, or have written from, but in which I'm not currently residing or visiting. As I endeavor to show in this book, through some of the places that I describe or encounter directly, there are many modes of knowing a place; it is possible to write while being there; it is possible to recount or reveal knowledge of a place through stories and published accounts; it is possible to pass down stories about a place from another's perspective and tell those stories anew, albeit with necessary care and sensitivity. I believe it is possible to move between these different but equally valuable ways of knowing places, as we honor and engage with the gifts that such places provide. Writing about place with gratitude and consideration is but one possible way of reciprocating these gifts. And as Boyle and Rice remind us, the joint relationship of a body in a place can inform such approaches to writing and can have implications far beyond that of the writer's immediate experience. It is thus my hope that in writing about some of the places that I know and love, and in doing so with care and gratitude, this book can help foster new ideas about our roles and responsibilities as humans residing in ecosystems that we must share with our more-than-human kin in a time of climate crisis.

With this chapter, I have endeavored to introduce some of the book's overarching themes, concepts, and arguments. In doing so, it is my hope that this local walk that I have shared with my readers has helped begin to reveal the gifts that are all around us, if we are mindful and respectful of their presence. At the same time, I know that my individual experience of this walk is hardly the only version of this place, and I have thus tried to show in this introduction that there are many ways to know, to story, or to generate knowledge about a place.

As Kimmerer tells us, and as I am learning myself, to listen to the language of our more-than-human kin is to become mindful of the languages of a place that are not our own, but that may shape our accounts of the ecosystems that we share. By receiving the gifts of our ecosystems and of our more-than-human kin, and by reciprocating those gifts in kind, we are presented with an alternative to an anthropocentric mindset—one that can instead introduce us to new ways of coexisting on a planet in crisis. To understand the world as full of gifts and to be receptive to the lively languages spoken by a place and all its kin is compatible with an approach that values empathy for our more-than-human kin—one that understands wildlife and nature not as "out there," or separate from humans, but as entangled and among us. The chapters in this book continue to explore these ideas through different accounts and stories.

Chapter 1, "What Counts as Home in the Anthropocene?," considers our relationship to the natural world and our possible ethical obligations to vulnerable species, and it does so largely through narrative that describes the challenges and the work of wildlife rehabilitation. I emphasize how entangled empathy and compassionate conservation play out through various nuanced, relational practices that can help mitigate the direct and indirect impacts of human intervention in ways that provide comfort, care, respect, and shelter for vulnerable species. I show how the artifacts that compose home and shelter can help illustrate and articulate the many possible constellations of what Cohen refers to as "elemental" relationships. I argue that these relationships take part in what Cohen and Ingold refer to as the "environmental meshworks" in which our in/organic entanglements with the material world take shape. In doing so, I suggest they may also participate in what Kimmerer calls a "culture of gratitude." Specifically, chapter 1 reveals some of the ways that the practices of wildlife rehabilitation participate in an environmental meshworks that can help foster more ethical contemporary relationships with our more-than-human kin.

In chapter 2, "Fire-Lost and Trying to Cross," I tell two recent stories about encounters between humans and mountain lions, and in doing so, allow us to imagine a world where encounters with our wild kin can be viewed as gifts that we humans may reciprocate. I first tell the story of a mountain lion who unwittingly wandered into an Oregon resident's home during the wildfires of 2018. In brief, I suggest that the homeowner's communicative approach in prompting the lion to exit her home implicitly demonstrates entangled empathy and the compassionate conservation principle of "do no harm," and makes use of peaceful modes of nonverbal, animate communication to which the animal was ultimately receptive. I then juxtapose this story with a narrative about a series of mountain lion sightings that took place in Santa Barbara, California, during the fall of 2019, when there were five reported sightings around the UC Santa Barbara campus. I reveal how discourses that perform an openness to respectful coexistence can inform ideas about what counts as home in the Anthropocene, and how humans and more-than-human animals can "story their places" together in an age of climate crisis. Building on the work of Gruen and Kimmerer, we see what kinds of encounters become possible when, in a world where our more-than-human kin are increasingly displaced due to climate change and other anthropogenic forces, we respond not with fear and reactivity but with generosity and empathy.

In chapter 3, "Storied Places and Species in Flux: Connectivity as Reciprocity," I begin with the story of a mountain lion named P-22 who wandered into and now resides permanently in southern California's Griffith Park. The park is essentially surrounded by freeways, and thus P-22 is unable to make his way out of the park due to lost habitat connectivity. I juxtapose P-22's story with that of the planned, nearby Liberty Canyon wildlife corridor, which is intended to help restore lost connectivity and prevent mountain lions like P-22 from continuing to get hemmed into urban areas without a feasible way out. At the same time, I complicate the idea of P-22's situation by considering a more posthuman perspective informed by urban ecologies—that "wildlife" is always among us, and thus P-22 is our "neighbor" with whom we may coexist. Informed by ideas about entangled empathy and understanding connectivity as an ethical obligation that humans have to their more-than-human kin, I consider how wildlife corridors can perform conservation practice grounded in an ethic of compassion and empathy and a culture of reciprocity. I argue that, working in the positive, wildlife corridors can be part of a culture of reciprocity—they are but one way of returning the gifts bestowed by our more-than-human kin, in the form of renewed and ideally sustained biodiversity.

In chapter 4, "At Home with Big Kin," I tell the story of the black bears who reside in Vermont's Green Mountain National Forest and consider their well-being in light of their reciprocal relationship with local beech trees and the recently completed Deerfield Wind Energy Project, which is the first wind farm to be built on national forest land. Or rather, I describe this storied place—where black bears and beech trees alike can be said to participate in a kind of communal generosity that helps sustain lives and habitats. The story of Vermont's black bears and the beech trees upon which they rely helps tell a story about home—one that helps reveal the possibilities for communal generosity and a culture of reciprocity. "Home" in the Anthropocene is thus, in part, about fostering sustainable habitat and doing what we can to decrease risk for our vulnerable kin. Part of a culture of reciprocity means understanding our own ethical responsibility to these vulnerable species as we embark on projects of human infrastructure, and as they seek safe passage through their home ranges and neighboring habitats.

In chapter 5, "Gratitude for the Trail and the Gift of Roadside Geology," I wind down the book in the Midwest, where I managed to travel to visit my brother in fall 2020. During a hike with my brother and my nieces and nephew, I reflect on all there is to celebrate in this complex elemental moment. Through narrative and storytelling, I consider our broader ethical obligation to share knowledge with our future generations and to model continued empathetic engagement with our more-than-human kin and the ecosystems we share. The sharing of knowledge through narrative, and the elemental experiences of these storied places, are small steps in this direction. At the same time, this hike prompts me to consider how children's engagement with the natural world is something that we, as adults, may learn from ourselves. Children's innate curiosity, lack of preconceived judgment, and ability to engage with new ideas are ways of being in the world that we can return to—these are gifts to behold and to reciprocate, especially in the Anthropocene and in an age of climate crisis, when coexistence with species and ecosystems is more important than ever before. While this concluding chapter is set during the time of the pandemic, it is important to note that not all of the chapters are anchored in this particular cultural context.

As mentioned earlier, however, the pandemic did make its way into this book in ways that I had not anticipated—either literally, through travel to places that I had not planned on traveling to, or more so behind the scenes, as I considered the themes that I was writing about, but now, through this unforeseen lens. As a result, I have also woven into this book what I am calling "interludes," or a couple of shorter sections, which serve as points of reflection or meta-narrative. These shorter interludes function as reflections that happen to be set during the time of the pandemic, and somewhat surprisingly, sync up fluidly with the themes of the book as a whole. I did not set out to write the book this way; rather, this approach emerged somehow, more organically. This is the best way I can think of to describe the overarching layout of the book. Taken as a whole, then, I seek a compassionate and respectful path forward as we negotiate our relationships with our more-than-human kin *in place, in the world,* and I consider how entangled empathy, compassion, and a gift mindset can play out through relational practices of connectivity, care, and home as they pertain to our contemporary relationships with vulnerable species.

CHAPTER 1

# What Counts as Home in the Anthropocene?

It's just before 7 a.m. on Sunday morning—it's Mother's Day, actually. It's early on a holiday weekend, so we have a slightly smaller crew than usual; that's okay, though, because while it's just a small handful of us getting things up and running this morning, we work well together. Having a great team is a large part of what makes wildlife rehabilitation work rewarding and also manageable, for it is physically and emotionally demanding work. Many of these birds are quite fragile and require a high degree of care from morning until evening; we always do the best we can, as this is part of the work. This morning, there is one fledgling mockingbird in particular who has been on my mind, and whose condition I hope has stabilized.

I enter what we more informally refer to as the "baby bird room." The room is still relatively dark and quiet; this is essentially the part of the wildlife center that houses all baby birds in need of care. To my right are three long metal tables arranged in parallel rows, which makes it easy to move between them. On each table are anywhere from eight to ten small plastic baskets; each basket houses a baby bird in need of care. In the coming months, several more tables will need to be set up around the perimeter of the room, for May is just the start of what we refer to casually as "baby season," or the time of year, in this region, during which most baby birds are born.[1]

These tables are the first thing I see when walking in the room, but the first thing I hear is the sound of quiet chirping coming from each of the baskets

27

arranged on them. The sound of muted chirping comes from the many baby birds in this room. Some are hatchlings, still in incubators, and most are fledglings, who are just waking with the sun. This will be the quietest and slowest part of the day—before feeding and cleaning have officially begun.

Each of these baby birds is here temporarily. Each is set up, or housed, you could say, in a small, white, plastic basket—similar to the kind you might find in a home and bath store. The baskets are lined with a layer of newspaper at the bottom, and a layer of paper towel over the newspaper. They are each outfitted with at least one branch that serves as a perch, and sometimes other organic materials like flowers, berries, and buds, depending on the species of bird, for the rehabilitation habitat should resemble the bird's natural habitat as much as possible. A lightweight cloth, fastened tightly over the top of the basket, lets in light but creates a complete and safe enclosure. This enclosure typically includes water, seed, fruits and vegetables, and meal worms or other insects, arranged in small bowls, all in combinations appropriate for the specific species being cared for. Hatchlings and fledglings who are not yet self-feeding must be hand-fed every half hour, sometimes more, essentially mimicking the schedule that a parent bird would feed the baby in its natural habitat.

These young birds have each wound up here for a variety of reasons. Sometimes a nest has fallen from a tree during tree-trimming and has subsequently been abandoned by the parent. Some birds have been "cat-caught"; in other words, they have been attacked by somebody's domesticated cat. Others have somehow been injured or have fallen ill and have subsequently been found by a good Samaritan or passerby. It isn't always possible to know a bird's full story coming in, even with a good intake exam. But they are all here because they've somehow been unable to thrive on their own in their natural habitat, to the point where they have become vulnerable enough to be discovered and brought in by a compassionate human.

Volunteering at a wildlife center has given me a newfound and more conscious appreciation for encountering thriving, healthy wildlife out in the world. As I write here at home on a Wednesday morning, an adult male, dark-eyed junco sunbathes in a patch of dried leaves on the ground behind my house. Upon first glance, some might think this bird to be injured, as he appears to lie listless in a pile of leaves under an oak tree, perfectly camouflaged with the ground. More steady observation reveals, however, that he quietly cleans his feathers, occasionally stretching his wings, moving around in the leaves to catch some good sun. I remind myself that these beautiful moments exist, too—and I hope that this little junco will continue to thrive in his natural ecosystem.

As rewarding as wildlife work can be, it can be difficult and challenging work at times. When viewed through the lens of compassionate conservation, which suggests that the life of every individual species matters in decisions about wildlife conservation and policy, the work of wildlife rehabilitation is often understood as part of our responsibility to coexist ethically with our more-than-human kin, and to mitigate, to the extent possible, the impacts of various modes of human intervention.[2] Such a vantage point would consider that wildlife rehabilitation work is one way of giving back to a community of wildlife often made vulnerable by the impacts of climate change and human intervention in the first place, and in fact, we might further complicate these ideas by considering that wildlife rehabilitation is, technically, one more mode of human intervention on top of that.

These questions about our relationship to the natural world—questions about how much to intervene and when, the related tendency to toggle between "hope" and "despair," as Donna Haraway has described, and the question of how we can arrive at a middle ground—constitute a theme that pervades not only this work but also my broader thinking about issues related to climate change, ecosystem and species vulnerability, and the role that humans ought to play in the general state of affairs regarding our planet and those vulnerable species with whom we share it.[3] What counts as help? What counts as empathetic and compassionate care? How do our perceived ethical responsibilities to our more-than-human kin influence our desire to participate in their lives? And more specifically, at a time when vulnerable species find themselves wandering farther to search for food or shelter due to a variety of circumstances not of their doing, and perhaps beyond the human purview as well, what counts as home?

With these ideas in mind, this chapter reveals how entangled empathy and compassionate conservation play out in ways that provide comfort, care, and shelter for vulnerable species. It considers how the artifacts that compose home and shelter can help illustrate and articulate the many possible constellations of what Cohen refers to, for instance, as "elemental" relationships.[4] As I mentioned in the introduction, these relationships also participate in what Cohen and Ingold call "meshworks," or the environmental meshworks in which our in/organic entanglements with the material world take shape.[5]

I suggest that these elemental sites of caregiving for injured birds participate in environmental meshworks that can help foster more ethical, contemporary relationships between humans and our more-than-human kin; such sites of caregiving may also then participate in what Kimmerer calls a "culture of gratitude." As Kimmerer writes: "In a culture of gratitude, everyone knows that gifts will follow the circle of reciprocity and flow back to you again."[6] The sites of wildlife rehabilitation arguably constitute one way of giving back to our fragile and fraught ecosystems with the hope of making them whole again for the benefit of all beings. As such, following Wright, these places are sites of belonging that "rely on attending and responding with care. They challenge and actively destabilize simplistic ideas of belonging," and as such they both complicate and constitute "practices of becoming together."[7]

When people call the wildlife center to inquire about a baby bird that they've found, we typically ask a series of questions to help determine the best course of action; for example, we ask whether the bird is fully feathered, whether the caller sees a parent nearby, whether the baby bird is in a dangerous location, or whether it is in a safe place. Sometimes, and often, in fact, the best course of action is to do nothing—leave well enough alone and the parent will likely be back soon enough. That is the ideal scenario, at least.

But if the baby bird does make its way to the wildlife center, this small enclosure will be its home until it is well enough and mature enough to move to an outdoor aviary, where it will continue to progress in foraging on its own, flying, and acclimating to spending twenty-four hours a day outside in its closer-to-natural habitat. Once it is strong enough to survive on its own, it will be released, ideally nearby the location where it was first found.

When residing at the wildlife center, the young bird, if it is a hatchling or fledgling, will be fed every half hour until it is self-feeding, or until the bird can and will eat on its own. For the time being, then, this place, and this small enclosure, becomes home to these vulnerable birds who have unwittingly made their way here through no effort of their own.

This Sunday is a particularly busy morning. It is the busiest part of the year here, as well as a holiday weekend, and the trailer that houses baby birds is currently home to quite a few species. In the incubators that house hatchlings not yet fully feathered are house finches, bushtits, California towhees, and European starlings. In baskets arranged on the tables are oak titmice, fledgling house finches, sparrows, scrub jays, Anna's hummingbirds, starlings, a spotted towhee, a dark-eyed junco, a Bewick's wren, and a particularly delicate young mockingbird who arrived just a few days earlier with a ruptured air sac.

Every individual body matters; do no harm. These are some of the guiding principles of compassionate conservation. Do no harm; every individual body matters—these are also some of the main philosophies underpinning wildlife rehabilitation.

We don't always know how it is that a bird has wound up in the condition that it's in. Sometimes the person who brings in an injured bird will convey what they know or describe what they've seen; other times, someone has found the bird but didn't see what happened. In the case of this little mockingbird, there were just a couple of clues to go on. The bird had apparently been chased by a cat, and it had a visible scab toward the top of its leg. It was a fledging—able to fly, but still young and learning the ropes, so to speak.

It isn't known what exactly causes a ruptured air sac in birds, but the condition can sometimes occur secondary to another injury. Air sacs are part of the reason birds are so lightweight and buoyant. As the Animal Medical Center of New York describes:

> Evolution made birds lightweight for flying. To lighten their bones, some bones contain air (pneumatic bones) as part of their respiratory system. Like reptiles and mammals, birds also have lungs, but bird lungs function differently than ours. With each breath, our lungs fill and empty with air due to movement of the diaphragm. Birds lack a diaphragm, and air moves through the lungs and into and out of the air sacs in two cycles as their sternum expands and contracts with each breath. While air is in the lungs, exchange of oxygen and carbon dioxide occurs. The air sacs help keep birds "light as a feather" and buoyant for flight.[8]

Birds have a series of air sacs, which are located in the neck (cervical air sacs), chest (thoracic air sacs), and belly (abdominal air sacs). If one of the air sacs ruptures, usually due to injury, "air will leak from the sac and accumulate under the bird's skin. This condition is known as subcutaneous emphysema."[9] When the ruptured air sac becomes visible, the bird may look as if it has a balloon under its skin, which was the case with this young mockingbird.

It is possible to treat the ruptured air sac with a procedure that involves inserting a small stent into the air sac to remove the accumulated air and reduce the swelling.[10] However, it is also possible for air sacs to "normally repair themselves," usually within a couple of weeks, if, for instance, the bird gets proper care and is no longer in danger and out of harm's way.[11] In this case, the young mockingbird is prescribed a common anti-inflammatory medication and kept in a calm, quiet, and clean environment. It is the hope that this young mockingbird will be able to make a full recovery with this care, and in this setting.

A bird with a ruptured air sac must be handled very carefully and as little as possible, so as not to aggravate or worsen the condition. This reminder is written visibly on the tag affixed to the bird's basket, such that any caregiver will be reminded of the situation before handling the bird. This fledging mockingbird poses a challenge because it needs to be hand-fed every thirty minutes; the good news, however, is that this little bird will readily "gape" for food, meaning it will open its beak widely when presented with food, much like it would do with its parent. Because the bird gapes for food, handling the bird during feedings is not necessary, and it readily accepts medication via the same means, thus greatly reducing the need for physical intervention, with the exception of exams and enclosure cleanings. This is a good thing not only because of its physical condition but also because these animal patients should not become too accustomed to seeing or interacting with humans.

It requires much care to handle this young bird when cleaning its enclosure—its body feels like a fragile balloon. I am hesitant to move the little bird, even quickly and delicately, and even with experience and proper training, but this is a necessary part of ensuring an environment conducive to healing. As I carefully pick up the mockingbird and quickly place it in another temporary basket while I clean its enclosure, I wonder, is this fledgling mockingbird even aware of its own condition? How and what is it feeling and perceiving right now? Does this little bird, on some level, understand that it is now safe and surrounded by other beings who are interested in and fully devoted to its care and recovery? Chased and possibly attacked by a cat, the young bird likely would not have survived without a safe environment in which to heal, and without some of the anti-inflammatory properties of the medication administered to it. But for this fledgling bird, its entire worldly experience, and the home it was beginning to understand, all changed in an instant. Here, perhaps the philosopher and animal activist Lori Gruen would suggest that I am in some way empathizing with this mockingbird.

In distinguishing between sympathy and empathy, Gruen writes that "sympathy involves maintaining one's own attitudes and adding them to a concern for another. Sympathy for another is felt from the outside, the third person perspective. . . . Empathy, however, recognizes connection with and understanding of the circumstances of the other."[12] Gruen acknowledges that this understanding may be incomplete and "often is in need of revisions. However, the goal is to try to take in as much about another's situation and perspective as possible."[13] Gruen has written extensively on the topic of how we empathize with other animals and has developed a concept that she calls "entangled empathy." Entangled empathy, or "being able to understand what another being feels, sees, and thinks, and to understand what they might need or desire," she says, "requires a fairly complex set of cognitive skills and emotional attunement."[14] Because entangled empathy focuses on "another's experiential wellbeing," this kind of empathy tends to lead to action based on an assessment of what seems to be the best, or most compassionate, choice in helping to pursue the well-being of another.[15] Such decisions are, nonetheless, often fraught and not necessarily clearly defined. Based on these ideas, though, it becomes clear that both compassionate conservation and entangled empathy are very much aligned with the philosophies, discourses, and practices underpinning wildlife rehabilitation.

If we consider more closely the environment and the physical condition of this young mockingbird, for instance, the nuanced complexities of its situation and the various possible lenses through which to view the healing scenario emerge. We might, for instance, consider that this bird's process of learning to survive on its own, in its natural habitat, has been disrupted, at first, by a domesticated predator, and now, by human healers, albeit with the most altruistic of intentions. Moreover, the young bird convalesces in this in/organic setting—this plastic, basket-like enclosure at a wildlife center designed to aid in the rehabilitation of sick and injured wildlife. This plastic basket, whose interior is designed with the accoutrements of a fledging bird's natural habitat in mind, becomes a paradoxical place of healing. This place of healing, this setting overseen by the most empathetic of wildlife caregivers, is both organic and artificial, founded on an ethic of care, and designed to encourage healing conducive to resuming life in its natural habitat.

A few years ago, I wrote a book called *Visualizing Posthuman Conservation in the Age of the Anthropocene,* which explored our perceived ethical responsibilities to and relationships with our more-than-human kin.[16] That book focused largely on the role of texts and images, such as photographs or maps, for instance, in shaping our understanding of how we might better coexist compassionately with vulnerable species, in at-risk ecosystems. In it, I devoted a chapter to the albatrosses that reside on Midway Island in the Hawaiian archipelago, who have been consuming and feeding their chicks plastic debris found in the ocean; as a result, many of the chicks do not survive, and these birds are thus dwindling in numbers. In considering how images shape knowledge and understanding about this issue, that chapter explored the work of photographer Chris Jordan, who has been documenting the plight of these birds through photography and filmmaking since about 2009. In that chapter, I also explored the work of literary scholar and ocean activist Stacy Alaimo, whose ideas about what she calls "transcorporeal bodies" align eerily well with how we might think about the fate of those albatrosses.

For Alaimo, "transcorporeality," or the "transcorporeal body," relates to the argument that "nonhuman life is a matter of concern"; more specifically, "transcorporeality" suggests that "even the smallest, most personal ethical practices in the domestic sphere are inextricably tied to any number of massive political and economic predicaments" that can then impact the lives—the embodied, visceral experiences—of other species.[17] In this case, these albatrosses die as a result of the plastic debris they ingest. Subsequently, to situate Jordan's photography in the context of Alaimo's ideas about transcorporeality reveals that the photos "disclose trans-corporeality"; we see images of these birds' bodies, "invaded by terrestrial, human consumerism, revealing the swirling natural-cultural agencies, the connection between ordinary terrestrial life and ocean ecologies, and the uneven distribution of harm."[18] The practices of human consumerism, then, are inextricably tied to the deaths of these birds, whose decomposing bodies continuously and sadly reveal that they are filled with plastic debris.

I cannot easily turn my thoughts away from what feels like the still-inevitable fate of these albatrosses, even now, as I write about this fledging mockingbird, whom I helped care for, and whose encounters with plastic present quite a different context. For this young mockingbird, plastic provides the substance of a makeshift home; it participates in the paradoxical offering of a second chance. This temporary home is artificial but composed of elemental artifacts; it is, in many ways, as Wright describes, "a site where contradictions must co-exist and may be partially reconciled."[19] How, then, do we make sense of this particular transcorporeal body and the vastly different environments it inhabits? An environment, moreover, that is born out of an ethic of caring, empathy, and compassionate conservation.

Despite the emotionally painful work of documenting the lives and deaths of the albatrosses of Midway, Jordan has expressed the nuanced view that plastic, in and of itself, need not be demonized, per se. In an interview about his photography of the albatrosses on Midway Island, Jordan acknowledges that he is not critical of plastic specifically, but rather some of the ways in which it is used: "There are some things that plastic is great for, like there's no better way to make a motorcycle helmet, or lots of medical devices or computer keyboards, etc., and we're not finding that stuff polluting the environment."[20] Rather, Jordan is more critical of single-use, disposable plastics and our tendency to use them in less mindful, or more disconnected ways.[21] I strive to reconcile these two vastly different contexts: plastic as toxic debris that harms environment and species, and plastic as participating in the practices of wildlife rehabilitation via its function as an enclosure for an injured bird.[22] Unless, that is, we, like Jordan, also consider a more nuanced view that departs from such a limiting and binary juxtaposition, and instead situates and understands this enclosure—this non-native habitat designed to aid in healing and born out of an empathetic ethic of care—as participating in larger, empathetic processes that are also elemental and in/organic in their own, Anthropocene way. In other words, as I argue throughout this book, anthropogenic forces need not preclude relational, empathetic practices of caring for vulnerable species. Or, put differently, the Anthropocene and a caring ethic are not mutually exclusive. This chapter helps illuminate how entangled empathy and compassionate conservation are practiced through various nuanced, relational, elemental efforts that can help mitigate the direct and indirect impacts of human intervention in ways that provide comfort, care, and shelter for vulnerable species in the Anthropocene.

## ENTANGLED EMPATHY AND ELEMENTAL RELATIONSHIPS

In *Visualizing Posthuman Conservation*, I argued that Chris Jordan's photos of the albatrosses of Midway helped convey to public audiences the gravity of these birds' complex, embodied entanglements with "the specifics of place, time, physiology, and culture."[23] I argued that these entanglements then configure and produce vulnerable, toxic bodies, inscribed with the plastic signature of our human consumerism.

Our entangled relationships with other species, however, need not necessarily bear such negative connotations. Each morning, for instance, I go to the wildlife center with the hope that the young mockingbird continues to heal. As I check the bird's progress and clean its enclosure, I am heartened to find that the young fledging continues to improve. By the end of May, the mockingbird's air sac has healed, and it no longer needs to be given medication. As I continue to help care for this bird and watch it regain its strength and continue to mature, I realize that in many ways, I have become entangled in a complex relationship with this young bird and am very much invested in its recovery. The entangled nature of our relationships with our more-than-human kin can work in the positive as well—these relationships are nuanced and paradoxical.

Gruen's theory of entangled empathy is also grounded in an understanding of the entangled relationships of humans with other animals. She argues that these relationships "co-constitute who we are and how we configure our identities and agency, even our thoughts and desires. We can't make sense of living without others, and that includes other animals."[24] We must therefore acknowledge the complexities of these "complex relationships" rather than deny them, and thus, she argues, "we would do better to think about how to be more perceptive and more responsive to the deeply entangled relationships we are in.[25] This, she writes, "is the entanglement of entangled empathy. We are not just in relationships as selves with others, but our very selves are constituted by these relations."[26] I would add that these complex relationships not only involve our more-than-human animal kin, but that they may also incorporate places, ecosystems, plant life, and other earthly matter.[27]

For Cohen, again, such entanglements constitute what he calls "elemental relations."[28] As Cohen describes, we are always in relationship with the elements in unpredictable and novel ways—they move us and humble us: "The elements are at once the most intractable, enduring, agentic and fundamental of materials."[29] In more detailed description, he writes:

> Thick stone is documentary, the material of our earliest surviving tools and the conveyor of human prehistory. Restless water is that which cannot be inscribed (except as ice), a substance enclosed within our bodies as memory of a briny origin, the force through which we domesticate landscapes. . . . [W]ithout elemental confederations we would possess no dwellings. Smaller than gods and larger than atoms, the elements offer a human-scale entry into nonhuman relations.[30]

Cohen's ideas help us consider how humans, more-than-humans, and other species coexist and interrelate through practices of care and rehabilitation, and through the various, elemental means by which elemental materials participate in these ethics of care.

Many of our entanglements with elemental matter play out through our relationships with both the physical environment itself and the species with whom we share those habitats. These plastic enclosures—these prescribed, temporary shelters designed to mimic natural habitats—can both foster and constrain these elemental relationships. As such, they help us better conceptualize what counts as habitat and home in these meshworked environments. I argue, then, that the artifacts that compose home and shelter may actually help illustrate and articulate the many possible constellations of these elemental relationships, and that these relationships participate in environmental meshworks that can help foster ethical relations with our worlds.

## EMPATHETIC, ELEMENTAL RELATIONSHIPS:
## AN ENTANGLED MESHWORKS

For anthropologist Tim Ingold, the concept of *meshworks* better accounts for how we make our way through and inhabit the world. As stated earlier,

Cohen's work on the elemental and Ingold's notion of meshworks can provide starting points for understanding and conceptualizing elemental, in/organic environments and habitats, especially as they pertain to what counts as "home" in the Anthropocene. Building on Cohen's ideas, as mentioned in the introduction, an Anthropocene ethics must acknowledge natural habitats more complexly as "interfactual, transcorporeal, and transmaterial,"[31] and as incorporating in/organic posthuman interventions.

Ingold's notion of meshworks also helps us to understand habitats and environments in more nuanced and fluid ways. His concept of meshworks is anchored in what he describes as an "animic ontology" in which "beings do not propel themselves across a ready-made world but rather issue forth through a world-in-formation, along the lines of their relationships."[32] Meshworks are thus highly context-dependent and always in flux. I align with Ingold's concept of meshworks specifically, although it is worth noting that his concept is also informed by and adapted from the biologist and animal behaviorist Jakob von Uexküll's earlier theory of the *Umwelt*.[33] With "meshworks," Ingold wishes to move beyond the more conventional notion of "a network of interacting entities," and instead argues for what he calls the "*meshwork* of entangled lines of life, growth and movement."[34] Such a meshwork, he says, "is the world we inhabit."[35] Drawing on anthropological and ecological perspectives, Ingold contends that "what is commonly known as the 'web of life' is precisely that: not a network of connected points, but a meshwork of interwoven lines."[36] In a meshwork, all of the interwoven lines describe "a flow of material substance" in "topologically fluid" environments.[37] Subsequently, all organisms, human and more-than-human, "should be understood not as a bounded entity surrounded by an environment but as an unbounded entanglement of lines" in fluid environments.[38]

Gruen's concept of entangled empathy similarly suggests that our relationships with other animals constitute unbounded, entangled relationships, which take shape in ever-changing places and contexts. These relationships, these practices and places of wildlife rehabilitation, also arguably constitute ways of belonging in the world. Following Wright, I suggest that "through belonging, people may work with others, including more-than-humans, to generate new pathways in the future, to bring themselves and the world into being in new, more inclusive ways."[39] Practices of wildlife rehabilitation can help generate such new pathways, as we work alongside humans and with more-than-humans, as we generate new ways of becoming together in the Anthropocene.

Practices of wildlife rehabilitation and the artifacts that help foster an ethics of care constitute elemental meshworks that help work against binary thinking about our ways of being in the world. Such shelters and enclosures participate in and perform these relatively brief moments of elemental relationality. Wildlife rehabilitation is paradoxical in the ways that it prompts human caregivers to participate in relational and entangled practices that help perform a culture of gratitude and reciprocity.

What emerges during these moments of caregiving, through the interventions of human caregivers, entails a merging of plastics with plant matter—artificial environment with natural habitat—branches brought in from "outside" and refashioned into perches made to fit with and create the in/organic world in which healing can ideally occur. "Thick stone" and "restless water," harnessed momentarily to create small platforms, troughs, and areas in which to drink and bathe, help craft calm but powerful shelters for healing; thus, the elements participate in momentary, posthuman interventions into the natural world. To arrive at this point in our thought, discourse, and action—and in our anticipating the needs of the other—we must also be able to empathize. Ideas about empathy and elemental, meshworked relationships are not mutually exclusive. They are part and parcel of both wildlife rehabilitation and compassionate conservation, and they necessitate and signify a shift in our thinking about what I argue are *posthuman* interventions into ecosystems we share with our more-than-human kin.

## POSTHUMAN INTERVENTIONS, WILDLIFE REHABILITATION, AND A COMPASSIONATE CONSERVATION ETHIC

As described by the National Wildlife Rehabilitators Association, "the goal of wildlife rehabilitation is to provide professional care to sick, injured, and orphaned wild animals so ultimately they can be returned to their natural habitat."[40] Wildlife rehabilitation is grounded in a philosophy of empathetic and compassionate conservation, which relies on the principle of "do no harm," first and foremost, along with the notion that every animal body matters, and that the individual lives of animals must be taken into account in matters of conservation policy and practice. Compassionate conservation seeks to promote a critical awareness of how we understand our relationships with our more-than-human kin, and to foster an ethic of peaceful coexistence in which all wildlife is valued, and in which decision-making about conservation practice and policy is grounded in a consideration of the most compassionate choice for all beings.[41] Of course, this is easier said than done, and we may easily complicate the notion that conservation practice is still, at the end of the day, a mode of human intervention into the natural world, albeit one that works from a place of gratitude and generosity to remediate damage done, often as a result of humans in the first place.

Wildlife rehabilitators, too, seek to foster a critical awareness about human interactions with wildlife in everyday practice. And, like conservation practices, wildlife rehabilitation also entails some level of human intervention into the lives of our more-than-human kin. In my previous book, I complicated these ideas about human intervention and conservation practice, and argued for what I called "posthuman conservation." I extend these ideas here to consider how entangled empathy and elemental, meshworked relationships participate in compassionate conservation practices related more specifically to shelter and home.

Ideas about posthumanism and compassionate conservation stem from different disciplinary camps in the humanities (philosophy and literary theory) and the sciences (biology and ecology), respectively, but they are not incompatible. Broadly speaking, a posthuman perspective would call into question the anthropocentric notion that humans are to be privileged over all other forms of life. As I also described in the introduction, posthumanism tends to align with a more ecological perspective that favors simultaneous coexistence with other species and resists the notion that humans are at the center of any given context. That said, as human beings who reside on this planet, make use of its resources, and create and consume goods without always anticipating the various costs associated with that consumption, some posthumanist thinkers, myself included, would argue that we have an ethical responsibility to engage with critical awareness about those practices; moreover, they might argue that we would do well to step outside of our sometimes human-centric vantage point to consider the implications of our technological undertakings from a perspective that looks even farther beyond the realm of the human in accounting for our relationships with our more-than-human kin.[42]

To practice conservation in the Anthropocene—to engage in a more posthuman conservation ethic, can, working in the positive, help recover marginalized or less amplified voices by destabilizing human exceptionalism in ways that subsequently account for the needs of otherwise vulnerable, more-than-human species. However, as I have argued elsewhere, the trickiness is that to account for the needs of the other, we must also be mindful of truly acting in the best interests of that other, in the most compassionate ways possible, and to avoid pitfalls such as bias or other kinds of self-interest that result in further risk to vulnerable species.[43]

To imagine and practice a posthuman conservation ethic requires that we necessarily shift our perspective from the perceived best interests and outcomes for humans and human needs, to the perceived best interests and outcomes for the more-than-human kin with whom we share our worlds. To these ends, a posthuman conservation ethic would be guided not by hierarchical mechanisms of control or transcendent systems of values but rather by a mode of thinking and acting steeped in compassion and consideration for and a sense of ethical responsibility to the worlds and bodies that are very much a part of us, and with whom we are inextricably interconnected. Such a mindset is hardly novel to scholars like Bekoff, for example, who has argued that

> we owe it to all individual animals to make every attempt to come to a greater understanding and appreciation of who they are in their world and in ours. We must make kind and humane choices. . . . There's nothing to fear and much to gain by developing deep and reciprocal interactions with our fellow animals. Animals can teach us a great deal about responsibility, compassion, caring, forgiveness, and love.[44]

As I consider my own relationship with the fledging mockingbird whom I helped care for, I realize that this little bird has indeed taught me a great deal about empathetic, compassionate care, while also prompting me to consider both the affordances and limitations of such interventions.

The conundrum of intervention. On the one hand, it seems safe to speculate that this intervention ultimately saved this mockingbird's life. This human intervention into this one young bird's life, arguably and implicitly carried out from the vantage point of posthuman perspectives about coexisting with our more-than-human kin. On the other hand, as Gruen also points out, we must keep our own projections in check as we consider the challenges and nuances of empathetic care for our more-than-human kin.

As I write at this moment, for instance, my domesticated cat of thirteen years sits on my lap. He knows and trusts me. We have our daily routine, and we have our specific ways of communicating with each other. Those readers who do not share a home with a companion animal may think these points odd, but those who do will surely relate. In the interest of not overidealizing our relationship, I will note that my cat also steadfastly detests riding in the car for any reason; likewise, I would rather go to the dentist than drive this cat anywhere. During the times that I've had to bring him to the vet, which he also readily detests for reasons too numerous to name, I have been there with him. Here, however, following Gruen, I must also be careful not to project my own desires onto my companion animal.

Gruen rightly points out, for instance, that "those of us who live with animals or work directly with them usually know a lot about the animals we spend time with, but we also have to keep an eye on our projections."[45] She notes that because dogs, to which I would also add cats, "are prone to pick up on our emotions, it is likely that projection can turn into a cycle."[46] Thus, for instance, if I am nervous about bringing my cat to the vet, my cat will likely pick up on my anxiety and become anxious himself; perhaps, then, my cat's anxiety is, in fact, at least to some extent, an extension of my own, which further indicates another permutation of our entangled relationship. That said, despite the unpleasantness of these car trips, my cat knows that he will eventually return home with me, which nonetheless, unfortunately requires enduring another ride in the vehicle of disdain while in his loathsome carrier. But during these moments, because we do know each other so well, I can communicate with him in what Natasha Seegert might call more "animate" terms, and I do sense that he receives comfort knowing that I am there for him. I raise these points because I am also aware that this sense of mutual knowing and comfort seems different in the case of working with sick or injured wildlife who are necessarily less accustomed to interacting with human caregivers. This does not mean that the challenges of projection are absent in the case of our more-than-human kin who are not companion animals or well-known to us; rather, it means that the contexts around which projection happens are various and nuanced, and that these moments of relationality provide opportunities to explore the idea of communicating *with* "rather than *about* animals."[47] In fact, perhaps those human relationships with other animals that are shorter in duration or less ingrained over time simply provide additional opportunities for learning and critical awareness.

For instance, Gruen notes that to genuinely empathize, we must "focus carefully on and take account of the specific context of the other, their idiosyncratic desires and personality, and the processes that shaped who they are."[48] This kind of position requires being open-minded to "learning and gathering information across differences," as well as a "commitment to critical reflection, and ideally consultation with people who have experience with and knowledge of the life-worlds of specific others."[49] Such openness to accounting for the specific context of the other, and an interest in learning about the processes that shaped who they are, helps work against projection and also anthropomorphization. I would add here that to be mindful about avoiding projection is also compatible with a posthuman conservation ethic.

In the case of both anthropomorphizing and projection—a variant of anthropomorphization—the focus is more on understanding the more-than-human other in terms of qualities or characteristics that are familiar or applicable to our own selves; in other words, anthropomorphization involves "the interpretation of what is not human or personal in terms of human or personal characteristics."[50] Some scholars have suggested that anthropomorphizing can provide an opportunity, or at least a starting point, for more closely identifying with more-than-human others, in that "we at first may see only a world in our own image," but what follows from that initial vision can offer myriad distinct variations and possibilities for connection.[51] Gruen, however, cautions that in the more nuanced case of projection specifically, the outcome tends to be less productive because projection can result in the needs of the other not being met, in favor of what wittingly or unwittingly makes the caregiver more comfortable on some level. In this way, to be aware of the challenges of projection resonates with the tenets of a posthuman conservation ethic, in which our attention is focused on better understanding the needs and vantage points of our more-than-human kin.

Gruen emphasizes that we must not become complacent in our assumptions or potential biases around even the most compassionate and altruistic of interventions, and that "being able to answer questions about the specific other with whom one is empathizing can help minimize the dangers of projection as well as the various biases that tend to be associated with empathy."[52] In handling the mockingbird with the ruptured air sac, for instance, I mustn't assume that just because I work quickly, I will avoid making the bird nervous or uncomfortable. A quick process is best, but it must also be carried out with the intention of compassion rather than complacency.

I cannot necessarily assume that this young mockingbird knows that my wildlife colleagues and I are there to help in the first place. Does this fledgling creature understand or sense human kindness? Surely, I cannot make such an assumption, although I do believe that our more-than-human kin do, on some level, perceive altruism, or attempts at altruism, and that they do communicate with us.[53] Moreover, as wildlife rehabilitator Ben Kilham has noted through his work with black bears in New Hampshire, such species will often display altruistic behavior toward each other.[54] The case of wildlife rehabilitation is tricky, however, precisely because we want to avoid habituation. We must try, then, to let go of bias and attachment, and make a concerted effort to empathize without projecting; this requires an arguably more nuanced and relational commitment to learning about and listening to our more-than-human kin, while knowing that we are making what seem the most compassionate choices possible in a given context.

By early July, the young mockingbird continues to progress in its healing. Its air sac has healed and it has been eating well. It now has the strength and stamina necessary to be moved to one of the larger, outdoor aviaries. Here, the mockingbird will learn to more fully forage on its own, and it will need to fly on a regular basis in order to retrieve food and water. It will also reacclimate to spending twenty-four hours a day outside, in its closer-to-natural habitat.

These enclosures, from the smaller, indoor baskets to the larger, outdoor aviaries are but temporary places of healing for these vulnerable species. For this young mockingbird, the wildlife center became a prescribed but unintended and relatively minor detour that eventually enables its recovery and allows it to resume its life unabated in its natural habitat.

The mockingbird arrived here because it had been cat-caught—an unfortunate but common injury for young songbirds; however, wildlife centers often care for animals that are victims of oil spills and natural disasters like wildfires. No matter the reason, however, the wildlife center constitutes a material and discursive manifestation of empathetic and elemental engagement with our surroundings; it is arguably a form of posthuman intervention born out of a caring ethic whose goal is to avoid projection and function from the vantage point of posthuman, compassionate conservation.

These enclosures are the material workings and places of compassionate conservation; they participate in and perform these relatively brief moments of elemental relationality. They are empathetic, posthuman interventions into a world shared with our more-than-human kin. I am aware that in situating the wildlife center as a posthuman intervention into the lives of our more-than-human kin, I am perhaps balancing on the edge of projection myself—putting my own, human-centric presumption on this place—this elemental, meshworked environment.

## DWELLING PLACE AS EMPATHETIC POSTHUMAN INTERVENTION

As I write about places like wildlife rehabilitation centers, while simultaneously questioning what counts as "home" in the Anthropocene, I am drawn to Ingold's notion of *dwelling,* which allows for an understanding of the wildlife center and its attendant aviaries and enclosures as a manifestation of empathetic engagement with our surroundings. Ingold's "dwelling perspective" draws upon and extends philosopher Martin Heidegger's juxtaposition of building and dwelling.[55] Ingold describes, for instance, that to understand a building as architecture is to presume more simply that "built form is the manifest outcome of prior design."[56] The notion of dwelling, on the other hand, "is intransitive: it is about the way inhabitants, singly and together, produce their own lives, and like life, it carries on. Critically, then, dwelling is not merely the occupation of structures already built."[57] Rather, "the forms humans build, whether in the imagination or on the ground, arise within the currents of their involved activity, in the specific relational contexts of their practical engagement with their surroundings."[58] Wildlife centers are indeed posthuman interventions—manifestations of empathetic, compassionate activity that arise out of specific relational, elemental contexts. More than a structure, a wildlife center is a place of compassionate conservation—an elemental and empathetic, yet paradoxical dwelling place for our vulnerable, more-than-human kin.

## NO SMALL FEAT AND NO SMALL STORY: NARRATIVE AS PART OF AN ENVIRONMENTAL MESHWORKS

By the end of July, the young mockingbird is deemed strong enough to survive on its own and is ready to be released back to its native habitat. For these past few months, this fledging bird has been able to heal and mature such that it can ideally make its way in the world and thrive on its own. It is important to note that not every story of wildlife work ends on such a relatively positive note, and that even these shorter-term "success" stories are not necessarily "easy." I have chosen to wind down this narrative about the mockingbird at the point of its release back to its natural habitat, but this is hardly the end of this bird's story; in fact, one might argue that the mockingbird's release marks the start of a new, hopefully even longer story. It will need to make its own way in the world, where it will hopefully thrive and avoid harm—this is no small feat for a young bird. That said, from the vantage point of wildlife rehabilitation work, this story does constitute a relative success, and I suggest that these "successful" rehabilitations and releases reveal possibilities for compassionate coexistence grounded in an ethic of empathetic care, in settings that, to the greatest extent possible, take into consideration the needs and individual lives of vulnerable, more-than-human kin. Moreover, perhaps these various points of interconnection with the individual lives of our feathered kin, from the point of "intake" to "successful release," for instance, also help humans build empathy by allowing us to better understand, for better or worse, the challenges that our more-than-human kin face in a world so inhabited by humans.

Such moments then illustrate how it is possible to engage with entangled empathy in the practice of a posthuman conservation ethic, and to participate in a culture of reciprocity. Stories of wildlife rehabilitation such as this one reveal posthuman interventions that are compassionate, participatory, elemental, and empathetic. Storytelling and narrative are necessary components of understanding these environmental meshworks—these empathetic, entangled, elemental relationships. Narrative gives shape to knowledge and can help generate meaning and ideas as it engages the imagination. As Cohen suggests, "within this complicated cosmos, then, we must through narrative and other kinds of action foster ethical relations" among humans and other animals, matter, and environments alike: "multifold, hesitant, consequence-minded interconnections that thicken, fructify, and affirm. Narrative is the intermediary by virtue of which these environmental meshworks, mangles and networks are articulated, documented, vitalized."[59] Cohen argues that we must "compose our stories and our ethics not *from* the elements," as though the elements were passive or "inert," but rather "with them (as agency-exerting partners possessed of unsounded depths and innate dignity)."[60] These enclosures, these temporary dwelling places, then participate in the relational, elemental practices of empathetic care for our vulnerable, more-than-human kin.

At a moment when we are seeing increased numbers of wildlife coming into contact with humans following events like wildfires and other natural disasters, and increased development of natural habitats and ecosystems, it is becoming increasingly necessary that we evaluate the nature of our relationships with vulnerable species and how we understand our responsibilities to them. As I described earlier, the fledgling mockingbird arrived at the wildlife center because it had been cat-caught—a generally more common injury for young songbirds that nonetheless ought not to be minimized for its relative frequency of occurrence. But such stories and narratives only become more complex from there. Again, injuries or illnesses sustained from wildfires or oil spills become more challenging not only in terms of the complexity and duration of care, but also in terms of the range of professionals and resources needed to consult and assist in these scenarios—issues this book will address in subsequent chapters.

This chapter has revealed how the artifacts that compose home and shelter can help illustrate and articulate the many possible constellations of elemental relationships that participate in the environmental meshworks in which our in/organic entanglements with the material world take shape. Specifically, it has shown how the practices of wildlife rehabilitation participate in such environmental meshworks and a culture of reciprocity in ways that can help foster more ethical relations with our worlds. But we need not stop here. As the habitats we share with other vulnerable species are in a constant state of flux, we must continue to think critically about what counts as home, and for whom. We must continue to think critically about the everyday practices that shape and constitute empathetic coexistence with other animals. And we must continue to think critically and empathetically about how we might coexist compassionately with our more-than-human kin in a time of climate crisis.

In chapter 2, for instance, I will first describe some recent responses to increasing mountain lion sightings, in different contexts, in areas of California and the Pacific Northwest. I will consider how our communicative practices can shape ideas about what counts as home in the Anthropocene. In the specific context of the displacements that happen to our more-than-human kin, increasingly due to climate change and natural disasters, I consider what kinds of encounters become possible when we respond not with fear and reactivity but with generosity and empathy—from a mindset that understands encounters with our more-than-human kin as gifts that we may receive and reciprocate in kind.

## CHAPTER 2

# Fire-Lost and Trying to Cross

To be native to a place we must learn to speak its language.
—Robin Wall Kimmerer, *Braiding Sweetgrass*

*She had wandered off course a couple of days ago. At first, the smoke intuitively prompted her to leave her den; she would keep heading away from the smoke. But then the sound of the helicopters had also spooked her, and so she kept wandering. Away from smoke, away from noise, but not necessarily toward food or water.*

•

The stretch of time from winter 2017 through the summer of 2018 constituted a particularly long and drawn-out fire season for California and the Pacific Northwest. In mid-July 2018, only about six months after the Thomas Fire ravaged central California in December 2017, and as the Carr Fire and the Mendocino Complex Fire burned in northern California, a lightning storm sparked several wildfires throughout southern Oregon. Two of these Oregon wildfires, the Taylor Creek Fire and the Klondike Fire, would eventually merge to become a "megafire."[1]

It seems safe to speculate that the term "megafire" is still relatively new for many readers; it is, at least, a fairly new term in my own personal lexicon. For Oregonians, however, the summer of 2018 marked the second year in a row that large wildfires had merged to form a megafire in the state. A megafire, as defined by the National Interagency Fire Center, is a fire that burns at least 100,000 acres.[2]

47

By late August 2018, these two fires had grown so large, with the Taylor Fire at over 50,000 acres and the Klondike Fire at about 68,000 acres, that they were divided into two separate management zones. By September 2018, the two fires had set a record, surpassing the acreage burned during Oregon's Chetco Bar Fire in 2017. The Klondike Fire had burned 140,232 acres and the Taylor Creek Fire had burned 52,839 acres, for a combined mega-total of 193,071 acres.[3]

The Taylor Creek and Klondike Fires merged near an area called Grants Pass, about an hour or so northwest of Ashland, Oregon. Ashland, one of Oregon's more well-known cities, is only about a half hour north of California's northern border. Ashland is located near the Cascade-Siskiyou National Monument (CSNM), which marks the crossroads of the Cascade, Klamath, and Siskiyou mountain ranges in southwest Oregon and northwest California. The monument is also considered a "landscape corridor designed to protect habitat and migration and dispersal routes for wildlife moving between the Cascade and Siskiyou mountain ranges."[4] This region of southern Oregon comprises over 10,000 acres of forest and grasslands, and the National Monument was established in 2000 to recognize and protect the region's unique ecological gifts. That is to say, the Department of the Interior references the area's diverse range "of biological, geological, aquatic, archeological, and historic *resources*," including songbirds, small mammals, deer, bears, and mountain lions.[5] However, following Kimmerer, I would encourage a reading that understands such resources, instead, as *earthly gifts*.[6]

As teams worked to contain the Taylor Creek and Klondike megafire, they were largely able to keep flames away from highways and other major routes such as Bear Camp Road, which is "a critical route that allows faster shuttles on the iconic 34-mile 'wild' section of the Rogue River," and an important throughway for recreation and tourism related to the Grants Pass economy.[7]

•

*She wasn't really following the path of the Rogue River anymore, and she was wandering farther from her home range each day.*

•

Containment of these fires was of critical importance for various and obvious reasons, and media outlets often understandably pointed to protection of local economies as a primary concern. As one local citizen commented: "Fires aren't something that are new to us, but when they get this close they threaten not only our community but our livelihood as well."[8] The threat of these fires to the local community is a point that I would obviously never contest; rather, in continuing to think about entangled empathy, I would simply extend the idea of "community" to more broadly and fluidly encompass humans *and* all wildlife.

Though wildlife are not generally privy to being directly quoted in media outlets, their voices emerge in such narratives in other unique ways, and their actions speak volumes when it comes to understanding the impacts of these natural disasters on their lives and livelihoods, as well as our own. To be mindful of the voices of our more-than-human kin provides an opportunity to learn and even speak the language of another. From such a vantage point, every encounter with our more-than-human kin may be understood as a gift that bears reciprocating. With these ideas in mind, to be at home in the Anthropocene means being receptive to the languages of our more-than-human kin. It means engaging more fully in policy- and decision-making that accounts for the well-being of wildlife, that helps foster entangled empathy, and that is rooted in a culture of gratitude and a "gift" mindset. Again, as biologist and Indigenous studies scholar Robin Wall Kimmerer describes, when we are mindful of the language spoken by a place and all its kin, we can truly be at home in a place.[9]

•

*She had grown up in this fire-prone ecosystem and was good at escaping fire. She knew how to do that. But she was also thirsty and in need of temporary shelter.*

•

For better or worse, fires are a natural part of the landscape in the western United States, and wildlife have long been dealing with fire in these regions.[10] How wildlife respond to fire and other natural disturbances depends on many variables, such as the species and age of the animal, the type of event, and how extreme that event might be. Not surprisingly, many kinds of wildlife will instinctively tend to move or fly away from smoke and flames, or in some cases even burrow underground to escape perceived danger. Amphibians and other small creatures, for instance, "will burrow into the ground, hide out in logs, or take cover under rocks," while other animals may seek refuge in streams and other bodies of water.[11]

On the one hand, it is relatively comforting to know that wildlife who live in these "fire-prone ecosystems" have evolved to deal with fire, and "will use their keen senses (such as hearing, smell, and sight) to escape fire." The US Fish and Wildlife Service has similarly reported that it is "uncommon for large mammals to die in wildfires and [they] do not need help escaping fire."[12] Sadly, though, some animals will not survive in smoke and fire if they are not fast enough or can't find shelter. Younger and smaller "animals are particularly at risk in a wildfire. And some of their strategies for escape might not work— a koala's natural instinct to crawl up into a tree, for example, may leave it trapped," as we saw during the recent wildfires in Australia.[13]

Any kind of habitat destruction that prompts species such as bears, coyotes, bobcats, and mountain lions to flee their territory in search of safety will likely result in the "temporary displacement" of these animals.[14] These displaced creatures, or "those that have lost their homes, will temporarily seek out food and shelter in non-affected areas, including both rural and urban areas."[15]

•

*It was late July, still relatively early in the movement of the nearby Taylor Creek and Klondike Fires, when an Oregon woman returned home to find a mountain lion napping quietly behind her couch.*

## FIRE-LOST

To be "fire-lost" refers to the displacement encountered by wildlife who leave their home territories or ranges when they perceive danger from smoke or fire; they often subsequently wander off-course and find themselves closer to areas of human habitation.[16]

•

*She was thirsty and had needed a rest—just a brief respite from the fires. She was fire-lost.*

•

Thirsty and looking for water, this mountain lion had discovered and taken a drink from the fountain outside this Oregon resident's home, and then unwittingly wandered into the home through the open front door.[17] With so many plants and flowers both outside and inside the home, this tired and displaced creature may not have even discerned the difference between indoors and outdoors when she wandered through the front door. As the homeowner noted in one media article: "The door was open and the room has huge plants [and] stairs built around real tree branches, so she likely didn't even realize she was walking indoors until she was inside."[18] And why would she, necessarily?

•

*There was water. It was quiet and she did not perceive danger. She merely continued on the path that felt safe.*

•

In this moment, the lives of two creatures, mountain lion and human, overlap—become inadvertently entangled. What follows suit is an unlikely opportunity for the kind of "exchange of intentional energy between humans and other animals" that Plec's internatural communication helps account for, and empathetic engagement from which we may all learn.[19] With this merging of places and habitats comes an unwitting posthuman intervention that provides an extended moment both elemental and relational: an opportunity to reciprocate the gift of a beautiful encounter, and to practice conscious, entangled empathy. This moment is composed of interwoven lives, lively practices, and communication in which, as Ingold reminds us, all animals and life-forms "should be understood not as a bounded entity surrounded by an environment," but as an unbounded meshwork of fluid environments.[20] At the same time, the elemental moment that this merging of environments allows for reflects a tension in how we try to reconcile what it means to belong in these places. We must not forget the overarching context here, which is that this mountain lion is weary and fire-lost; she is seeking a reprieve from the impacts of a climate crisis that is, in essence, due largely to anthropogenic forces. These encounters are paradoxical, in that they constitute manifestations of our climate crisis, as much as they also provide an opportunity to engage in a language of animacy. We may choose, then, what to make of these moments; this scenario is just one such example.

If we understand this moment of elemental relationality—this unwitting posthuman intervention in which lives, bodies, places, matter, and languages intersect, as an opportunity to engage in what Kimmerer calls a language or "grammar of animacy," then we may arguably explore a more recuperative aspect of this context. A grammar of animacy, as Kimmerer describes it, could move us closer to recognizing and honoring modes of communication other than our own; it would be receptive to more subtle kinds of nonverbal cues, communications, and energies that frequently but sometimes unnoticeably or ineffably take place among species other than humans, and even between humans and other species.

In this way, a grammar of animacy offers a more mindful and empathetic approach to conceptualizing our relationships with our more-than-human kin, and can illuminate "new ways of living in the world, other species a sovereign people, a world with a democracy of species, not a tyranny of one."[21] A grammar of animacy also implies what Kimmerer refers to as an "indigenous worldview," in which, as she describes, we may view the ecosystem not as "a machine," but rather as "a community of sovereign beings, subjects rather than objects."[22]

Moreover, as mentioned earlier, views of posthumanism that are ecologically informed and grounded in an ethic of entangled empathy for all life-forms are not incompatible with the Indigenous worldview that Kimmerer describes. And as Jennifer Clary-Lemon reminds us, scholars who study rhetoric and communication "may or may be not be shocked to note that a holistic ontology and an emphasis on the non-rational, the embodied, the affective, or the power of things not only resonates with Indigenous knowledge, but it is emerging from it directly in non-attributed ways."[23] Such an alignment not only adds depth and richness to how we may conceptualize our relationships with our more-than-human kin, but also, to Clary-Lemon's point, these resonances can work toward "unseat[ing] the colonial attitude that to invoke Indigenous ways of knowing is to place Indigenous people within the realm of the past, the shamanistic, the mystical instead of the present, the political, the rhetorical, the material."[24] These resonances between aspects of posthumanism and an Indigenous worldview may also help create a fuller picture of the range of perspectives that can inform our relationships with places and how we understand our participation in the projects of human development. Such perspectives can then work together in ways that are culturally and ecologically beneficial for all life-forms.

•

*The energy shifted and the lion realized there was another unfamiliar creature in close proximity. There was a loud noise, and with no easy exit in sight, she hid as best she could and went back to sleep. For she was still so tired.*

•

Once the mountain lion realized she was inside, as the homeowner described, "she immediately tried to leave through a closed window" and became frightened when somebody screamed, thus prompting the lion to then hide behind the sofa. After that point, she settled down again and went to sleep.[25] The woman generously allowed the mountain lion to continue sleeping behind her couch for about six more hours, while she remained outside until just before dawn.[26]

With an exhausted mountain lion sleeping behind her couch, the homeowner was now faced with the prospect of how to best handle the situation. How she then describes communicating with and ultimately prompting the mountain lion to exit her home not only implicitly values the principles of compassionate conservation and entangled empathy, but also arguably draws upon the grammar of animacy for which Kimmerer advocates. In doing so, this homeowner clearly empathizes with the mountain lion; moreover, she implicitly understands this encounter as an opportunity to engage peacefully and respectfully with this creature:

> When she was so quiet and it was obvious from the position of her feet on the wall that she was laying down, I went outside to see through the window what she was doing. She was sleeping! When I made noise, she woke up and looked startled so I consciously raised my frequency, gazed lovingly into her eyes, and communicated using feline-speak eye blinking to calm her. It was amazing to realize that this worked. I gazed lovingly then blinked hard and then she did it back! Then, she went back to sleep.[27]

•

*This was a new environment that the lion did not recognize, and the energy was different, but she was not scared by the presence of this other creature. She felt at ease, and was comfortable enough to go back to sleep.*

•

While it is relatively uncommon to hear of humans communicating with other animals such as mountain lions by using nonverbal cues like "slow-blinking," such a communicative approach is not as outlandish as some might think. There has been much documentation and discussion among veterinarians and animal behavior specialists about how cats recognize slow eye-blinking as a sign of friendliness, as opposed to aggression.[28] In fact, those readers who share a home with a domesticated feline companion and who have tried to calmly and intentionally "slow-blink" to their cats may happily discover that their companion returns the gesture in kind.

By learning and practicing this basic tenet of feline-speak, we may engage on an entirely new communicative, more "animate" plane with our companion species and our "wild," more-than-human kin. Again, as Seegert describes, an animate approach to communication "explores the prospect of speaking *to* rather than *about* animals. Animate rhetoric allows for the possibility that everything *might* be speaking. It is not claiming that everything is speaking or that it is speaking to us, merely that there is the *possibility*."[29] An animate approach to communication, she says, "opens up the space of opportunity for an encounter with animal others rather than shutting it off or forcing them to speak in human terms."[30] This kind of animate communication is arguably one mode of engaging more empathetically with our more-than-human kin—of "being able to understand what another being feels, sees, and thinks, and to understand what they might need or desire," as Gruen reminds us.[31]

## ENTANGLED EMPATHY AS CO-EMERGENT MOMENTS OF BELONGING

Entangled empathy, as Gruen describes, is concerned with "another's experiential wellbeing." This kind of empathy tends to lead to action based on an assessment of what seems to be the best, or most compassionate, choice, in helping to pursue the well-being of another.[32] In this moment, there exists an opportunity to give back to a struggling community of wildlife—an opportunity for empathetic engagement with our more-than-human kin. Here, the homeowner recognizes both the lion's exhaustion and need for rest, as well as the need for this creature to eventually exit her home. Her home has thus become a temporary shelter for this displaced creature, and, as such, a complex site of belonging. For this Oregon resident, home has just taken on new meaning—it has become imbued with new possibilities for comfort and care. Home in this instance is a "site for establishing and producing connections that encourage a sense of belonging," where she and the mountain lion act upon each other "as relationally co-constituted beings that co-emerge together" in this moment of understanding.[33] In this way, home "is both a place/physical location and a set of feelings. . . . It is both material and imaginative, a site and a set of meanings/emotions. Home is a material dwelling and it is also an affective space, shaped by emotions and feelings of belonging."[34] And as Kimmerer writes, "to become native to this place, if we are to survive here, and our neighbors too, our work is to learn to speak the grammar of animacy, so that we might truly be at home."[35] Being open to a grammar of animacy, then, is one step toward learning and practicing entangled empathy, engaging in relationally co-constituted, emergent moments of belonging, and acting with compassion in our encounters with vulnerable species. To be at home in the Anthropocene thus means being receptive to a language of animacy as we engage empathetically with our more-than-human kin.

As dawn approached, the woman acknowledged that it was time for the lion to be on her way; she wanted to prompt the lion to leave without alarming her.[36] Notably, she managed to prompt the mountain lion to exit her home with a peaceful intervention that again draws upon compassion, empathy, and a language of animacy. The woman described creatively visualizing the lion exiting her home and heading back into the hills by imagining or picturing "routes out of the house via open doors and the route out the backyard, across the creek, through an open field, and back up into the hills."[37] Then, as the homeowner weighed the possible options for prompting the lion to exit her home, she and her housemates also drew on an approach that involved peaceful, nonviolent communication. After opening some more doors, they "started lightly tapping a drum from a safe vantage point at the top of the stairs."[38] The homeowner then used "her energy to coax the wild cat out of her home."[39] The mountain lion seemed receptive to this communicative gesture—one that implicitly performs entangled empathy and that values a language of animacy.

At that point, the lion woke up and seemed to know what to do; she exited the home through the open doors and headed out through the yard, as the homeowner had hoped.[40] And with this peaceful intervention, the creature was soon on her way. The homeowner successfully prompted the mountain lion to exit her home through the empathetic and animate use of nonverbal communication and drumming. The use of drumming in particular is a variation on the theme of what departments of fish and wildlife typically recommend in the event of a mountain lion sighting: stay calm, avoid running, and make loud noises. Through this mode of relational, nonverbal, animate communication, the homeowner sought to convey to the lion that she intended not harm but rather assistance. To be mindful of the different languages of animacy is a worthy and necessary part of any posthuman, empathetic engagement with our more-than-human kin—such communication about relationship is something from which we may all learn.

## ENTANGLED EMPATHY AS PEACEFUL COMMUNICATION AND A LANGUAGE OF ANIMACY

Many species, human and more-than-human alike, make use of sound and rhythm to communicate in various ways, for various purposes. Communication scholar Byron Hawk looks at how sound functions in the musical composing process; he is particularly interested in the different objects that factor into how music is organized, such as the recording technologies that capture "the science of sound waves" or "the mathematics of pitch." For Hawk, music is a set of "performative acts" that also require "participatory modes of listening."[41] He draws on David Byrne's recent book, *How Music Works*, when describing that how music functions depends very much on the context in which it is made, performed, and received; the reception of music depends in part on "what surrounds it, where you hear it and when you hear it."[42] Hawk recounts, for instance, that some "African drums and complex polyrhythms work perfectly in open outdoor spaces but would become indistinguishable noise in a larger, reverberating hall."[43] He writes that "music doesn't progress technically or in terms of complexity; it evolves and adapts to fit material conditions and sonic spaces, which include technologies and audiences."[44] I would add that these material conditions and sonic spaces may include and account for audiences both human and more-than-human; this latter point is meant to be more in dialogue with Hawk's ideas than an extension of them, per se.

In this case, the context and space in which the drumming happened seems central to the successful outcome of this communicative scenario. The woman's use of drumming and rhythm as a mode of communication is meant to strike a balance between not causing alarm on the one hand, but sending a message that creates enough of a disturbance to prompt the lion to exit, on the other hand. While the woman's drumming is a peaceful and nonviolent invitation to exit, other species use drumming and rhythm as a means to gain attention, or to present an invitation for a mate to stay.

When we are attentive to a grammar of animacy across species, we see that many species make use of rhythm and music to communicate about place, shelter, safety, danger, and matters of home, in a variety of ways and toward different ends. In the conclusion of *Visualizing Posthuman Conservation*, for example, I described the palm cockatoo of northern Australia's use of sticks and natural objects to "drum regular rhythms."[45] In doing so, they are the only known more-than-human animal to combine the two skills of sound production and tool use to create musical compositions.[46] Palm cockatoos mate for life; they can survive between forty and sixty years in the wild, and up to ninety years in captivity.[47] The male's drumming ritual is thus not only a vital part of this species' ability to thrive but also an embodied practice that is intimately connected with place-making and relationship. The birds use sticks and seedpods to create musical rhythms in order to impress potential mates, and "even have their own signature cadences," or musical styles.[48] A rhetorically successful musical composition would then result in courtship and breeding—an invitation not to exit but to be there for the long haul.

In both cases, that of the mountain lion and the palm cockatoo, drumming reveals a language of animacy that plays a role in these creatures' lively experiences as living beings in the world. The drumming helps weave a narrative and a context for specific, attentive, and conscious ways of *being there*. In this way, as anthropologist Thom Van Dooren reminds us, "place" is not an abstract entity but rather something that is "nested and interwoven with layers of attention and meaning."[49] Moreover, the story of this displaced mountain lion and her encounter with the Oregon homeowner reveals the ways that these two beings were able to story their place together, or create a sense of storied place, through their shared experience of *being there, in place*, at this singular, challenging moment of climate crisis. In this context, the homeowner implicitly recognizes and respects both the mountain lion's vulnerability and the need for the creature to move on, and the lion seems receptive to the communicative gesture. As Susan McHugh describes, "certain engagements with narrative configure people and animals as working together to do things that do not add up to a sum of individual efforts."[50] As such, these engagements with our shared places and ecosystems invite us to think more critically about animate communication and how we and our more-than-human kin story our places together.

## THE ENCOUNTER AS PARADOXICAL GIFT

To understand the use of drumming as an invitation to exit also helps us to understand species as "flight ways," as Van Dooren invites us to do. The mountain lion's need to move on emphasizes "the 'embodied temporality' of species," which, in this case, we may understand as related to the displacement wrought by wildfires.[51] That is, even though the lion showed "clear signs of being comfortable in [the] home," the homeowner was confident that the creature was in flux and just passing through. As one media article reiterated: "There have been wildfires in the area recently, and it's likely that's what pushed her to wander into the neighborhood."[52] The wildfires had, paradoxically, prompted not only the lion's displacement but also what we may perhaps understand as the gift of this temporary encounter.

As the homeowner described, "It was a perfect ending to a *blessed encounter* that could have been dangerous if approached from a lower frequency [of energy]. May she stay safely in the hills to enjoy a long life as a wild and healthy lion."[53] The homeowner's reference here to the mountain lion's visit as a "blessed encounter" is significant for how we might understand our relationships with our more-than-human kin. This perspective is also aligned with Kimmerer's own understanding of the world as full of gifts to be discovered.

Not unlike the wildlife center, the home of this Oregon resident is a safe place for the mountain lion, but it is not a permanent home. Home is still in flux for this vulnerable creature, and the solution is, as yet, only partial. Nonetheless, this homeowner has done what she can to provide the gift of a dwelling place, a temporary shelter, at a challenging time. We may consider, then, that in return for the gift of what the homeowner understands to be this "blessed encounter," she was willing and able to reciprocate with the gift of safe, temporary shelter.

Kimmerer describes how, when picking wild strawberries for her father's birthday, she first had the experience of understanding the world as "full of gifts simply scattered at your feet."[54] Moreover, it was this encounter with picking these wild berries that gave her a sense of place and purpose in the world: "It was the wild strawberries, beneath dewy leaves on an almost-summer morning, who gave me my sense of the world, my place in it."[55] While she describes the idea of the world as "full of gifts" in a slightly different context, her ideas may easily apply to our encounters with our more-than-human kin as well, and so I borrow from and extend them here. For instance, Kimmerer writes:

> A gift comes to you through no action of your own, free, having moved toward you without your beckoning. It is not a reward; you cannot earn it, or call it to you, or even deserve it. And yet it appears. Your only role is to be open-eyed and present. Gifts exist in a realm of humility and mystery—as with random acts of kindness we do not know their source.[56]

If we wanted to unpack and apply these ideas more literally or directly in the case of encounter between the Oregon woman and the mountain lion, we could reasonably make the point that, in this case, we technically *do* know the circumstances prompting the encounter: the wildfires were, as mentioned above, paradoxically the catalyst that prompted the gift of this temporary encounter. However, perhaps we need not go so far with such a literal interpretation.

Rather, taken more fluidly, and understood with more nuance, we may understand the fires as likely having prompted many species to flee, but this *one* mountain lion, in this instance, wandered into this Oregon woman's home without her beckoning. And how wonderfully fortunate for this displaced lion to have happened across such an empathetic and generous human in this time of need. Conversely, how fortunate for this woman to have had the opportunity to engage with this creature—to be open-eyed and present—to engage in peaceful communication and contribute to the lion's well-being and perhaps even save her life. For, when this mountain lion arrived at the Oregon woman's home, she was thirsty—likely dehydrated—and exhausted.

Clary-Lemon suggests that "when we acknowledge gift-relations with non-human others, we are also forced into contemplative relationships with the suffering of those others—both human and more-than-human—advanced from a language of capitalism and a history of colonialism: with genocide, with extinction of species and languages, with a rapidly changing climate—all that we have inherited as a part of being-with."[57] The ability of the Oregon homeowner to provide this gift of water and shelter in this creature's time of need is really a reciprocation that began when the mountain lion gifted this woman with such a "blessed encounter" that paradoxically happened in the context of one vulnerable creature's suffering, and one compassionate human's ability to engage empathetically with this creature. Moreover, the woman was able to share her experience of this encounter with local and social media, and in doing so, implicitly promote an approach to empathetic, compassionate encounters with wildlife. In many ways, then, this encounter was a gift for many more than just the woman and the mountain lion.

This story allows us to imagine a world where encounters with our wild kin may be viewed as gifts that we humans may reciprocate. We see what kinds of encounters become possible when, in a world where wildlife are increasingly displaced due to climate change and other anthropogenic forces, we respond not with fear and reactivity but with generosity, animacy, and empathy.

The connections, then, between entangled empathy and the gift are perhaps in the giving back—in the reciprocity—in the ability to understand the needs of the other and to be able to help provide for those needs in the moment. In this particular scenario, it is the ability to give the gift of water and shelter—a brief respite from the fires—and to engage in a language of animacy such that the invitation to move on is presented with care and consideration. This is a moment where entangled empathy arguably aligns with an Indigenous worldview that understands the ecosystem as a community of beings, all equally deserving of compassion and respect. Entangled empathy and an Indigenous worldview likewise create room for understanding such encounters as reciprocal gifts: the gift of the "blessed encounter," as the homeowner puts it, and the ability to reciprocate with a generosity of spirit that does not respond in fear, but rather in kindness, understanding, and peaceful communication in this moment of elemental relationality, through the ability to provide water and shelter in a moment of need.

Gruen writes that empathy "recognizes connection with and understanding of the circumstances of the other."[58] And in juxtaposing Kimmerer's ideas with Gruen's, I would add that a language of animacy is part of that connection; it is one step toward learning and practicing entangled empathy, and acting with compassion in our encounters with vulnerable species. To be at home in the Anthropocene, in this context, thus means being receptive to the many languages of our more-than-human kin. It means engaging in decision-making and a language of animacy that helps foster entangled empathy and starts from a "gift" mindset.

We may ask, then: What might environmental policy and conservation projects look like when approached from a more empathetic and generous vantage point—if more encounters with wildlife were understood as gifts to be received and reciprocated in productive, animate ways, however that may be defined, given the context? What if we approached *all* projects of compassionate conservation from such a "gift" mindset? The gift of respite; the gift of water and of rest; the gift of having room to roam and the space to find one's way?

●

*EMERGENCY NOTIFICATION*

*UCSB Alerts (Do Not Reply) alert@alert.ucsb.edu*
*Tuesday, September 17, 4:48 PM*
*UC Santa Barbara*

*A mountain lion was spotted on campus at Campus Point near the lagoon and service road turnaround. Police are in the area. Avoid area until further notice. California Fish and Wildlife have been called to respond. Update will be provided when information is available.*

●

It is a Tuesday afternoon in mid-September, and the solar glare bounces off the ocean during that part of the day when sunglasses are an imperative in central California. It is the end of a busy workday at the start of a busy week. Many UCSB employees are getting ready to leave the office and walk to nearby parking lots and bus stops. Students are leaving campus for the day, and many head to the gym or to their part-time and work-study jobs. It is not surprising that a text message and email alert such as the one just issued, and shown above, would unnerve the campus community and invoke a fear response in relation to this sighting—not exactly a gift mindset.

My phone lights up with text messages from friends and colleagues: "Oh no! Did you see this??! Should we go out?? Do you think it's safe?? ☹"

I am somewhat more concerned for the lion: "Ohh, the poor lion . . . she is probably scared . . . they are probably coming closer to campus because so much of their territory was burned during the fires. Poor thing. I don't think mtn lion wants to bother anyone . . . I think it's probably okay to go outside. Oh, I hope people will leave her alone . . . 😔"

"Yeah, you're right . . . mtn lion is probably lost! I hope nobody hurts her . . . Hope teaching went well!"

Between September 17 and October 8, 2019, there were five reported mountain lion sightings around the University of California Santa Barbara (UCSB) campus where I work. In each instance, UCSB sent out a text message and email "emergency alert," or "emergency update," to keep members of the campus community apprised of the latest information. Some of these alerts also included information from the California Department of Fish and Wildlife (CDFW) about how to best coexist with mountain lions. The Tuesday afternoon message was the first of several that were issued by UCSB, either to provide updates, or in this case, to report a sighting.

Along the eastern edge of campus, at a point where a singular span of scenic vista affords a panoramic view of both Campus Point Beach and the neighboring Lagoon Island, and in an area frequented by students, surfers, and other visitors to campus, a mountain lion had been seen roaming the area.

Campus Point is, admittedly, not my favorite part of campus. This stretch of beach is heavily trafficked and typically full of people; it is a go-to spot for tourists and prospective students, and those students and even faculty who have family in from out of town. I have walked there with my own parents when they have visited. It is aesthetically beautiful but energetically frenetic at times. As I consider my own feelings of overwhelm when I think about my many visits to Campus Point over the years, I realize that I am also projecting my feelings on to how I imagine the experience of this mountain lion: simultaneously roaming in an area of heavy recreation and yet trying to avoid humans (a point to which I can relate), this lion is likely looking for food and following the path of these waterways as best as possible. Food and water would be easier to come by here, and a hungry mountain lion would likely find a variety of prey including rodents, brush rabbits, and even raccoons. Nonetheless, I imagine a stressed-out lion wandering out in the sun, in search of food, water, shade, and quiet.

The adjacent Lagoon Island, closer to where the lion was actually spotted, however, is one of my favorite places on campus. One of two lagoons on campus, Lagoon Island is adjacent to and extends just northwest of Campus

Point Beach. It is tucked into the campus a bit more and is thus protected from the additional cars and foot traffic, although it is easily accessed on foot from within the main part of campus. Called "Tiptip" by local Chumash tribes, Lagoon Island appears on maps "dating back to at least 1870."[59] Lagoon Island provides the gift of a beautiful walk along a coastal marsh that looks out over the ocean. Full of plant life, shorebirds, and seabirds, it is also a popular birding hot spot that often shows up on the Cornell Ornithology web app, eBird—a contemporary indicator, perhaps, for what counts as sought-after nature. During a recent visit here, my mother, a seasoned birder, spotted an assortment of least sandpipers, greater yellowlegs, killdeers, and black-necked stilts, along with a selection of egrets, grebes, and ruddy ducks, to name a few.

Lagoon Island and Campus Point are "coastal mesas" situated between the campus and the Santa Barbara Channel. These sites are "characterized by nearly vertical bluffs on their oceanward side, and steep vegetated slopes that descend into the campus lagoon." Much of this area is carpeted with an exotic succulent called "iceplant"—technically an invasive species that "competes with native plants by forming thick mats that cover the landscape." Where the iceplant has not taken over the landscape, brome grass and coyote brush are dominant.[60] The visual result is what one might imagine if *Wuthering Heights* had been set in Santa Barbara.

As I wander this coastal mesa myself, it is easy to imagine a mountain lion roaming here. They have lived in the mountains of Santa Barbara County and in California for tens of thousands of years—a humbling juxtaposition with the eight or so years I have resided here. Mountain lions are also known as "a keystone species that act as 'ecosystem engineers.' They keep prey populations—especially rodents—in check and their kills provide food for scavengers like the critically endangered California condor. Their presence helps maintain diverse habitats that support a multitude of fish, amphibian, reptile, bird, mammal, insect, and invertebrate species."[61] That said, it is not uncommon for them to venture closer to areas of denser human habitation, especially in these past few years since the Thomas Fire. And what better place to get one's basic needs met relatively efficiently.

## COMMUNITY MESSAGING AND A LANGUAGE OF ANIMACY

I was having trouble reconciling the tenor of these email and text message alerts with my own empathy and concern for this mountain lion, given the increasing challenges they face, especially in this region. The emergency alert systems, the police response, the stark warnings to avoid the area. It is understandable enough to need to keep the community informed, although such emergency alerts hardly instill a gift mindset or encourage a language of animacy. This lion is merely traversing an area that these creatures have inhabited long before humans; today, though, the lion's movements are the catalyst for a series of emergency notifications issued from the same system that alerts the community about burglaries and other crimes and issues of concern.

While the hope was that the lion would move on by that Wednesday morning, this creature remained in the vicinity for a good three days, keeping the campus community on its toes and alive with vigilance. Just a couple hours later, by that Tuesday evening, the campus police had posted warning notices and started patrolling the area. There had been no additional sightings so far that evening.

•

EMERGENCY NOTIFICATION UPDATE

UCSB Alerts (Do Not Reply) alert@alert.ucsb.edu
Tuesday, September 17, 6:35 PM
UC Santa Barbara

UPDATE: No additional sightings of the mountain lion reported. Warning signs have been posted in the area. Officers are conducting frequent patrols. Continue to avoid Campus Point. While UCPD continues to monitor the situation, an all clear is not anticipated until morning.

•

By late Wednesday morning, there were still no new sightings since the previous evening. UCSB sent out an update asking members of the campus community to be aware of their surroundings and report any new sightings. This update also included a set of safety tips provided by the California Department of Fish and Wildlife, included below. The CDFW's recommendations for what to do in the event of a mountain lion sighting in many ways draw upon ideas about compassionate conservation. These recommendations are, overall, grounded in an ethic of "do no harm" and respectful coexistence. In some places, as shown below, they even implicitly reflect a language of animacy and a gift mindset.

•

*EMERGENCY NOTIFICATION UPDATE*

*UCSB Alerts (Do Not Reply) alert@alert.ucsb.edu*
*Wednesday, September 18, 9:58 AM*
*UC Santa Barbara*

*Update: There have been no mountain lion sightings since it was first reported at 4:30pm yesterday. Warning signs remain in place at Campus Point, and officers continue patrols. Be aware of your surroundings and report sightings. Safety tips provided by the California Department of Fish and Wildlife can be found here: https://www.wildlife.ca.gov/Keep-Me-Wild/Lion*

*The following Safety Tips are provided by the California Department of Fish and Wildlife:*

*Mountain lions are quiet, solitary and elusive, and typically avoid people by nature. However, as human population expands into mountain lion habitat, more frequent sightings may occur and human/mountain lion encounters may increase.*

*Mountain lion attacks on humans are extremely rare. However, attacks have occurred in California. Understanding mountain lion behavior and how to act responsibly in mountain lion country may greatly reduce potential conflict with these majestic animals.*

*The following safety information is a compilation taken from wildlife managers, wildlife officers and scientists that study mountain lion behavior. Although no strategy in the event of an encounter is guaranteed to be successful in every situation, these tips will help keep you safe in lion country.*

- *Do not hike, bike, or jog alone. Stay alert on trails.*
- *Avoid hiking or jogging when mountain lions are most active—dawn, dusk, and at night.*
- *Keep a close watch on small children.*
- *Off leash dogs on trails are at increased risk of becoming prey for a mountain lion.*
- *Never approach a mountain lion. Give them an escape route.*
- *DO NOT RUN. Stay calm. Running may trigger chase, catch and kill response. Do not turn your back. Face the animal, make noise and try to look bigger by waving your arms, or opening your jacket if wearing one; throw rocks or other objects. Pick up small children.*
- *Do not crouch down or bend over. Squatting puts you in a vulnerable position of appearing much like a 4-legged prey animal.*

- *Be vocal; however, speak calmly and do not use high pitched tones or high pitch screams.*
- *Teach others how to behave during an encounter. Anyone who runs may initiate an attack.*
- *Carry and know how to use bear spray to deter a mountain lion. Bear spray has been shown to be successful in emergency situations with mountain lions. Have the spray readily accessible. Carry in a holster belt or attach to a mountain bike. Talk to the folks at your local outdoor store. Make sure you know how to properly use bear spray. People have been known to spray their own faces when attempting to use it.*
- *If a lion attacks, fight back. Research on mountain lion attacks suggests that many potential victims have fought back successfully with rocks, sticks, garden tools, even an ink pen or bare hands. Try to stay on your feet. If knocked down, try to protect head and neck.*
- *If a mountain lion attacks a person, immediately call 911.*

•

The CDFW's acknowledgment, included in the message above, that mountain lions are "quiet, solitary and elusive, and typically avoid people by nature" helps allay fears and stereotypes that mountain lions seek out confrontations with humans. The safety recommendations also implicitly reflect a posthuman, nonanthropocentric perspective by noting that mountain lions were here before people—that "human population" is "expand[ing] into mountain lion habitat."[62] For this reason, "more frequent sightings may occur and human/ mountain lion encounters may increase." To note, rightly, that mountain lions have resided in this place long before people is an important point that the CDFW has made with subtlety, and one that is also implicitly aligned with an Indigenous worldview. As Kimmerer also notes, an Indigenous worldview would view people as the youngest of all species, with the most to learn. When recounting the Anishinaabe story of how the Original Man came to live on Turtle Island, Kimmerer aptly points out that, according to this story, "we humans are the newest arrivals on earth, the youngsters, just learning to find our way."[63] Indeed, we have much to learn from our more-than-human kin who have managed to thrive in this region long before humans. And yet, here we are, reacting fearfully to the presence of our mountain lion kin, leveraging the resources of technoscience to communicate about this creature's whereabouts.

That said, the CDFW's recommendations do help allay the public's fears by reminding us that "mountain lion attacks on humans are extremely rare." While "attacks have occurred in California," the CDFW again notes with subtlety that humans have some responsibility to learn "how to act responsibly in mountain lion country," and that doing so "may greatly reduce potential conflict with these majestic animals."[64]

The CDFW acknowledges that their list of safety recommendations is generalized across possible scenarios, and represents "a compilation taken from wildlife managers, wildlife officers and scientists that study mountain lion behavior." Moreover, all encounters are specific, contextual, and nuanced, and thus "no strategy in the event of an encounter is guaranteed to be successful in every situation."[65] The CDFW then presents a bulleted list of general safety recommendations, many of which apply across possible scenarios and encounters involving a range of creatures; they recommend not hiking or jogging during dawn or dusk, or at night; watching small children closely; and keeping track of domesticated dogs when they are off leash. This last point is in fact relevant to encounters with rattlesnakes as well, in the Western region. Most rattlesnakes also do not want to be bothered and will run and hide from humans; when we hear of encounters with rattlesnakes, there is often an overly curious, off-leash dog involved.

The CDFW recommends that humans "never approach a mountain lion." Importantly, they note, we must "give them an escape route."[66] I might suggest that, framed more empathetically, we might also "give them the gift of space."

The CDFW's next set of recommendations in many ways represent a more generalized variation on the theme of the Oregon woman's specific approach to dealing with the mountain lion in her home. On the one hand, the CDFW's suggestion to "stay calm," avoid running, "make noise and try to look bigger by waving your arms," for instance, seems to encourage a more peaceful approach to such encounters. On the other hand, the CDFW's suggestion to "throw rocks or other objects" perhaps seems more confrontational than necessary. We might consider here the tension between acknowledging that the human population is ever expanding into mountain lion habitat—that mountain lions have resided in this area long before humans—and yet articulating a response to an encounter that implicitly perpetuates human dominance over more-than-human animals. While it is unlikely that the CDFW explicitly seeks to promote this kind of human mastery over nature, these recommendations illuminate the tensions and challenges of creating messaging that is, at the end of the day, more fully relational and nonanthropocentric.[67]

Moreover, the CDFW's recommendation to "be vocal; however, speak calmly and do not use high pitched tones or high pitch screams" is also compatible with the Oregon woman's approach. The CDFW suggests that we "teach others how to behave during an encounter." This was, in essence, what the Oregon woman did. By sharing her story with news outlets and on social media, she performed a variation of this teaching, by showing others what is possible when approaching a mountain lion encounter from the perspective of entangled empathy, a language of animacy, and a gift mindset.

The CDFW's recommendations are, overall, implicitly grounded in an ethic of respect for and peaceful coexistence with our more-than-human kin; however, that messaging is not without its tensions. Moreover, the delivery mechanism for this information—a series of emergency text and email alerts—has the likely but unintended rhetorical consequence of lessening the potential for empathy. And, by mere feature of a delivery mode called an "emergency alert," such messaging instills an "us" versus "them" mindset that reinforces an anthropocentric view that inadvertently perpetuates a hierarchy of species.

All remained seemingly quiet throughout the day on Wednesday. But then, later that afternoon, the lion was spotted once again. This time, the lion was seen near the Devereux Lagoon, which is the second of the two lagoons at UCSB—this one on the quieter, west side of campus.

•

*EMERGENCY NOTIFICATION UPDATE*

*UCSB Alerts (Do Not Reply) alert@alert.ucsb.edu*
*Wednesday, September 18, 2:05 PM*
*UC Santa Barbara*

*UPDATE: A mountain lion was spotted in the area of the Devereux Lagoon. Police are in the area. Avoid area until further notice. California Fish and Wildlife have been called to respond. Update will be provided when information is available.*

•

The area where this second sighting took place is a much quieter and less frequently traveled part of campus. Devereux Lagoon sits next to some of UCSB's original faculty housing, a childcare facility, and some buildings that are now used for campus conferences or to house visiting scholars and researchers. It is easy to imagine a mountain lion wandering this area; it is peaceful, if not eerily so at times, as several buildings here are either underutilized or sit empty for much of the year. Devereux Lagoon is also located within the

Coal Oil Point Reserve, which is part of the University of California Natural Reserve System.

Devereux Lagoon, more commonly referred to as Devereux Slough, sits in the heart of the reserve. The slough is a "seasonally flooded tidal lagoon that dries out in the summer to form salt flats and hypersaline ponds, and channels."[68] In the winter and spring, it becomes a shallower body of water.[69] Referred to as "Uksholo" by the Chumash, the slough originally "connected with the much larger Goleta Slough," which is now home to the Santa Barbara Airport.[70] Despite the presence of the airport, it is easy to picture the region before it was connected with roads and runways. Like Campus Point and Lagoon Island, Devereux Slough is a popular spot for birders; my most recent walk around this area yielded sightings of acorn woodpeckers, coots, lesser goldfinches, sandpipers, barn swallows, and a pair of red-tailed hawks. Great blue herons often sail over the lagoon and wade along the shoreline to hunt for frogs.

By Wednesday evening, all seemed quiet once again, and the hope was that the lion had gone on its way. But on Thursday morning, however, it became clear that the mountain lion was still in the area, and had unfortunately wandered near the UCSB childcare center just east of Devereux Slough. This understandably caused some tension. It seemed that the lion had stealthily located the nearest childcare facility and had planned its next move accordingly.

•

*EMERGENCY NOTIFICATION UPDATE*

*UCSB Alerts (Do Not Reply) alert@alert.ucsb.edu*
*Thursday, September 19, 8:01 AM*
*UC Santa Barbara*

*EMERGENCY NOTIFICATION UPDATE: A mountain lion was spotted in the area of the West Campus Child Care Center this morning. Police are in the area. Avoid area until further notice. California Fish and Wildlife have been called to respond. Update will be provided when information is available. Be aware of your surroundings and report sightings. Safety tips provided by the California Department of Fish and Wildlife can be found here: https://www.wildlife.ca.gov/ Keep-Me-Wild/Lion*

•

I write with some sarcasm above to make the point that, while I do not wish to disparage any specific agency or institution for its messaging, and while I do understand the need for a large institution to think and act in terms of what is perceived to be in the best interests of the surrounding community, I again found myself wondering if it was necessary to frame this message in terms that could potentially be inferred by an uneasy reader to suggest that the lion was targeting a specific group as prey, and thus inadvertently reinforce common stereotypes about mountain lions. The message did not explicitly suggest a correlation between the lion's location and its interest in a specific group; however, a concerned, fearful, or uninformed reader may understandably make such an inference. Mountain lions are, "in fact, afraid of humans and even children."[71] Moreover, as UCSB evolutionary biology professor Samuel Sweet noted, "People don't really understand that mountain lions are around campus all the time."[72] As long as people follow the suggestions of the CDFW, "these animals are fairly harmless" and "will likely be on their way soon."[73] If we take to heart Kimmerer's suggestion that "to be native to a place we must learn to speak its language," we might consider that knowledge of our more-than-human kin is a necessary part of learning to speak their language. In doing so, we also become more at home in a place, and more receptive to engaging with empathy and compassion.

## A MATTER OF PERCEPTION

By the end of the week, the situation had seemed to calm down. By Friday afternoon, UCSB felt it was safe to discontinue the messages, and issued the following update: "There have been no reported mountain lion sightings since Thursday morning. At this time we do not plan to send additional Emergency Notifications. Continue to be aware of your surroundings and report sightings."[74]

I was relieved that the text and email alerts would soon wind down. But with a background in technical writing and environmental studies, I will admit that I again imagined editing the CDFW's list of safety recommendations. Rather than: "Never approach a mountain lion. Give them an escape route," my revised bulleted list might simply read, "Give them the gift of space." For Kimmerer, it is "human perception that makes the world a gift." Indeed, such reframing is a matter of perception, which, as she says, if developed, also has the potential to benefit the well-being and survival of species, perhaps in part through the practices of compassionate conservation.[75]

Again, all remained quiet for about a week, and it seemed that perhaps this possibly young lion had found its way and moved on, when another lion was apparently again spotted over at Campus Point, back on the eastern side of campus. A new emergency notification was then issued: "On October 7, 2019, at 7:45PM, a mountain lion was spotted near campus on the beach below the cliffs at Campus Point. Police are in the area. Avoid area until further notice. California Fish and Wildlife have been notified. Update will be provided when information is available."[76]

On the following day, however, it seemed that the mountain lion had returned to the area on the *west* side of campus, near the childcare facility. UCSB issued another emergency notification and again included the list of safety tips from the CDFW (not included here for purposes of concision): "A mountain lion was spotted on campus west of the Orfalea Childcare Center located on West Campus. Police are in the area. Avoid area until further notice. California Fish and Wildlife have been called to respond. Update will be provided when information is available.[77]

This latest sighting seemed a bit odd—the mountain lion had not been around for over a week, but was now spotted near the cliffs by Campus Point, on the other side of campus? And then, that next day, the lion was back near the childcare center, on the west side of campus? In fact, this sighting turned out not to be a lion, exactly. Rather:

•

*EMERGENCY NOTIFICATION*

*UCSB Alerts (Do Not Reply) alert@alert.ucsb.edu*
*Tuesday, October 8, 2:39 PM*
*UC Santa Barbara*

*Officers confirmed, in this instance, the reported animal was a bobcat who has lived in the area for many years without issue. We have previous confirmed mountain lion sightings in the area. Continue to be aware of your surroundings and report sightings.*

•

That's right, nothing to see here—just your friendly neighborhood bobcat who has a long history of positive relations within the community. To be fair, to the untrained eye, a bobcat may be mistaken for a mountain lion easily enough, although bobcats are generally much smaller. Both species have lived in Santa Barbara County for many years, however, and it is not uncommon for them to come down from the mountains outside of the city, especially in times of drought and during wildfire season. And so, with this final lion, er, bobcat sighting, the alerts concluded and the lion did not return—or, at least, our friend was able to stay out of the fray enough not to encounter additional humans.

## LEARNING THE LANGUAGE OF A PLACE: HOW TO EXIST WITH OUR MORE-THAN-HUMAN KIN IN THE ANTHROPOCENE

The story of these mountain lion sightings, as told through the lens of this thread of email and text alerts, provides a useful example for analyzing how different discourses about our encounters with our more-than-human kin produce and encourage different vantage points and perspectives. It is often through comparison that we discern meaning, and so it may prove useful to compare the UCSB lion sightings with the Oregon woman's encounter with the mountain lion, to help examine what these stories reveal about our encounters with our more-than-human kin.

Both of these stories, in different ways, help us address the question of what counts as "home" in the Anthropocene. We may recall that for the ancient Greeks, *oikos,* or "home," typically refers to a more traditionally structured notion of family, or the house and the household.[78] Subsequently, when we begin to complicate ideas about what counts as home in the Anthropocene and for whom, it quickly becomes clear that this more boundaried notion of home is constraining—especially when we begin to consider a more posthuman perspective, where the distinctions between inside and outside, and in/organic matter, become blurred. We may then question what, then, is *oikos,* and for whom? The mountain lion wandered into the woman's home presumably because she was displaced—fire-lost—an increasingly common dilemma, and the catalyst for many such encounters in an age of climate change. The homeowner noted that "the door was open and the room has huge plants [and] stairs built around real tree branches, so she likely didn't even realize she was walking indoors until she was *inside.*"[79] The mountain lion was now technically "inside" the home; however, "home" here arguably involves a merging of worlds, a more empathetic and relational understanding of *oikos*—one that relies on "attending and responding with care," and that involves the "emergent co-becoming" of humans and more-than-humans.[80]

The homeowner's approach also implicitly values the compassionate conservation principle of "do no harm," and engages with entangled empathy in a language of animacy through feline slow-blinking. The woman was successful in conveying to the lion that she was not a threat to the animal's safety. She also used drumming as a mode of nonverbal communication—a peaceful but clear way of trying to communicate, again through a language of animacy, and with empathy and compassion, that the animal should exit the area.

To be native to a place, then—to truly be and feel at home, as Kimmerer says, we must learn to speak the language of a place.[81] To be at home means engaging in a language of animacy; it means understanding every encounter with our wild kin as a gift to be received, learned from, and reciprocated. Such a mindset is easy to recognize through the story of the Oregon homeowner and the mountain lion.

A gift mindset and a language of animacy are also implicitly embedded in many aspects of the CDFW's "Keep Me Wild" campaign and the related recommendations that UCSB's text alerts draw upon.[82] The advice of the CDFW, is, in essence, compassionate and empathetic, especially for a large, state-run agency: do no harm; give these creatures room to move; stay out of the way and leave them be. And we should indeed remember that the CDFW is a governed body that must communicate a generalized message to a public audience, whereas the Oregon woman's drumming took place in a specific context in which decision-making was able to happen on a smaller, more independent scale. The CDFW is concerned with broad, generalizable language, policy, and recommendations, and they plainly state that "no strategy in the event of an encounter is guaranteed to be successful in every situation." That said, the need for a generalizable message does not necessarily negate the potential for making empathetic recommendations. And perhaps such messaging could potentially go even farther in helping to allay fears about these creatures, and attempting to communicate even more directly ideas about entangled empathy and a language of animacy, especially following a fire season that burned much of these lions' home range. Again, what if, instead of: "Never approach a mountain lion. Give them an escape route," such messaging read: "Give them the gift of space"?

At the same time, I acknowledge that not all of these ideas may be possible, and I do not make these points to critique the already wildlife-inclusive work of any one organization; rather, I am interested in exploring what such ideas might look like, and whether such a shift could change how we imagine engaging with our more-than-human kin in the context of such encounters.

In fact, we might also consider that the Oregon woman's drumming is not actually that dissimilar from the CDFW's recommendation to make loud noise or make oneself look big in the event of a mountain lion encounter. Both approaches engage a language of animacy, albeit to different extents, and in different presumed contexts. The drumming, however, was more intentional and took rhythm into account—it was done consciously, and "produced," if you will, as an intentional, percussive composition.[83] Moreover, the drumming seemed to emerge from a place of compassion and empathy, and not from a place of fear and panic or a sense of hierarchical presumption. In some ways, then, the goal was similar: make noise and create a disturbance. However, the Oregon woman's mode of delivery was carried out more expressly with clear compassion, intentionality, and empathy. Moreover, it is also notable to remember that this encounter happened in the larger context of ongoing, nearby wildfires that threatened the homes and communities of humans, more-than-human animals, and the broader ecosystems in which we all live. Empathetic practice can help offset the damage incurred during such unsettling times, and it helps renew our faith in the possibilities for peaceful coexistence, but our ecosystems remain vulnerable to the continued threats characterized by an age of climate crisis. Perhaps, as Rush suggests, it is through grappling with these "efforts and losses that we are made whole."[84]

Finally, this story could have easily taken another turn. The homeowner could have called the authorities; she could have easily taken the more human-centric position and called the police or the Oregon Department of Fish and Wildlife, and they may have then tranquilized and relocated the mountain lion—a common practice in similar cases.[85] Instead, though, she was interested in taking what she perceived as a more compassionate, empathic, or inclusive approach that is arguably in sync with a more ecological, embodied understanding of place and entangled empathy related to our relationships with our more-than-human kin.

The text message alert system leveraged by UCSB during the mountain lion sightings does, in essence, convey a more human-centric message that places human safety first. That said, it is understandable that a large institution like UCSB, responsible for the safety of its community of students, staff, and faculty, would need to issue such a series of alerts related to mountain lion sightings. The emergency alert delivery system does not exactly inspire a gift mindset, but perhaps it is not meant to; rather, it is associated with the need to be vigilant, as seen through the eyes of an institution responsible for policies and guidelines related to the safety of its community. It is the same alert system, after all, that is used to warn the campus community of crimes, trouble with buildings, and other such issues. I should again note that it is not my intention to critique the policies of institutions that aim to provide sensible information for a public audience seeking advice and safety in such matters. Rather, I make these points because I am interested in engaging in a kind of reframing exercise, such that we may begin to imagine some different possibilities for a more fully empathetic engagement with wildlife.

Such empathetic modes of engagements—a language of animacy and a mindset in which we may reciprocate the gifts of these encounters—are compatible with a posthuman, relational vantage point that, moreover, shares commonality with and even derives from an Indigenous worldview. To be at home in the Anthropocene thus means, following Gruen, recognizing "connection with and understanding of the circumstances of the other."[86] Following Kimmerer, I would add that a language of animacy is part of that connection; it is one step toward learning and practicing entangled empathy, and acting with compassion in our encounters with vulnerable species. Being at home in the Anthropocene, then, means being receptive to and willing to engage with the full range of wisdom that surrounds us. It means knowing, respecting, and even speaking the language(s) of a place. Put into practice, then, we may imagine policy- and decision-making that accounts for all species and that engages in a language of animacy—that helps foster entangled empathy and starts with compassionate conservation.[87] Taken together, these perspectives may help us understand the ecosystem as a community in which we reside and coexist respectfully with our more-than-human kin in an age of climate crisis.

# From Climate Anxiety Emerges the Gift of a Whisper Song

Part of the previous chapter was set in the context of the wildfires that plagued the western US during the summer of 2018. It is now summer 2020, and in central California, we are once again essentially surrounded by wildfires seemingly too numerous to list. In September 2020 alone, California saw the Oak Fire in Mendocino County, the Glass Fire in Napa and Sonoma Counties, the Creek Fire in Fresno County, the San Antonio Fire in Santa Barbara County, the Snow Fire in Riverside County, the El Dorado Fire in San Bernardino County, and the Valley Fire in San Diego, to name but a handful.[1] The list is exhausting but hardly exhaustive.

Moreover, the ongoing pandemic prevents people from gathering in indoor spaces, and yet by late August and mid-September of 2020, it is not easy to be outdoors in parts of California, either, as the air quality is often rated "unhealthy for sensitive groups," and at times "unhealthy" in general.[2] By mid-September, temperatures now sometimes climb into the 90s, making the most mundane of daily tasks untenable for many. I am tempted to type something akin to "these are some of the challenges of this time," but in doing so I realize that such words have begun to feel rote, and they do not adequately account for my ongoing sense of *solastalgia*. Solastalgia is a concept coined by philosopher Glenn Albrecht, which refers to "the pain or distress caused by the ongoing loss of solace and the sense of desolation connected to the present state of one's home or territory," and it specifically relates to "the lived experience of negative environmental change" that impacts one's sense of place.[3] Animal studies and communication scholar Emily Plec further contextualizes solastalgia in her recent essay, "Presence and Absence in the Watershed," when she describes how engaging with environmental issues that we care deeply about "can produce the kinds of insights and intimate relationships that can bring an end to the agony caused by careless anthropocentric contamination in the form of dams, pollution, habitat destruction, deforestation, and intensive agriculture," or the kind of emotional pain caused by human-wrought environmental degradation that constitutes solastalgia.[4] In other words, the emotional pain associated with solastalgia need not necessarily be a permanent state, especially if we can engage in work that bears some personal and broader environmental recuperative power.

Moreover, to acknowledge the ongoing challenge that is our climate crisis is not to concede or uncritically accept that the current state of affairs is a foregone conclusion, or to understand these times as something altogether new or unprecedented. Rush describes how climate change undoes our ability to weave narratives or tell stories in any sort of conventional way; climate change, she writes, is among the "moments and phenomena that test and ultimately rend our ability to arrive at a narrative line."[5] Even so, as she points out, "we keep trying to tell this story in a straightforward manner, with conventional narrative techniques and news reporting. Climate change has entered into our contemporary culture as a never-ending set of 'record-breaking' statistics—record-breaking storms, record-breaking heat waves, record-breaking rain. . . . Many ask if this is the new normal."[6] I agree with Rush that we must push back against such implicit acceptance, for there is, in fact, nothing normal about it; however, when we write about our climate change "with the same tired vernacular, we dull readers to the dynamism at the heart of such transformation. Put another way: we have plenty of climate change news, but this reporting tells the story straight, and so we think the conclusion is foregone."[7] When we implicitly or unwittingly normalize climate change, we "steal from ourselves the possibility that we might be transformed, and not just for the worse, by this disruptive force."[8] Rush asks how we may tell such stories in ways that constitute "more than elegy alone."[9] Likewise, I am interested in finding the recuperative power in these increasingly pervasive accounts of the ongoing damage done to our vulnerable ecosystems by way of largely anthropogenic forces.

To implicitly normalize climate change as a foregone conclusion can also have the unintended outcome of exacerbating what is now alternatively referred to as "climate anxiety," "eco-anxiety," or "climate grief." Briefly put, climate anxiety and eco-anxiety refer not only to the "anxiety that shows up when we're waking up to the climate crisis," but also to the sense of fear and dread associated with those realizations.[10] Climate anxiety refers to the "fear that the current system is pushing the Earth beyond its ecological limits," and this form of anxiety is becoming an increasingly common sociocultural phenomenon, at least in our more immediately mainstream culture.[11] It is important to note, however, that while many Americans have more recently begun to acknowledge climate change and its attendant anxieties, as Nishnaabeg scholar Leanne Betasamosake Simpson writes: "We should be thinking of climate change as part of a much longer series of ecological catastrophes caused by colonialism and accumulation-based society."[12] Thus, as anthropologist Joseph Weiss similarly reminds us, when we engage in discussions of climate anxiety and the Anthropocene, we must also be mindful of the deeper roots of what is often viewed uncritically as a "new" era of climate crisis.

Additionally, it is fair to say that human impact to the planet also predates academic discussions of the Anthropocene, which, as Weiss points out, "are of a much more contemporary vintage, emerging in the early 2000s and becoming ubiquitous within the last ten years."[13] Anthropocene discourses of climate crisis have, on the whole, arguably emerged in sync with the public's ongoing and cumulative experiences of natural disasters "in places like the continental United States, where the real-life impacts of global environmental shifts are becoming increasingly difficult to dismiss," and yet equally difficult to grapple with.[14] But as Haraway suggests, we ought not to conflate or mistake the seeming unpredictability of climate change with "unknowability itself."[15] More specifically, Haraway writes, the Anthropocene is a time of "multispecies, including human, urgency: of great mass death and extinction; of onrushing disasters, whose unpredictable specificities are foolishly taken as unknowability itself; of refusing to know and to cultivate the capacity of response-ability . . . of unprecedented looking away."[16] However, she adds, "Surely, to say 'unprecedented' in view of the last centuries is to say something almost unimaginable," especially in light of the fact that we are complicit in "webs of processes that must somehow be engaged and repatterned."[17] As we consider our accountability to our vulnerable ecosystems in Anthropocene times, we must understand that, "recursively, whether we asked for it or not, the pattern is in our hands."[18] We must avoid the pitfall of inadvertently perpetuating the idea that climate change is our new norm, or a foregone conclusion, or that these increasingly unpredictable times are therefore unknowable or preclude any necessity for critical thought, accountability, and careful response.

It is important to recognize that human intervention in the environment has indeed been taking place long before this now crisis-level situation has made its way on to our more collective, public radar. Moreover, to understand Anthropocene discourses as potentially or inadvertently perpetuating capitalist or colonialist practices makes it all the more necessary to illuminate and extend these concepts with those perspectives that are less anthropocentric and more rooted in compassionate, empathetic, and relational understandings of our shared ecosystems.

Again, my goal is not at all to disparage these more recent discourses about climate anxiety for their relative newness or more frequent appearance in the mainstream public sphere, for the acknowledgment of such concepts is arguably useful for many people who struggle to articulate feelings of climate grief at this cultural moment. Many of my own students, for instance, have sought solace in being able to identify a forum and a framework for discussing what they are more frequently understanding as their own climate anxiety. For this reason alone—having had what I think of as invaluable discussions with my students based on some of the very resources that I cite here—I think it is important to keep all of these conversations going. But we must keep the conversations going in ways that are relevant to and inclusive of the constellation of perspectives that underpin them. Certainly, I do not claim to outline all possible paths forward in this regard, though I was heartened to read, recently, that beginning in 2020, for instance, all New Zealand schools will "have access to materials about the climate crisis written by the country's leading science agencies—including tools for students to plan their own activism, and to process their feelings of 'eco-anxiety' over global heating."[19] The curriculum will apparently be offered in all schools that teach students who are eleven to fifteen years of age.[20] Perhaps coincidentally, this announcement came about one month after the young climate activist Greta Thunberg critiqued New Zealand's climate policies for not being strong enough; either way, to integrate curricula about the climate crisis at the elementary and high school levels seems a productive starting point for moving in a direction that favors acknowledgment of and regular dialogue about issues that we cannot necessarily assume younger generations would otherwise have access to, and it is a move that other educational systems might do well to emulate.[21] In these ways, we may perhaps help younger generations, especially, grapple with the challenges of finding a middle ground someplace between hope and despair, and participate in these conversations in ways that can illuminate productive frameworks for understanding and addressing our climate crisis.

It is not only our younger generations who now grapple with such climate anxiety, however. According to researchers at Yale University and George Mason University, in the past five years alone, "the number of Americans who are 'very worried' about climate change has more than doubled, to 26 percent. In 2020, an American Psychiatric Association poll found that more than half of Americans are concerned about climate change's effect on their mental health."[22] According to Dr. Lise Van Susteren, psychiatrist and cofounder of the Climate Psychiatry Alliance, climate anxiety, or what she calls "eco-distress," can manifest in a number of ways, "from anguish over what the future will hold to extreme guilt over individual purchases and behaviors. . . . Though its symptoms sometimes mirror those of clinical anxiety, she said she saw eco-distress as a reasonable reaction to scientific facts—one that, in mild cases, should be addressed but not pathologized."[23] Psychologist and communications scholar Renee Lertzman also notes that "loss and mourning, when unattended to and unresolved," can contribute to what she calls "environmental melancholia," or "a condition in which even those who care deeply about the well-being of ecosystems and future generations are paralyzed to translate such concern into action."[24] She argues that rather than "an exclusive focus on solutions," we may view "loss and ambivalence as psychosocial 'achievements' not to be avoided but integrated for more authentic modes of engagement with a dynamic, uncertain world."[25] Again, as Rush similarly notes, perhaps "through our losses we will be made whole."[26] I too can relate to climate anxiety and the sense of solastalgia that Rush and others describe, and this book contends implicitly and explicitly with the dissonance of acknowledging climate anxiety, while simultaneously reckoning with how to distill any recuperative power from these moments. I suggest once again that we may find some recuperative power in the recognition of the myriad earthly gifts that still surround us, and that we may endeavor to reciprocate those gifts in ways that are informed by entangled empathy and a language of animacy, for starters.

Part of the climate anxiety I have come to know involves the dissonance over longing to be elsewhere at a time when wildfire smoke, for instance, has become so pervasive in Santa Barbara. That is, I feel conflicted for heading out of California, but I am also grateful to have the option to seek out a reprieve. Though the wildfire smoke and unabating heat wave are some of the variables prompting my decision-making at this time, I hesitate to use the term "displacement" in this context, because I have the privilege of thinking about and planning my destination in advance, and thus my decision to head from the West Coast to the Midwest, for example, was a choice carefully considered. From these moments of climate anxiety, then, perhaps more optimistically, emerges the gift of the opportunity to experience a new place. The grief associated with mourning the environmental losses of one place, in this moment, yields new opportunities for experiencing the joys of another place. This is some of my thinking as I encounter and seek to reciprocate the earthly gifts of the varied ecosystems in which we coexist with our more-than-human kin.

My partner is from the Midwest, and I am a dyed-in-the-wool New England, still *becoming with* the West Coast. We reside in central California, but by early fall, as mentioned above, we needed a reprieve from what was, at the time, unrelenting smoke and heat that pervaded the region. In seeking this reprieve, I again recognize that in doing so, we had the privilege to be able to work remotely and to move ourselves elsewhere, even for a brief period of time. And so, we packed up some companion creatures and drove east toward family, and toward the Midwest.[27]

I am soon enough writing from Omaha, Nebraska, where my experience of this place is at once filled with anxiety and joy. I write from the Midwest, but with concern for my home in California. My current "body-place collaboration of emplacement"[28] sparks a sort of dissonance that resonates with my broader feelings about what counts as home and belonging right now and for whom. It serves as an unanticipated catalyst for much of my current thinking about climate grief and the associations we form with newer places.

I am grateful for the somewhat spontaneous and less thoroughly planned opportunity to get to know this place. As such, I find myself immediately reaching for analogues: Omaha reminds me a little bit of Minneapolis, a place where I once spent much time while in graduate school and that I still think of quite fondly. Omaha also reminds me a bit of its southwestern neighbor, Colorado; specifically, the downtown region's architectural mix of industrial and mid-century modern styles reminds me quite a bit of Boulder. I suspect that I reach for analogues to earlier places because this place is newer to me and I try to situate it in my existing schema for the places I already know—akin, perhaps, to a sort of "given-new strategy" of place.[29] I do not know Omaha like I know some of the other places that I describe in this book; this is the first time I'm visiting this place. I did not grow up here, nor have I lived here for a longer span of time, as I now have in California, and so I do not have longer-term points of reference or memories that inform my sense of place. Instead, my experience of Omaha is informed at this moment by what I would describe as a combination of gratitude and curiosity.

My gratitude and curiosity are perhaps one variation on the theme of belonging; this is not quite home, exactly, but in this moment, it is nonetheless possible to recognize and appreciate the co-constitution of humans, more-than-humans, and the ecosystems in which we all coexist.[30] This site for establishing and producing new connections quite literally takes the form of a rented house in a quiet south Omaha neighborhood. Here, for instance, I can stand in the front yard and watch an early morning thunderstorm— a powerful and humbling feature of a landscape that I am glad to know at this moment. This thunderstorm does not produce the anxiety that it might in Santa Barbara, for in this moment, rain does not produce the threat of impending mudslides. But as I am soon reminded, this is not to say that Omaha is impervious to the natural disasters or landscapes in flux to which Santa Barbara is so accustomed.

Nevertheless, the earthly gifts of this place are ephemeral. Of course, climate change emphasizes and performs the seeming ephemerality of *all* ecosystems at this point, but here, in addition, I understand ephemerality as even more salient by mere fact of my own travel choices. As Rush describes when considering the migration routes of the birds she observes at H. J. Andrews Experimental Forest in Oregon, perhaps we are all "in from out of town." I too consider that "we are not that different from the rufous [hummingbirds] and the other birds overhead" that she observes, for "we too fly in an endless loop. . . . No singular home, pulling harder than the rest."[31] This is true enough; I am in from out of town and will soon loop back to California; moreover, New England is never far from my mind. In the meantime, though, my gratitude for and curiosity about this place have taken the form of a particular captivation with the local waterways here, and with the joys of light precipitation that I did grow up with in New England, and that I so long for in California.

On this rainy fall morning in Omaha, joy wins out over anxiety. As I drink coffee on the front porch and watch thunderstorms roll in from the west, the sound of intermittent thunder in the distance is punctuated with the calls of Eastern blue jays. I am trying to think of the last time I was in the company of Eastern jays—it has been well over a year, maybe longer. I do love the California scrub jays that I have come to know well in Santa Barbara, but Eastern jays have been my kin since childhood. The black, white, and blue checkered pattern of their shoulders looks like decorative stained glass, and the bold black ring of feathers that descends from their blue head crest creates a portraiture effect; these are the most visually classic of the jay species. To be in the company of Eastern jays is a gift in itself, but this morning, I am in for an extra treat. Perhaps the greatest gift, and yet relatively small in scale, is hearing for the first time what I now know is called the "whisper song" of the Eastern blue jay.

Since arriving at our house in south Omaha, I've been hearing a bird call that I haven't quite been able to identify. I'd look around the backyard, and up into the oak tree canopy overhead. There, I spotted some red-bellied woodpeckers—a species I hadn't seen in person before. Their call is as boisterous and celebratory as the wide red racing stripe that runs down the middle of their heads, but what I was hearing was somewhat different; I would describe this mysterious vocalization as a sort of "quiet burble." I couldn't quite tell where it was coming from. On this morning, I heard the quiet burbling in the tree canopy above and was finally able to spot the avian vocalist—it was, much to my surprise, an Eastern jay. I couldn't quite believe it—there in the tree it perched, mumbling sweetly to itself as it briefly cocked its head to acknowledge my presence, its song much more subdued than one would expect from a typically raucous jay. My research later revealed that male jays will sometimes produce what are called "whisper songs" as part of courtship behavior, while solitary jays sometimes produce their whisper song for reasons not immediately discernable to humans. The bird will quietly turn its head from side to side and sing these subdued, rolling, gurgling-type of songs.[32] Some ornithologists have described whisper songs as "a soft, quiet conglomeration of clicks, chucks, whirrs, whines, liquid notes, and elements of other calls," noting also that "a singing bout may last longer than 2 minutes."[33] I have known Eastern jays all my life, but here in Omaha, my connection with these feathered kin yields new knowledge and a new language of animacy; I am privy to aspects of their communication in a way I have not been before. While it seems that multiple species of jays indeed produce whisper songs across the various ecosystems in which they reside, I associate hearing their whisper song with this yard in Omaha. This little yard bears great gifts and fosters new earthly connections with my jay kin. I feel privileged to hear my first whisper song here.[34]

While also new to the whisper songs of jays, my partner has grown up here and knows this neighborhood and city better than I do, and kindly provides many driving and walking tours of the area. My knowledge of this place is thus limited, on the one hand, yet also intricately entangled with that of someone who knows this place exceedingly well, on the other. Perhaps this is yet another paradox of place—learning through the perspective of another person whose knowledge is entangled with specific contexts that are truly known only to them. Moreover, I am not interested in arriving at any singular conclusions about this place, so much as I am curious to listen for the new ideas that emerge from these encounters.[35]

Among the many locales[36] that I visit and learn about here is Haworth Park. Haworth Park is a public park about fifteen miles south of Omaha, in the city of Bellevue, which is considered a southern suburb of Omaha. Haworth Park is situated along the banks of the Missouri River. This park has long been home to a large and popular campground, but the campground has been closed to the public since the flood of 2019, or the Heartland flood. The area is beautiful but now eerily vacant, and if I had not known we were in fact driving through a campground, I might not have identified the area as such. Rather, we follow a winding road through a large expanse of field that is actually the campground and eventually drive right up to the boat ramp, where we get out and walk around.

We stand at the edge of the concrete boat launch, the Missouri River a perhaps deceptively calm sheet of water that offers both a translucent view just beneath its sepia-tone surface and an imperfect reflection of the contrastingly clear sky above. On this notably warm September afternoon, the slow and steady currents of the river at times appear more like a curated science museum exhibit than a naturally occurring body of water. Standing here at this moment, it is hard to believe that just a year and a half ago, this entire area was completely submerged by floodwaters. I imagine this is how visitors might experience Santa Barbara; they may see the previous burn areas along a trail or along the route of a scenic drive—evidence of past wildfires—but in the moment of their visit, they experience these idyllic vistas most prominently.

Likewise, as we survey the grounds in more detail, we notice stacks of picnic tables, gathered up in piles and chained together in groups. These tables were obviously rounded up at some earlier time and removed from the flooded campground. These are the picnic tables that once helped define the footprint of each individual campsite. At this moment, though, the park is peaceful; piles of picnic tables provide just scant evidence of the previous extreme weather event that took place just a little more than a year ago.

In March 2019, thousands of Nebraskans were forced to evacuate their homes following a "bomb cyclone" weather system that brought vast amounts of precipitation to a region already inundated with ice and snowmelt. As a result, dams and levees became overwhelmed, many roads were washed away, and local neighborhoods, farms, and military bases became submerged in up to eight feet of water.[37]

Perhaps, along with "fire-lost" and "megafire," we can add "bomb cyclone" to our ongoing new lexicon of climate crisis terminology. A "bomb cyclone" refers to a storm that intensifies very rapidly. This kind of storm forms when "air near Earth's surface rises quickly in the atmosphere, triggering a sudden drop in barometric pressure—at least 24 millibars within 24 hours."[38] In the month leading up to the Heartland Flood, more than a foot of snow was already on the ground in parts of Nebraska. In February 2019 alone, the National Weather Service had recorded twenty-seven inches of snowfall in Omaha. On March 12, 2019, Winter Storm Ulmer moved out of the Rockies and dropped twenty-four millibars in only thirteen hours, and then continued to move across Nebraska from March 13 to 14, bringing with it rain, wind, and heavy snow.[39] The Missouri River at Plattsmouth, just about eighteen miles south of Haworth Park, recorded a crest of 40.62 feet, which was nearly four feet over the previous record that was set during the last major flood, in 2011.[40] By the time the storm had moved through the area, a total of 104 cities, eighty-one counties, and five tribal nations in Nebraska received state or federal disaster declarations based on the flood events.[41]

Haworth Park, which sits along the Missouri River, incurred extensive damage to the campground and surrounding park area, and was among those areas submerged in floodwaters. Two months following the flood, the Missouri River was still expected to rise, thus making it impossible to estimate when the park could reopen.[42] The river would need to go down at least ten feet before the damage could be assessed or FEMA could be involved.[43] Local officials estimated that repairs could cost up to three million dollars; they subsequently considered that since the park had a history of flooding, and since flooding could become a yearly event, the city may in the future decide to remove the RV campsites and "let the park return to nature." In the months following the Heartland flood, discussions would continue about whether the campground should reopen, and whether the park itself should be "restored again or allowed to sit undisturbed in the floodway."[44] On the one hand, the idea of letting such public places return to a more natural state references traditional ideas about protected spaces, which picture wildlife as *over there,* in areas defined by human absence. On the other hand, however, when viewed through the lens of the Anthropocene, such ideas may be likened to a resiliency strategy that Rush describes as "organized retreat."

Rather than continue to restore areas of human development damaged from repeated natural disasters, Rush writes, "real resiliency might mean letting go of our image of the coastline, learning to leave the very places we have long considered necessary to our survival."[45] Organized retreat, as she notes, is among a handful of adaptive strategies that begins to acknowledge the scale of our climate crisis. For Rush, then, organized retreat is not necessarily about keeping humans separate from nature, per se, so much as it is about reconsidering our perceived need to continually repair ecosystems following natural disasters, especially when the reasons for such repairs privilege the perceived needs of humans. Moreover, Rush notes more generally that organized retreat can potentially make room for other vulnerable, more-than-human species to move in to climate-damaged regions as well.[46] In this way, for instance, we can acknowledge organized retreat, and what some may describe as "letting a place sit undisturbed," as a way of letting go of the human-centric emphasis on recreation, and instead allow breathing room for other life-forms that can make do without the accoutrements of human infrastructure.

I again juxtapose this once-flooded landscape with the comfort I have felt in the light rain and morning thunderstorms here. The sound of distant thunderstorms has been a comforting accompaniment to coffee on an overcast morning—one that is reminiscent of East Coast summers. My experience of the rain here is one that, in this moment, sparks joy rather than anxiety. But I am a temporary visitor to this place. Again, I imagine that these more immediately idyllic perceptions of place are what people might experience when they visit Santa Barbara. On the night of the Montecito mudslide in January 2018, the rain fell at a rate of thirteen millimeters, or 0.54 inches, in just five minutes. In nearby Carpinteria, rain accumulated at a rate of twenty-two millimeters, 0.86 inches, in fifteen minutes.[47] When rain falls at that rate in an area with so little vegetation left, then there is risk of debris flows. These places are simultaneously beautiful and fragile, comforting and anxiety-producing. My visit to Omaha underscores the ways that experiences of place are contextual and ephemeral. When we are in from out of town, perhaps we experience the immediate beauty of a place more readily.

I am hopeful that Haworth Park will recover from the Heartland flood in time, but what such a recovery might look like is as yet unclear. As of September 2020, the Haworth Park campground loop and old marina remained closed to the public; however, the city of Bellevue plans to maintain the campground portion of the park, and to help manage the costs, the city formed a public-private partnership with a local resident to help rebuild it.[48] Thus, perhaps in time, people will be able to enjoy the campground once again, while perhaps other portions of the park may see more of an organized retreat. All of these scenarios will likely invite new ways of understanding this place. Whatever the future of Haworth Park, I am grateful for the privilege of being able to experience these different ways of knowing this place. And I feel grateful to be able to convey this dissonance through writing; it is but one small way that I feel able to return the gifts that these encounters provide. I had not at first anticipated how this interlude might become a catalyst for writing about climate anxiety. Nor had I anticipated the experience of writing from and about one place while simultaneously experiencing concern for another. That is, as I imagine the possible futures of Haworth Park, and as I listen to the whisper song of the Eastern jay, I am still thinking of California.

## CHAPTER 3

# Storied Places and Species in Flux

## *Connectivity as Reciprocity*

P-22 is doing well these days; that is, he's reported to be in good physical health, at least.[1] We know this because in spring 2019, biologists with the California Department of Fish and Wildlife temporarily captured him to replace the batteries in his radio collar; during this time, they also conducted a general physical exam. At about nine or ten years old, this 118-pound male mountain lion appears to be doing well. But the details of his personal circumstances might prompt us to question whether he's living his best life, whether his physical wellness extends to his emotional well-being, and what the broader implications are for this mountain lion who has in fact adapted to a home that is less optimal and more public than some feel it ought to be.

P-22 resides in Griffith Park—one of the most well-known parks in the Los Angeles, California, area. Home to the famous Griffith Park Observatory, the park is essentially surrounded by highways. It is flanked by the infamous 405 to the east, the 101 to the south and west, and the 134 to the north—none of which are for the faint of heart or those unaccustomed to driving in southern California. These are the same freeways that are responsible for the stereotypes about what it's like to drive in Los Angeles.

We don't know exactly how or when, because his arrival in Griffith Park happened pre-radio collar, but P-22 somehow managed to traverse the 405 and the 101 freeways to make his way into the park. It is possible he was "searching for an unoccupied space with food," or that he was seeking out his own territory, as adult male lions will do, and venturing away from other male mountain lions in the region; we don't really know for sure.[2] Adult male lions "can occupy up to 250 square miles," but P-22's home range in Griffith Park is a mere eight square miles.[3] He was first spotted on the park's security cameras sometime in 2012—a sight that surprised even the most seasoned National Park Service professionals. Since then, he has lived in the park, mostly unseen.

P-22 spends most of his time in the remotest sections of Griffith Park. He keeps to himself for the most part and suffers no shortage of mule deer to hunt—typical prey for a mountain lion. He is regularly monitored by officials with the Santa Monica Mountains National Recreation Area but is rarely seen by the public, even though his territory is only about a third of what a typical adult mountain lion requires and "the smallest recorded home range of any adult male mountain lion ever studied."[4]

Over the past eight years or so, P-22 has dealt with several challenges. In 2014, he had a troubling case of mange, for which he was successfully treated. Perhaps most concerning, however, was his exposure to anti-coagulant rodenticides, which may have actually been related to the mange.[5] P-22's blood tested positive for two kinds of rodenticide, diphacinone and chlorophacinone, adding fuel to the ongoing debate in California about the use of these toxic chemicals.[6] While P-22 survived exposure to these poisons that are commonly used in rodent bait stations and that easily move up the food chain, two other mountain lions are known to have died from rodenticide poisoning, according to the National Park Service.[7]

Despite these human-induced adversities and his relative lack of room to roam, P-22 has seemingly adapted to his home in Griffith Park. He is not at all viewed by park officials or biologists as a threat to human safety; in fact, it is arguable that humans pose more of a threat to his own well-being.

> Mountain lions are our *"neighbors."*
> —Beth Pratt[8]

One might think that the presence of a mountain lion in such close proximity to areas of human habitation would give local residents cause for concern and thus reason to fear P-22. Rather, just the opposite seems to be the case; thanks in large part to a public education campaign led by Beth Pratt, California regional executive director for the National Wildlife Federation and leader of the #SaveLACougars campaign, people have, for the most part, come to empathize with what they understand to be the challenges P-22 faces and to which he has adapted. As Pratt has compassionately put it, local citizens have largely embraced P-22 as their wild kin—as their "*neighbor.*"[9] For better or worse, then, Griffith Park has become home for P-22, by way of unintentional displacement via his attempt to traverse a fragmented habitat.

The local public's acceptance of P-22 has been due in large part to the efforts of the #SaveLACougars campaign, which educates the public about how to coexist with wildlife in urban spaces. The #SaveLACougars campaign was founded by Pratt and is a joint effort of the National Wildlife Federation and the Santa Monica Mountains Fund. Its mission is to "Save a population of mountain lions from extinction; Reconnect an entire ecosystem for all wildlife; Set a worldwide model for urban wildlife conservation; [and] Create a conservation legacy for the next century."[10] As I describe in more detail below, the campaign also supports the "conservation, education and fundraising" for the related Liberty Canyon wildlife crossing, which, as of this writing, is still scheduled to break ground in 2021.[11]

P-22 has in many ways become the face of the #SaveLACougars campaign. In the Los Angeles area, for instance, the campaign sponsors the well-attended "P-22 Day" and "Urban Wildlife Week." During the inaugural Urban Wildlife Week in 2016, Pratt led a much-publicized, four-day hike from the Agoura Hills in the Santa Monica Mountains about fifty miles east to Griffith Park, to retrace the journey that P-22 would have completed in order to wind up in Griffith Park.[12] The hike, which crossed two freeways just as P-22 would have done, began at the Liberty Canyon trailhead near the 101 freeway, at the site of the proposed wildlife corridor. Pratt, who led the hike, carried with her a life-size P-22 cutout to call attention to the need for people and wildlife to coexist.[13]

The life-size cutout of P-22 has gained some local popularity, and people often take selfies with P-22's likeness at events like Urban Wildlife Week. Moreover, P-22 now has his own Facebook page, in which discussions of local events are often written in P-22's point of view. These public events and discourses arguably allow humans to relate with or better identify with P-22, and may help foster a sense of empathy for him.

On the one hand, some scholars have critiqued a communicative approach that leverages anthropomorphization for its potential to speak on behalf of another species, and have subsequently begun to explore the question: "Who benefits, cui bono, when species meet?"[14] More specifically, when people anthropomorphize, or project their own human assumptions or voice on to more-than-humans, they interpret "what is not human or personal in terms of human or personal characteristics."[15] Some scholars have also, for instance, critiqued selfies with actual, living animals, suggesting that they can perpetuate a distance between the human and the animal, or reinforce boundaries of "us" and "them."[16] I have similarly argued elsewhere that when we make species more visible, we may run the risk of making them more vulnerable in the process. On the other hand, however, I would also suggest that in this context of the selfie with P-22's *likeness* (certainly not with a living mountain lion), the selfie, taken specifically in the context of a festival meant to educate about peaceful coexistence with wildlife, may in fact help to foster a sense of compassion and empathy for vulnerable species—empathy that can then help garner support for broader, related conservation efforts.

In this sense, then, as philosopher Jane Bennett argues, anthropomorphism can also function more productively to draw our attention to the mundane in more meaningful ways, and as a result, "an anthropomorphic element in perception can uncover a whole world of resonances and resemblances."[17] Where we "may at first see only a world in our own image," we may soon also see points of "vibrant" uniqueness.[18] While context matters greatly, anthropomorphization can, then, be a useful tool for establishing common ground or a point of identification with a perceived other. When we anthropomorphically see another in ourselves, myriad possibilities arise for compassion and entangled empathy—for seeing and understanding in a way that can make a productive difference in the world.

Moreover, as this chapter argues, entangled empathy can move us closer to understanding conservation and connectivity restoration projects through the lens of a culture of reciprocity—as gifts that we may give back to our more-than-human kin who were here long before us. This chapter ultimately helps reveal that, in the Anthropocene, "home" not only means being receptive and open to a language of animacy and a culture of reciprocity, but also, by extension, it means an openness to rethinking our assumptions about where humans and wildlife "belong." Such a mindset is, again, in many ways akin to what Kimmerer refers to as an "Indigenous worldview," in which, as she tells us, we may view the ecosystem not as "a machine," but rather as a community of entangled beings, "subjects rather than objects."[19] Such perspectives can help illuminate moments of elemental relationality and empathy for our more-than-human kin.

Largely as a result of #SaveLACougars campaign, then, P-22 has come to be "seen as a neighbor—as part of the LA community." As Pratt has described, "people like having him around." And perhaps most important, P-22 is helping people shift their perceptions about "where nature should be."[20] In many ways, the #SaveLACougars campaign promotes a message of coexistence, empathy, compassionate conservation, and a posthuman approach that complicates our assumptions about the perceived need for boundaries between people and wildlife.

While Pratt is clear that P-22's home in Griffith Park is far from ideal, she is humbled by how he has managed to adapt to a home in an urban setting, and she wonders if we may also adapt to these less boundaried ideas about who belongs where. As geographer Jamie Lorimer reminds us, "wildlife lives among us. . . . Risky, endearing, charismatic, and unknown, wildlife persists in our post-Natural world."[21] Moreover, Lorimer points out that "knowing wildlife well requires . . . curiosity and the open-ended care for difference it engenders."[22] Likewise for Pratt, "there is very little 'wild state' anymore."[23] Pratt, whose work has always taken place in national parks, describes the first time she hiked around Griffith Park; as she juxtaposed the surrounding views of the Hollywood sign and LA's smog with the knowledge that a mountain lion lived right there in her midst, it occurred to her that "this cat has more imagination than I do," thus prompting her to ask: "Why *can't* a mountain lion live in the city? Why is the human-built environment always seen as off-limits to wildlife? If it's good enough for a mountain lion, who are we to judge?"[24] She anticipates the human response to such questions: What about safety, and what about risks to humans? Of course, living among wildlife comes with risk, she says bluntly, "but if mountain lions wanted to eat us, they would. They're stealth predators. . . . And I can tell you, the risks of living with wildlife is minimal, compared with some of the human threats we face."[25] In Los Angeles County alone, says Pratt, "automobiles have killed an average of over 700 people a year," whereas "mountain lions have been responsible for just three deaths since 1986."[26] What's more, we already live with mountain lions—we just don't realize it. Instead of thinking about urban spaces as just for humans, we need to change "our perceptions of nature and where wildlife can be."[27] Pratt argues that humans tend to want to place these animals in a landscape we are more comfortable with, "like a forest or a meadow, or something free of human intrusion."[28] But clearly, sometimes "wildlife can adapt to human spaces. The real question is: Can *we* adapt to wildlife?"[29] Lorimer takes a similar view, suggesting that "a reappraisal of urban ecologies is part of a growing interest in nature outside protected areas. . . . In short, conservationists are finding that wildlife is poorly understood and governed by drawing and policing boxes."[30] Again, wildlife and nature do not exist solely in places where humans are absent; rather, we live among wildlife, and our more-than-human kin live among us. Moreover, writes Lorimer, wildlife is also "on the move—

transgressing national, regional, and other territorial boundaries, performing diverse and discordant animal, plant, and other nonhuman geographies."[31]

The traditional view of conservation has been to put people "over here," and wildlife elsewhere—in protected spaces. As Lorimer suggests, some have argued that the "biogeographies for the conservation of Nature tend to purify space and stabilize time. Protected areas map the modern Nature-Society binary to establish and police fixed and ranked territories for Nature"; they perpetuate a "separation of the urban from the wilderness/countryside."[32] Viewed in this way, says Lorimer, "conservation is caught in a 'territorial trap' in which nations, nature reserves, and other politicized units become the bounded containers for Nature."[33] Not dissimilar from this view, Pratt argues in her TED Talk that we do need to keep protecting places like our national parks—that wildlife do need these places; however, this approach *alone* does not entirely work. Even in our most protected places, like national parks, wildlife is having a hard time.

Pratt argues that "we need to challenge these notions of boundaries, because what science is telling us now, is nature needs to be connected to work across large landscapes."[34] And connectivity is really about fostering "a new paradigm of conservation, which is coexistence."[35] Moreover, coexistence is "not about habituating wildlife—it's about habituating *ourselves* to the wild world." Taking P-22 as a case in point, Pratt reminds us that wildlife "have proven themselves willing to compromise"; rather, she asks, "*What will we do?*"[36]

The case of P-22 is in many ways a quintessential example of how entangled empathy can function in the public sphere, and how anthropomorphization, in specific contexts, and working in the positive, can play a role in fostering empathy and promoting a message of coexistence. The #SaveLACougars campaign has arguably leveraged anthropomorphization in a productive and specific context to help educate the public about coexistence with mountain lions. The campaign has helped identify perceived points of commonality between P-22 and his human neighbors: he, too, has faced the challenges of LA traffic and fragmented freeway systems; he, too, lives on his own amidst a crowded urban population. As a result, local residents have come to view P-22 as part of their community. With the understanding that mountain lions rarely attack humans, that they prefer and seek out solitude, and with knowledge of what to do in the event of a mountain lion sighting—namely, don't run but instead make noise and calmly leave the area—people who live in the neighborhoods around Griffith Park have come to view P-22 as part of the community.

> The stories we tell change the way we act in the world.
>
> —William Cronon[37]

P-22 has unwittingly become part of the community—not by choice, however, but rather because he is essentially trapped *in place*. He has *storied his place* through the fact of his own displacement. For P-22, Griffith Park is an unintentionally "storied place" that is the outcome of a fragmented home range divided by human infrastructure. In considering the notion of a storied place, as described in the introduction, we may think of "a story" not only as a noun, but also as an adjective, "a storied place," and as a verb, "to story" a place. As anthropologist Thom van Dooren describes, to consider how species "story" their places can help us understand "the ethical significance of destroying places" that species "are in an important sense tied to."[38] He asks: "What kinds of ethical obligations might be opened up by a new sensitivity to the storying and place-making practices" of our more-than-human kin?[39] Storied places are "invested with history and meaning."[40] For mountain lions and other species, stories can help us think about the implications of human development and infrastructure for places upon which these more-than-human kin rely. Storied places can also help us contextualize the ethics of reestablishing places that species must reconnect with in order to thrive.

As Lorimer similarly points out, "to choreograph landscape dynamics and to seek to modulate such rates of change," conservationists must become open to and mindful of "animals' geographies—thinking like an elephant, an insect, or even a molecule" can help us better understand the perspective of our more-than-human kin, and "the diverse ways in which nonhuman life inhabits the novel ecosystems of the Anthropocene planet."[41] An empathetic perspective informed by storied places may then help illuminate "interspecies dependencies and conflicts. It makes manifest the consequences of differential mobilities and degrees of landscape permeability in the face of a changing climate" and helps us empathize with the different and "more-than-human ways of being on this planet."[42]

Building on these ideas, I am interested in the kinds of ethical obligations that are opened up by an attentiveness to the place-making practices of vulnerable species; subsequently, then, we might ask: Do we have an obligation to help displaced species story *new* places? To help them *re-story their lost places*? If so, how might we leverage our own place-making abilities in ways that are sensitive to and productive of the vibrant lives of vulnerable species?

P-22 has learned the language of his own place and adapted to it—he is both native to a place now inhabited by humans, and he has had to relearn and adapt to his native environment by navigating its margins to remain unseen, or rarely seen. When we pay attention to the lives of vulnerable species like P-22, we learn many "'unspoken' stories," and in the process, we learn "an appreciation for more-than-human practices of meaning and place-making in a disappearing world."[43]

The #SaveLACougars campaign also provides a useful example of how different groups of stakeholders can work together to garner public advocacy for urban wildlife conservation. On the one hand, it might initially seem difficult to picture the life of P-22 in terms of the "gift mindset" and the "culture of reciprocity" that Kimmerer describes, as P-22 has little to no chance of ever leaving the park, or, by extension, finding a mate, because of the fragmented habitat that the LA freeway system has created in this area. On the other hand, P-22's presence in the park is arguably a gift from which humans can learn empathy and understanding. It might seem harder to argue that humans have given him a gift in return—unless, that is, we consider more broadly the ways that we may reciprocate the gift that his presence has bestowed.

To this end, plans for the nearby Liberty Canyon wildlife corridor could help prevent such displacement scenarios from happening in the future. P-22 resides too far east of the planned wildlife crossing to directly benefit from it himself, but this corridor project can help prevent his situation from repeating. It can help protect the genetic biodiversity of mountain lions and other wildlife in the region by preventing them from getting hemmed in to a place, and it can also help prevent mountain lions in this region from risking their lives while trying to cross these dangerous sections of freeway in the future.

Thus, if we understand projects such as the Liberty Canyon wildlife crossing as part of a culture of reciprocity—as a way of giving back to a community of wildlife by fostering new pathways for biodiversity and working against the damage wrought by human development over time, then perhaps we may return the gift of P-22's presence after all.

Broadly defined, wildlife corridors are "spaces in which connectivity between species, ecosystems, and ecological processes is maintained or restored at various scales."[44] They are essentially large tracts of habitat linked in ways that allow species to move safely across or through areas of human use. Wildlife corridors are not meant to move species away from humans, per se; rather, it is just the opposite: they are meant to foster and sustain coexistence and connectivity. They are meant to give wildlife options so that they don't get hemmed in to specific areas without a way out. Corridors can be built in urban spaces as well as in more remote areas. Moreover, connectivity projects need not involve huge overpasses; sometimes, fostering connectivity can involve as minimal an adjustment as leaving a gap in residential fencing to give species a way out of a human's yard. As Lorimer further describes: "Connectivity is a multifaceted concept, configured by the nature of what is being connected and the spatial and temporal scope of analysis. In its most straightforward framings, it provides an index of spatial linkage and informs demands for 'conservation corridors' and 'ecological networks' to link together protected areas."[45] Lorimer also acknowledges the more "hands-on forms of connectivity management," which this chapter does not discuss, such as practices of assisted migration, as well as "translocating and reintroducing organisms that are unable to move or for whom such networked ecologies would be too expensive."[46] It is also worth noting that in California, it is illegal to physically relocate mountain lions.[47]

Connectivity projects are often viewed as necessary, because when land is set aside or used for human activities, habitats that were once fluid and connected can become fragmented. If species are unable to move between these fragmented areas, they become at risk for inbreeding or extinction. Wildlife corridors attempt to remediate such fragmentation by restoring connectivity and creating "bands of forest habitat that are large and intact enough that they provide animals with an important bridge between larger blocks of habitat."[48] Providing such linkages between habitats reduces these risks and helps maintain genetic diversity and a population's health; at least, this is the more posthuman and less anthropocentric rationale for wildlife corridors. That is, connectivity projects like the Liberty Canyon crossing constitute spatial, infrastructural, posthuman interventions that intervene, ideally productively, in the lives of vulnerable species and reconfigure our relationships with them, as well as their relationships with place. They also illuminate the different value systems and rationales that inform how we conceptualize and practice dwelling *with* our more-than-human kin.

While rationales for these projects vary, biodiversity conservation is one of the overarching arguments for wildlife corridors; others argue, however, that wildlife corridors are good for humans, in that they help prevent traffic accidents, for example, by giving wildlife other pathways for traversing areas of significant human use, ultimately helping to avoid such incidents. Of course, both rationales are sensible enough, and they often overlap when it comes to discourses about the need for wildlife corridors. The discourses around the need to keep mountain lions off California freeways, for instance, both to prevent their displacement and to protect lives (both theirs and humans'), are one example of such intertwined rationales. But Kimmerer productively and necessarily pushes our thinking a bit further, suggesting that we consider instead a more Indigenous worldview. Again, she asks: "What if we took an indigenous worldview" about restoration? Here, she rightly understands "the ecosystem is not a machine," but instead suggests that we are part of a collective—a "community of sovereign beings, subjects rather than objects." She asks: "What if those beings were the drivers?"[49]

Moreover, Kimmerer provides an apt example of how a culture of reciprocity not only pertains to an Indigenous worldview but also relates to wildlife corridors more specifically. To do so, she tells the story of salamanders who make an annual trek across a busy stretch of road in her hometown in Onondaga County, upstate New York. During this yearly salamander migration, she goes out at night to help carry individual salamanders safely across the road, such that they do not get hit by fast-moving vehicles. In doing so, she contends: "Carrying salamanders to safety also helps us to remember the covenant of reciprocity, the mutual responsibility that we each have for each other. As the perpetrators of the war zone on this road, are we not bound to heal the wounds that we inflict?"[50] I'm not sure I could pose this question any better myself. In other words, these acts of restoring connectivity, whether they be at a smaller, individual scale or at a larger scale, are part of a human ethical obligation to act with empathy as we consider the ways that contemporary human development and infrastructure have impacted the lives of our more-than-human kin.

Such a perspective not only calls into question anthropocentric, hierarchical rationales for conservation projects, but also, as chapter 2 suggested, it helps illuminate the possible connections between an Indigenous worldview and a more posthuman perspective, by positing a relational and ecological vantage point that also suggests we ought to think in terms of a "community of sovereign beings," all equally worthy of value and respect. Viewed from this vantage point, connectivity projects become about storied place, nuance, coexistence, and a culture of reciprocity, rather than about questions of which rationales make a project most worthwhile for humans.

P-22 is not the only mountain lion to traverse these infamous California freeways—he is perhaps just the most well-known to do so. The National Park Service (NPS) has actually been studying mountain lions in this region of the Santa Monica Mountains since 2002. Researchers with the NPS currently monitor over seventy-five lions in the region in order to better understand how they have managed to survive in such fragmented and developed habitats.[51] In late August 2019, the mountain lion P-65 successfully traversed the 101 freeway in southern California. The lion crossed the 101 around 2 a.m. near Agoura Hills, just north of the Santa Monica Mountains, near the planned crossing; from there, she headed north toward the Simi Hills—an area more populated by humans. Rangers for the NPS noted that "she's just the second radio-collared female to cross the 101 in the National Park Service's 17-year study of cougars in and around the Los Angeles area," and that prior to her movement, "P-65 had been tracked living in or around the perimeter of where the Woolsey Fire erupted last November [of 2018]. She was first collared in the mountain's central portion in March 2018."[52] The Liberty Canyon crossing thus hopes to address these safety issues affecting both people and wildlife; in doing so, it will also purportedly be the largest wildlife corridor in the world.[53]

In addition to showing that the freeway infrastructure in this region is deadly for mountain lions, research by the National Park Service over the past two decades has demonstrated that the fragmented habitat has curtailed their biodiversity.[54] For example, Seth Riley, a wildlife ecologist with the NPS, describes a single litter of mountain lion kittens, referred to as P-36 and P-37, in which "P-12 was the father and the grandfather and the great grandfather. That's what happens when you have all these animals basically stuck in this small area and they're not able to get back and forth."[55] Of course, fragmented habitats affect more than just mountain lions, and the planned crossing at Liberty Canyon should help species such as bobcats, deer, coyotes, lizards, birds, and other small fauna as well.

## THE PROMISE AND THE PARADOX OF CONNECTIVITY

Liberty Canyon is, in essence, the second act for this storied place—or what architect Clark Stevens has described as "storied Land."[56] Stevens created the final design plans for the crossing, and he is also the executive officer of the Resource Conservation District of the Santa Monica Mountains. This connectivity project is born out of a sensitivity to the lives and land of vulnerable species in need of mobility but trapped in place. Invested with history and meaning, Liberty Canyon and the surrounding region constitute already storied land that has potential to participate in the ethical re-storying of lost connection, lost place—lost inhabitation. For Stevens, "'authentic' inhabitation, 'while not restricted to the local or regional, depends on the clarity and precision that comes from sustained attention to the particular.' The process finds *global* truth through *ground* truth."[57]

Sustained attention to this particular ground truth gained "renewed urgency" in 2013, when a male mountain lion was killed on the 101 freeway.[58] In this case, according to Riley, the lion had apparently "made it across eight lanes of traffic but then was stopped cold by a 10-foot-tall concrete retaining wall topped by several feet of chain-link fencing on the south side of the freeway." By the point in time of this lion's death, the project had largely stalled due to lack of funding, and the California Department of Transportation "had twice sought federal funding" to build a crossing near the Liberty Canyon exit.[59] In November 2014, however, following the death of the mountain lion, "the California Wildlife Conservation Board unanimously approved $650,000 in voter-passed grant funds to complete Phase 1 of the planned safe wildlife crossing of the 101 freeway at Liberty Canyon in Agoura Hills."[60] Then, in 2015, the board of the California State Coastal Conservancy "voted unanimously" to donate one million dollars "to the California Department of Transportation to conduct the environmental assessment and develop initial designs for a possible crossing through the 101-Freeway at Liberty Canyon Road in Agoura Hills."[61]

The crossing itself will be about 165 feet wide and 200 feet long.[62] It will be built in a region of southern California called the Agoura Hills, and will connect the Santa Monica Mountains to the south with the Simi Hills to the north. The Simi Hills is a critical habitat area that lies between the Santa Monica Mountains and core habitat areas of the Santa Susana and Sierra Madre. The overpass will cross the ten lanes of freeway that P-22 once navigated and that P-65 recently traversed. This whole region, however, has in essence become an ecological island, bounded by the Pacific Ocean to the south and west, "and surrounded elsewhere by urban development and freeways."[63] While the corridor will essentially be a land bridge over the two sides of the freeway, it is not meant to attract more wildlife; rather, it is intended to make sure that current wildlife, namely mountain lions in the region, will not become extinct.[64]

While the Liberty Canyon crossing will appear to be a typical overpass, it will be covered in native plants such as scrub oak, with the goal of making it feel like and resemble native habitat. The structure is designed to "resemble an extension of the mountainside, and will be made of concrete and the soil that had been removed from that site to build the freeway."[65] Fencing will help guide wildlife toward the crossing. And while locals may know of its presence, it is not meant to be any kind of wildlife viewing area—just the opposite, in fact; it is "unlikely that people will be able to view wildlife on the bridge," as there will be much vegetation and plant life preventing a direct view from the freeway.[66] Visual and sound barriers will also be built along the perimeters of the structure "to block noise and headlights from scaring away wildlife."[67]

The Liberty Canyon site is promising for two reasons: "First, data from wildlife cameras and collared animals showed that they were already using the area. It's the spot where the male mountain lion was killed in 2013," and it's also the place where, in 2015, a female lion "successfully emigrated out of the Santa Monicas."[68] For Stevens, these points signal that the mountain lions are seeking to move from that region and are looking for ways to do so; as he puts it: "They're moving in there. They're interested."[69]

Next, as Pratt describes, the wildlife crossing will be built "in the last 1,600 feet in the area that possesses protected land north and south of the 101," and in doing so, "will re-establish a key connectivity path in the Santa Monica Mountains, and link to critical open space to the north," in the Simi Hills, Santa Susana Mountains, and Los Padres National Forest.[70] Stevens agrees, and sees the surrounding landscape as ideal for helping to connect this fragmented habitat: "The eastern connector runs [from the Santa Monicas] up through the Las Virgenes Open Space, a big patch of good habitat in the Santa Susana Field Lab, the Chatsworth-Simi Divide, and to the 118 where there's an existing crossing."[71] If a mountain lion makes it to that point, they would be in "the Santa Susana Mountains, just one step away from the cougars' promised land: Los Padres National Forest."[72] Moreover, this linkage "is relatively wide. An effective wildlife corridor isn't just a narrow strip of green between parks."[73] As Stevens points out: "Really what we're talking about is linkages where you can feed and breed."[74] In other words, we are not simply talking about a new overpass; rather, we must think more holistically about the more expansive, surrounding ecosystems and habitats that will be reconnected as a result of this project.

To reconnect this fragmented habitat achieves more than just drawing attention to the impact of fragmentation on vulnerable species. Sustained attention to the "ground truth" of Liberty Canyon in Agoura Hills and the surrounding region also reveals the complexities of "storied Land," or as Stevens further defines the concept, the "condition of Land relationships," beyond that of these vulnerable species.[75]

## BURRO FLATS PAINTED CAVE: A STORIED PLACE AND LOST SITE OF BELONGING

The area about twenty miles or so north of the planned wildlife crossing has some fascinating history and interconnections across time and place. Just north of the Las Virgenes Canyon Open Space Preserve and about twenty miles north of Liberty Canyon Road lies the Santa Susana Field Lab.[76] The Santa Susana Field Lab has an intriguing, slightly eerie, and somewhat checkered Cold War–era history; in addition, it is also situated in close proximity to an ancient Chumash site called Burro Flats Painted Cave. About thirty miles northwest of downtown Los Angeles, the field lab is a 2,850-acre site formerly used to test rocket engines and conduct nuclear research. The facility was built in 1947 and operational for over fifty years; nuclear research ceased in 1988 and the testing of rocket engines ended in 2006.[77] In 1996, Boeing acquired much of the site from Rocketdyne, and has since engaged in cleanup efforts and restoration of the area.[78] Nonetheless, as is imaginable, years of nuclear research and rocket fuel testing have resulted in contaminated soil and groundwater, and residents of nearby Simi Valley have since questioned whether incidents of cancer in fifty children in the area may be related to the environmental contaminants. Despite ongoing efforts to clean up the area, the site is still considered to be heavily contaminated, and a 2012 report from the Environmental Protection Agency found that "approximately one out of every seven samples contained 'concentrations of radioactive materials exceeding background levels.'"[79] More recently, the Woolsey Fire of 2018 burned a significant portion of the site, causing concern about whether additional radioactive substances may have been released into the environment.[80]

In addition to the detrimental environmental impacts of years of Cold War–era research on the land and its inhabitants, the site also has some more fascinating and celestial connections with local Chumash culture. Like much of central and southern California, the area around Liberty Canyon, the Santa Monica Mountains, and the Simi Valley is native Chumash land. Liberty Canyon itself was once the site of a Chumash village named Talopop, which is today the name of the loop trail that circles the vicinity.

Recently, the Santa Ynez Band of Chumash Indians and local environmental groups have become interested in protecting what are called the "Coca Test Stand Areas" at the Santa Susana Field Lab site, given the cultural significance of that place for the Chumash. These test stands were large, visually imposing structures—scaffolded towers, really, that were used by NASA to test rocket engines from the mid-1950s until the early twenty-first century.[81] The test stands were set up at multiple sites, or "firing positions," within the field lab area; "nearly all the stands were built between 1954 and 1957 and named Alfa, Bravo, Coca and Delta," but after the 1960s, most of the tests happened at the Coca stands.[82] The test stands are also situated in close proximity to the nearby Burro Flats Painted Cave site.

In April 2020, NASA announced that it would demolish the Bravo and Coca Test Stand Areas. The Santa Ynez Band of Chumash Indians and the nonprofit organization Save Open Space, Santa Monica Mountains (SOS), which "concentrates on maintaining open space, protecting wildlife, and preserving natural resources" in the Santa Monica Mountains, both disagreed with the decision, maintaining that "the Coca Stands are far more historically important and much more majestic as a possible future attraction in a National Monument."[83] Moreover, Save Open Space points out that environmental studies of these test stands show that contamination is mostly limited to the soils, and that soil cleanup "can be done without touching the stand structures themselves." The test stands contain leaded paint, which "is flaking off the structures," but this cleanup can apparently also be completed without fully dismantling the stands.[84]

## TWO CULTURES, BOTH STUDYING THE SKIES

The Santa Ynez Band of Chumash Indians and Save Open Space worked together to advocate for the protection of the Coca Stands, in part because of their close proximity to the nearby Burro Flats Painted Cave site. As SOS and the Chumash describe, the Coca Stands

are the ones in closest proximity to the Burro Flats Painted Cave site. This is the only place in the world where celestial paintings done by ancient man are located in the exact same spot where 20th century man actually took the steps to reach the stars. After the cleanup, The Burro Flats Cave and the Coca stands could be considered key features of a future National Monument/NASA Landmark celebrating that fact.[85]

For the Chumash in particular, then, the Coca Stands and the Burro Flats Painted Cave sites represent a merging of worlds, of temporality and spatiality, that speaks to the cultural importance of this place. Burro Flats Painted Cave "is a cave in a mountainous area located between Simi Valley, California and Chatsworth, California, containing Chumash Indian pictographs. The cave is located on private land owned by Boeing-Rocketdyne (formerly operated at Rocketdyne's Santa Susana Field Laboratory used to test rocket engines) and is not accessible to the public."[86]

The famous and somewhat mysterious pictographs at Burro Flats are considered to be some of the most well-preserved Indian pictographs in southern California, largely because they are, paradoxically, situated on restricted land. They are estimated as being several hundred years old, and are described in literature as depicting "two human stick figures wearing headdresses with lines radiating from the heads. There are also stick-figure animals with four fingers, a circle with a star inside, a plant resembling a cornstalk, and more abstract groupings of circles and lines with a tail." The cave is described as a "small, hollowed-out portion of a long, low rock set into a grassy slope," although its location is not public.[87]

Different theories exist as to the significance of the cave's location and the meaning of the pictographs. The predominant thinking is that the cave was used by the Chumash as an observatory and to celebrate the winter solstice.[88] As astronomer Edwin Krupp writes in his study of the area: "An astronomical element in the paintings at Burro Flats was first noticed in early 1979 by John Romani, a graduate student in archaeology at California State University, Northridge. He thought a natural cut—a kind of bottomless window—in the overhang above the western end of the panel paintings looked like it might let sunlight pass through and strike a part of the otherwise shaded panel—at about the time of the winter solstice."[89] And interestingly, the paintings, "which record the involvement of the Chumash with the sky, are separated by just a ridge from the stands on which the huge moon-rocket and Space Shuttle engines were test fired."[90] It is quite paradoxical that the Burro Flats Painted

Cave site has essentially been "protected" all these years because it is situated on land now owned by Rocketdyne and Boeing. That is, the land around the Santa Susana Field Lab has been restricted for so long that it is still "protected" to an extent, depending on how we define the concept. The land is arguably protected in the sense that it has not been further developed, but not in the sense that the land has been shielded from past environmental contamination. More recently, in 2017, "Boeing recorded a conservation easement covering its nearly 2,400 acres of the site to ensure Boeing's property is never developed for residential or agricultural use, and is forever preserved as open space habitat."[91] This open space habitat will then allow for the reconnection of the land to the north and south of the planned wildlife crossing at Liberty Canyon.

Thus, this storied place, once implicated in the sort of technological and nuclear research that is today deemed ethically questionable, and also considered a significant aspect of Chumash culture, may now participate in a culture of reciprocity through a contemporary project meant to reconnect these once-fragmented habitats. Paradoxically, these Cold War–era, restricted test sites—this multilayered, storied land, significant also to Chumash culture— are now part of a new technoscientific endeavor that is the Liberty Canyon wildlife crossing.

This merging of Chumash culture with the projects of technoscience, old and new, constitutes both an erasure and a rediscovery. The Burro Flats Painted Cave is an ancient site of belonging at once isolated yet preserved via the paradoxical mechanisms of technoscience. That is, the site can now participate in a culture of reciprocity, paradoxically because it was once unwittingly interconnected with Cold War–era, technoscientific endeavors. The projects of technoscience, however, ought not to be grouped under a single umbrella. Rather, they must be understood in the context of their overarching goals and also in the context of the philosophies that inform those goals. Grounded in an ethic of compassionate conservation and in a culture of reciprocity, the Liberty Canyon crossing has the potential to story this place anew. Part of the success of the Liberty Canyon crossing rides on species' ability to move easily through these areas. As species make use of these new connections, they will create new storied places. These long-forgotten connections between northern and southern regions, and between earth and sky, are not, however, the only currents of storied land, of storied skies, that this connectivity project invokes.

> It matters what stories we tell to tell other stories with.
> —Donna Haraway[92]

During a design workshop for the Liberty Canyon crossing, Beth Pratt, along with engineers, landscape architects, and other subject matter experts, came together to brainstorm their ideas and plans for the project.[93] An important outcome of the planning session, especially from the vantage point of this chapter, is how the wildlife crossing may help us to better conceptualize what counts as "home" in the Anthropocene. One discussion in particular that emerged during the workshop has some distinct synergies with such questions. Pratt had invited Alan Salazar to provide his input on the project; Salazar has been "involved with protecting Native American cultural sites for 20 years"; has served as a "consultant/monitor on sites in Ventura, LA, Santa Barbara, San Luis Obispo and Kern counties"; and is also a traditional storyteller.[94] Pratt describes how "the power" of Salazar's storytelling and perspective during the workshop "transformed that discussion," and moved engineers and those involved with the corridor's design to think with more nuance about its larger implications.[95] Salazar helped convey a perspective informed by Chumash culture to describe "what the wildlife crossing meant, beyond the structure" itself, specifically by telling the Chumash story of the Rainbow Bridge.[96] For Pratt, the story of the Rainbow Bridge is a "perfect way to represent the wildlife crossing," and so to help convey these ideas, she recently invited Salazar to share some stories, including that of the Rainbow Bridge, on her video series, "P-22 Presents."[97] During this video segment, Salazar, who is a descendent of the Chumash and Tataviam people and an elder in the Ferdandiño Tataviam Band of Mission Indians,[98] describes the Rainbow Bridge as a Chumash creation story that is meant to impart a lesson through its narrative.[99] As Salazar describes, the main lesson of the Rainbow Bridge story is that the "Chumash people believed that we came from the Earth, and this is our *home*."[100] I gratefully acknowledge permission from Alan Salazar to quote from and summarize his telling of the Rainbow Bridge story below. In doing so, I have used a combination of direct quotation and paraphrase to help convey his account of this story, and I have done my best to retain its meaning and essence; however, readers may also appreciate listening to the full version of his story, as he tells it online.[101]

## THE STORY OF THE RAINBOW BRIDGE

Alan Salazar tells the story of how the Mother Earth spirit, Hutash, created the Chumash people: "She took seeds from a special plant . . . and she cast them all over the island of Limuw," which is today called Santa Cruz Island. And "when the plant grew, instead of flowers or fruit blooming from the plant, the Chumash people bloomed from the plant."[102] As Salazar describes, "when the Sky People saw the Chumash people, they thought they were wonderful people, and the Sky Snake saw that they didn't have any fire, so the Sky Snake sent down a bolt of lightning, and started fire for the Chumash people, so they would be warm, so they could cook their food." Once the Chumash had fire, they were able to cook and to stay warm. They then "went out about the island and started families." Soon their families grew, and over the course of several generations, the island began to get too crowded.[103]

When the Mother Earth spirit saw how crowded the island was becoming, she told the Chumash people that "in three days, there will be a rainbow bridge," and it will reach "from the island, over to the big land over there," referring to the main land, near Santa Barbara. On the main land, there would be plenty of room "for families to start villages, and they won't be as crowded." And so the Mother Earth spirit gave the Chumash people three days to decide who would stay on the island and who would walk over the rainbow bridge. When the rainbow bridge appeared three days later, half of the Chumash people lined up and began walking across the bridge. The Mother Earth spirit told them that everything would be okay if they just walked over the bridge and did not look down, and that is what most of the people did.[104]

But, as Salazar describes in his telling of the story, some of the people were curious: "How can we walk on a bridge made out of a rainbow?" And as they crossed the bridge, "halfway between the island and the mainland," they started to look around and check out the bridge. And "it was very windy that day—the fog was rolling in and out—and as they were trying to check out the bridge, some of them got dizzy and fell off the bridge, and fell into the ocean. They fell down into the ocean and were drowning." At this time, Hutash, the Mother Earth spirit, called out to the Sun, the leader of the Sky People, and asked the Sun to save the people as they fell.[105] The Sun looked down and "saw these people in the ocean drowning, and he changed their bodies, and made them sleek and slender, and strong and powerful, and he gave them the ability to hold their breath for a long time. For he turned those people who were drowning into dolphins. And that's why even today, the dolphin is a very respected animal to the Chumash people."[106] Salazar tells this story of how the Chumash people came to inhabit Santa Barbara and the surrounding regions of California, and how they came to honor the dolphin in particular as a respected animal.[107] At this point, Salazar also adds a clarification to his telling of the story. He makes mention of another book about the rainbow bridge story, which he says "pretty much follows the story in its true manner." But in that story, notes Salazar, the author says that "the Chumash believe that the dolphin is like a brother or sister." Here, Salazar clarifies that he always says "that the dolphin is a very respected animal. Because we still hunt dolphins. We hunt bear. We hunt deer. But we would do ceremonies to honor those animals. . . . Our attitude is, those animals are giving their lives so we can survive. The least we can do is sing songs about them. Honor them. Be respectful to them. Only take what you need." The story of the Rainbow Bridge then helps reveal a worldview in which all beings are worthy of our respect and provide wisdom in troubled times. In this way, storytelling becomes part of how we understand our relationship to place, and part of how we articulate and conceptualize our relationships with and responsibilities to our ecosystem. As Kimmerer suggests: "We need a different kind of science—and we have one. It has existed for millennia. It is called traditional ecological knowledge, which is rich in teachings about how people can give back to land."[108]

## A NARRATIVE LENS FOR CONTEXTUALIZING LIBERTY CANYON

Alan Salazar tells the story of the Rainbow Bridge, in this context, to help us understand the connection between the history and meaning of this storied place and its significance for the Liberty Canyon project. In the context of this story, it becomes possible to understand the Liberty Canyon crossing as a connectivity project rooted in a culture of reciprocity. The knowledge that Salazar conveys through storytelling illuminates some analogues between the native Chumash's story of the Rainbow Bridge and how we may understand the Liberty Canyon crossing as storied place—as land imbued with meaning and history, and as fostering new means of connectivity for those who were here before us. Moreover, the story of the Rainbow Bridge, as Salazar helps us understand, is also about connectivity between the celestial and the earthly, and between our ecosystem and the beings who inhabit it. For Salazar, the Liberty Canyon crossing, like the Rainbow Bridge, is about providing safe passage across dangerous terrain in order to seek a home; it is, as he suggests, a "rainbow bridge of modern times."[109]

Considered in this light, the Liberty Canyon crossing is, then, very much about what counts as home in Anthropocene times—it understands land not as a resource to be exploited but as a means for giving back. It is one possible way that humans can participate in a culture of gratitude and reciprocity, and, as Salazar says, it is "the least we can do" for these creatures who were here before us.[110] The Liberty Canyon crossing helps us understand what land *means* from a more relational vantage point that honors the lives of our more-than-human kin. As Kimmerer writes:

How we approach restoration of land depends, of course, on what we believe "land" means. If land is just real estate, then restoration looks very different than if land is the source of a subsistence economy and a spiritual home. Restoring land for production of natural resources is not the same as renewal of land as cultural identity. We have to think about what land means.[111]

The Liberty Canyon crossing is about understanding land as offering the possibility of coexistence, connectivity, and renewed biodiversity—it is, then, a way of honoring the "moral covenant of reciprocity," which "calls us to honor our responsibilities for all we have been given, for all that we have taken."[112] Liberty Canyon is, in essence, a project of love, created from storied land, storied place. It can, functioning in the positive, help reconnect lost and fragmented habitats, rebuild biodiversity, and allow vulnerable species to story their places anew. As Van Dooren describes, "living well with others can never be about just learning to tell new stories; it must also involve learning new kinds of attentiveness to the stories of others—even if they are unspoken or told in other-than-human languages."[113] P-22 storied his place by way of his unintended displacement, but other mountain lions in this region may now have a chance to story their places by regaining an abundance of place and biodiversity. This comes from a sensitivity toward knowledge of and respect for the land and its inhabitants.

By approaching conservation and restoration projects from this vantage point, we may understand projects like Liberty Canyon not only as "imperative for healing the earth," but also as "imperative for long-lasting, successful restoration."[114] For, as Kimmerer reminds us, "like other mindful practices, ecological restoration can be viewed as an act of reciprocity in which humans exercise their caregiving responsibility for the ecosystems that sustain them."[115] As we imagine the future of the Liberty Canyon project, we may look to other connectivity projects that are thematically similar, yet contextually and geographically different, if only to get a glimpse of what a completed crossing at Liberty Canyon might provide.

## THE CROSSING AT PARLEYS SUMMIT

About 700 miles north, just east of Salt Lake City along Route I-80 in Parleys Canyon, Utah, is the recently completed Parleys Summit wildlife crossing. Completed in winter 2018, the crossing at Parleys Summit is the largest in Utah. The bridge is fifty feet wide—about one third of the planned width of Liberty Canyon, and 320 feet long, spanning six lanes of I-80.[116] Three miles of fencing along both sides of the highway create a pathway that guides species to the overpass. Along the overpass, the apparatuses of technoculture record the sights and sounds of "migrating moose, elk, deer, and other animals" as they traverse the freeway that has fragmented their local ecosystem. The overpass has also been used by some unexpected species, such as "bobcats, cougars, coyotes and a yellow-bellied marmot," and one Utah Department of Transportation (UDOT) spokesperson notes, "It's great to see so many different animals using the overpass."[117]

While the site is still too new to provide any long-term data, species' initial responses to the crossing has been encouraging. Local media articles about Parleys Summit convey different perspectives on the project, and are typically quick to note, however, that the crossing was designed with the safety of both humans and animals in mind. The local organization Save People Save Wildlife had advocated for the crossing since 2016, largely out of concern that "the moose population was beginning to dwindle and drivers were at risk along I-80."[118] Similarly, a spokesperson for UDOT expresses: "It's exciting to have this done. . . . This has been the most talked about UDOT project of the year, rightfully so. It is unique and it is really going to improve the safety of drivers in Parleys Canyon by cutting down on the wildlife and vehicle collisions. I think it is really going to make a big difference."[119] While UDOT also acknowledges the benefits to wildlife, they ultimately emphasize the benefits to humans:

> We have a lot of wildlife in that area, including deer, elk and moose. . . . We obviously want to ensure their safety. But, the real purpose of this crossing is to ensure the safety of everyone traveling in the canyons. They are the real beneficiaries. They are going to be able to drive in that area and not have to worry about wildlife coming onto the freeway.[120]

The Utah Division of Wildlife Resources has also been sending out videos that show animals using the overpass. In one tweet, the division says: "We're excited to see #wildlife using the new Parleys Summit overpass! The overpass and roadside fencing are providing safer migration routes and reducing collisions."[121] Thus, although there is clearly an expressed interest in insuring the safety of wildlife, we see that the primary motivation for the corridor seems to be driver safety.

My goal in describing the Parleys Summit crossing is not to delve as deeply into the context and history of this project as we have done with the Liberty Canyon project, but rather to tell enough of the story to illuminate some emergent perspectives and questions that may apply more broadly to wildlife corridor projects. For instance, perspectives about the need for the Parleys Summit overpass again raise questions similar in scope to concerns about mountain lions on California freeways. At the very least, we see a recurring theme in these discourses that prompt us to consider our relationships with our more-than-human kin: If driver safety is part of the UDOT rationale for creating a wildlife overpass, do such human-centric motivations necessarily negate the benefits for wildlife? Is a human-centric rationale the best that wildlife gets? After all, we can't expect to compare the Oregon woman's intuitive and directly empathetic approach in helping the mountain lion exit her living room with the perspectives and practices that inform larger-scale connectivity projects. Or can we?

As the forces of human development and climate change bring humans and more-than-humans in closer proximity to one another, we must contend with the implications and consequences of our decision-making and rationales about how to best coexist in challenged ecosystems. Again, Kimmerer's suggestion that we take an "indigenous worldview" about conservation and restoration—one that understands all creatures as equals, and the ecosystem as "a community of sovereign beings" worthy of our respect, begins to destabilize these different rationales."[122] She asks that we imagine the possibilities of

> walking through a richly inhabited world of Birch people, Bear people, Rock people, beings we think of and therefore speak of as persons worthy of our respect, of inclusion in a peopled world. We Americans are reluctant to learn a foreign language of our own species, let alone another species. But imagine the possibilities. Imagine the access we would have to different perspectives, the things we might see through other eyes, the wisdom that surrounds us. We don't have to figure everything out by ourselves: there are intelligences other than our own, teachers all around us. Imagine how much less lonely the world would be.[123]

On the one hand, of course, wildlife would likely not face fragmented ecosystems and habitats if it were not for the projects of human development in the first place. To understand all creatures as a "community of sovereign beings," however, quickly moves us past the anthropocentric arguments about whose needs are most pressing, and brings us to a more compassionate, empathetic perspective that similarly illuminates the more ecologically oriented aspects of posthumanism. Moreover, rather than surrender to "despair," we should embrace a "gift mindset" and view wildlife corridors as part of a culture of reciprocity. Kimmerer writes: "Restoration is a powerful antidote to despair. Restoration offers concrete means by which humans can once again enter into positive, creative relationship with the more-than-human world, meeting responsibilities that are simultaneously material and spiritual. It's not enough to grieve. It's not enough to just stop doing bad things."[124] Such a view takes a recuperative stance, and encourages us to think holistically about our ethical responsibilities to our more-than-human kin.

## HONORING A CULTURE OF RECIPROCITY

In the face of such human development, then, wildlife corridors are one way that we can work to create productive worlds, to help create storied places or re-story lost or disconnected places, in which compassionate, empathetic coexistence and an abundance of biodiversity is the goal to strive for, or the gift to give back to our more-than-human kin. In doing so, however, we need to develop and sustain such projects in ways that honor a language of animacy and a culture of reciprocity, and that incorporate a multitude of perspectives about working with and respecting the natural world and its species. Part of honoring a culture of reciprocity means helping foster the gift of coexistence. As we considered in the previous chapter: What if all conservation projects were to proceed from a vantage point that perceives encounters and coexistence with our more-than-human kin as gifts to be received and reciprocated? Or, as Kimmerer asks: "How, in our modern world, can we find our way to understand the earth as a gift again, to make our relations with the world sacred again?"[125]

In the previous chapter, we saw how the approach of one person in a specific, smaller-scale context had a lasting impact on the well-being of one displaced mountain lion. The Oregon resident's approach to the encounter with the mountain lion in her home can teach us something about "living in gratitude and amazement at the richness and generosity of the world."[126] In that moment, both beings had something to offer one another; together they created a storied place—they redefined what counts as "home" in a strained habitat.

The Liberty Canyon project reveals another perspective on what becomes possible when we can apply such a "gift" mindset at a larger scale—when we approach conservation and restoration in a way that understands "multiple meanings of land": "Land as sustainer. Land as identity. . . . Land as connection to our ancestors. Land as moral obligation. Land as sacred. Land as self."[127] And, I might add, land as "home" in the Anthropocene.

The Liberty Canyon project also reveals the ways that entangled empathy and a culture of reciprocity can inform contemporary conservation projects. We may see the nuance and depth of knowledge that comes with a greater understanding of and appreciation for storied places and a view that understands our vulnerable, more-than-human kin as our neighbors. In this way, we and our more-than-human kin are "relationally co-constituted beings that co-emerge together" in these ever-changing moments of understanding and belonging, and these reimagined ideas about what counts as home and belonging in the Anthropocene.[128] As Kimmerer reminds us, "if we are to survive here, and our neighbors too, our work is to learn to speak the grammar of animacy, so that we might truly be at home."[129] To be at home in the Anthropocene, again, requires an openness to a language of animacy as we engage empathetically with our more-than-human kin.

To understand connectivity projects like these as part of a culture of reciprocity requires empathy, a language of animacy, and an appreciation for the land and species who share that knowledge and those stories. Such an understanding also reveals how we might understand "home" in the Anthropocene, when making or storying a "home" entails the reestablishment of disconnected habitats and lost storied places. To be at home in the Anthropocene also means starting from a point of empathy for species, and entails a respect for and attentiveness to the co-emergent histories and meanings of storied places crafted by humans and more-than-humans alike. P-22, for instance, has adapted to a home that a mountain lion would not ordinarily find optimal; he has adapted to an eight-mile territory and life amidst a significant human presence. It is unlikely that he will ever be able to leave this area, and unlikely that he will ever find a mate. He has had to learn the language of this place—this predominantly human-built, iconic place, Griffith Park—and he has had to learn to coexist with species other than his own. To extend the gist of Pratt's earlier question, then, "can we do the same for him?"

In the Anthropocene, "home" not only means being receptive and open to a language of animacy and a culture of reciprocity, but also, by extension, it means an openness to adaptation and a willingness to rethink our assumptions of boundaried places, and instead think about conservation practice as encompassing an environmental "*meshwork* of entangled lines of life, growth and movement."[130] We inhabit a world of meshworks, which can illuminate moments of elemental relationality and empathetic, posthuman interventions into a world shared with our more-than-human kin. Openness to environmental meshworks means rethinking the places that we have always imagined as "just a home for humans," and making space for our "wild" kin; it means giving the gift of space and giving the gift of abundance, of biodiversity.

P-22 has become an unwitting ambassador for wildlife and the Liberty Canyon corridor project. To place P-22 in the spotlight in such a way has involved a degree of anthropomorphism, but as Bennett and others have argued, anthropomorphism need not be viewed in an entirely pejorative light; especially in the case of public advocacy and the need to educate publics about coexistence, it can help build a bridge that allows people to identify with our more-than-human kin. Anthropomorphism may allow us to start from a point of identification, and from there, we may come to better understand the nuanced differences between our different ways of being in the world. Understood in such a light, P-22 becomes our neighbor. We may empathize to an extent with his challenges, with how human development has shaped his way of existing in the world. We thus understand the Liberty Canyon crossing as a means of trying to foster coexistence and renewed and sustained biodiversity.

Working in the positive, then, wildlife corridors can be part of a culture of reciprocity—of returning the gifts that wildlife gives to all of us—biodiversity, and the gift of knowing another. Incorporating traditional ecological knowledge, in part through storytelling, is part of our ethical responsibility to ensure that historically marginalized voices and perspectives are heard, valued, and respected. To be receptive to such modes of knowledge-making can, in turn, also help contribute to and foster a culture of reciprocity.

In the Anthropocene, "home" also requires close and active listening, for, as Kimmerer reminds us, "to be native to a place we must learn to speak its language." This means being mindful of all the languages and histories of a place—those of species, land, peoples. The incorporation of traditional ecological knowledge and storytelling is one way of learning the language of a place and participating in a culture of reciprocity, but we can also be attentive ourselves at any time to the voices and stories of our vulnerable kin and the places they choose to inhabit.

## INTERLUDE II

# Fostering a Culture of Reciprocity during the Anthropause

When I took my usual walk through the Santa Barbara foothills in early March 2020, the situation with the global Covid pandemic was just beginning to escalate. I recall being distracted by the news, yet trying to focus on the walk that I had done so many times on my own, but now wanted to be able to describe for my reader. While this book is not intended to be about the pandemic, per se, I have written much of it within the context of changing stay-at-home orders and the anxieties that now inform and have altered many of our daily routines and broader decision-making. As a result, the pandemic made its way into the introduction, and occasionally seeps into this book in ways that I would not have anticipated, even if I had tried.

In the introduction, I mentioned the coyote with whom I crossed paths during one of my many walks through Franceschi Park. She and I have each storied that place differently over time—the very place that constitutes a mode of daily exercise for me is a relatively safe urban corridor for her. Moreover, that coyote and her family—her generations of kin—have likely made a home in this region for far longer than I have. I sometimes wonder whether my daily walk through that area is an encroachment on her storied land, and I hope that my respect for her and her home can at least help offset such a potential disturbance. To think of my own relationship to the environment in this way is humbling and prompts me to tread lightly in this place, especially when I consider how climate change and human development have played a role in fragmenting the home ranges of so many of our more-than-human kin.

As I continued in subsequent chapters to write about the challenges of coexistence in these shared and fragmented habitats, I never would have anticipated that within just a few months, in the midst of writing about the need to coexist with vulnerable species, no less, I would be reading news articles about wildlife wandering into seemingly abandoned urban centers and empty residential streets and neighborhoods, likely in response to humans' retreat into the relative safety of our homes, in an effort to flatten the curve of contagion during a global pandemic. Reports of Great Orme Kashmiri goats wandering into the deserted streets of a seaside town in Wales; coyotes walking brazenly through residential neighborhoods in San Francisco; macaque monkeys searching for food in the streets of Lopburi, Thailand; and deer being spotted around Baltimore City, Maryland, are among just a handful of examples of wildlife moving into areas normally dense with human habitation.[1]

As I write this brief interlude between chapters during the summer of 2020, scientists have just coined a term to help account for this seeming influx of wildlife into places typically frequented by humans: the "Anthropause."[2] In an article just published in the journal *Nature Ecology & Evolution,* a group of scientists and researchers write: "We noticed that people started referring to the lockdown period as the 'Great Pause,' but felt that a more precise term would be helpful. We propose 'anthropause' to refer specifically to a considerable global slowing of modern human activities, notably travel."[3] The Anthropause, then, marks a time of global slowdown of human development and activity, with a particular emphasis on travel and mobility.

More specifically, the researchers of this study describe how the Anthropause, or "this period of unusually reduced human mobility . . . may provide important insights into human-wildlife interactions in the twenty-first century. Anecdotal observations indicate that many animal species are enjoying the newly afforded peace and quiet, while others, surprisingly, seem to have come under increased pressure."[4] The researchers also view this period of "reduced human mobility" as a valuable learning opportunity, and argue that the international scientific community can tap into these circumstances "to gain unprecedented mechanistic insight into how human activity affects wildlife." Subsequently, they suggest that "scientific knowledge gained during this devastating crisis will allow us to develop innovative strategies for sharing space on this increasingly crowded planet, with benefits for both wildlife and humans."[5] To this end, for example, the researchers mention the newly formed "COVID-19 Bio-Logging Initiative," which is "a global project to track animals' movements, behavior and stress levels with small electronic trackers called 'bio-loggers.'" Such projects may then contribute to efforts to study "global patterns in animal behavior" during this time.[6] While such research may prove valuable for the scientific community, I would add that it is not only the scientific community but also the broader population who have an opportunity and responsibility to learn from these unique circumstances.

At first glance, the more immediate and perhaps more hyperbolic conclusion about increased wildlife sightings during stay-at-home orders might be that wildlife have opportunistically infiltrated urban places in response to the recent exodus of people from outdoors to indoors. But such a conclusion is arguably overly simplified and also based on the flawed presumption that all humans have the relative luxury of life indoors. The more measured interpretation, which must also acknowledge a range of variables not yet wholly understood, is that our more-than-human neighbors are flexible and adapting to these changes in their environment, which, once again, are actually wrought by changes in patterns of *human* behavior.

Many more people have been largely confined to their home during the pandemic, and as such, people have been redefining their own ideas about what counts as home during this time. This book does not necessarily focus on the interior spaces of contemporary homes in the sense that some newer habits of working from home allude to or address. However, it bears noting that recent increased time spent at home, and the different uses of space that have followed, may change our perspectives quite literally, thus prompting people to notice things around their homes they would not ordinarily pay as much attention to. We might consider, for instance, the recent surge in bird-watching that has been documented during the pandemic. The *New York Times* recently reported on increased birdseed sales at birding supply stores, and noted that the Cornell Lab of Ornithology's popular eBird site has seen record-setting numbers of observations logged in its database.[7]

In addition, we must be mindful not to overdetermine the outcomes of the movement of wildlife into places newer to them and more visible to people. For as the new study about the Anthropause also describes, while human development often puts wildlife at risk for displacement or extinction, some modes of human intervention also help protect vulnerable species. And when those protections are absent, new vulnerabilities may arise.

The researchers, note, for example, that "reduced human presence in more remote areas may potentially expose endangered species, such as rhinos or raptors, to increased risk of poaching or persecution."[8] Moreover, as the researchers describe, "various urban-dwelling animals, like rats, gulls or monkeys, have become so reliant on food discarded or provided by humans that they may struggle to make ends meet under current conditions."[9] If species are ultimately again adapting to humans, we might ask ourselves how we, too, may coexist compassionately alongside our more-than-human kin in these challenging times.

What is our ethical obligation to our more-than-human kin in such circumstances? First, perhaps a more equitable, ecological, and compassionate mindset is to suggest that we are *all* storying our places differently right now—that we are *all* observing each other in different contexts. We might also consider the gift that, for better or worse, is the glimpse we are getting into a different kind of world—a world in which our more-than-human kin have just a bit more flexibility to story their places in new ways. We are curious to know what they are up to, and it is possible that they are curious to explore new places as well. Again, though, we must be cautious not to over-romanticize this cultural moment but rather to look for ways to learn from it and to participate in a culture of reciprocity in the various ways that we can.

Interestingly, as the researchers of this study note, the "COVID-19 anthropause has transported us back to levels of human mobility observed a few decades—not centuries—ago. That means that we may discover that relatively minor changes to our lifestyles can potentially have major benefits for ecosystems and humans. For example, small modifications to the topology and operation of our transport networks may drastically reduce unintended disruptive effects on animal movement."[10] For all of these reasons, then, this new and unanticipated glimpse into the lives of our fellow kin, born once again out of human intervention into the environment, is one that we ought to learn from and reciprocate.

A culture of reciprocity and a language of animacy require that we do our best to ensure the well-being of these creatures, despite the sometimes detrimental impacts of human action. This likely requires some reframing of our default mindsets and assumptions, toward a more compassionate and attentive vantage point that understands these potential encounters as unexpected gifts, which we may reciprocate through our own willingness to learn from and coexist with our more-than-human neighbors. While these recent changes in the behavior of vulnerable wildlife have caught the attention of the scientific community, we can all play a role in helping to ensure the well-being of our more-than-human kin.

In Bellows Falls, Vermont, just a couple hours south of my family's home in Stowe, Vermont, a black bear has recently been seen roaming a downtown area locally referred to as "The Square." Black bears are the only species of bear to reside in Vermont, but it is nonetheless unusual to see one in this area of Bellows Falls. As of spring 2020, the bear apparently began "frequenting the downtown area regularly, in the evenings around 8 or 9 p.m."[11] The bear's presence in downtown Bellows Falls is very likely the result of the Anthropause and the related "stay home, stay safe" order that has limited outdoor activities within the state—well, at least for humans.

Bellows Falls is a small but populated village in Rockingham, Vermont; it is situated along the Connecticut River and sits parallel to the border with New Hampshire to the east. It is home to one of the first canals in the United States, the Bellows Falls Canal, and is one of many small, former mill towns in this region of New England. In the early 1900s, the development of water-powered mills allowed Bellows Falls to become one of the nation's largest paper manufacturers.[12] Today, much like many former mill towns in Vermont and northern Massachusetts, this place still looks and feels like it is set back in time. If it is possible for a place to be "paused" in two eras, then Bellows Falls provides an apt case in point: set back in time in the early 1900s, it seems that time has paused here once again, in 2020.

The urban and suburban streets here have been quieter since the pandemic, creating more of an invitation for wildlife to venture closer to areas normally dense with human habitation. The Vermont Fish and Wildlife Department (VFWD) attributes the recent black bear sighting to this "wider trend of wild animals straying into urban areas as the COVID-19 pandemic leaves urban and suburban streets a little quieter."[13] Local experts like game warden David Taddei, and Forrest Hammond, a bear biologist with the Fish and Wildlife Department, feel that black bears venturing closer to more urban areas of Vermont could become an issue if they become "increasingly less worried about running into humans."[14] As Hammond describes: "What is most concerning about this situation is that bear behavior in urbanized areas tends to become worse over time as the bear gets less wary of humans with each meal of garbage or birdseed." Taddei adds: "At some point, the 'stay home, stay safe' order will be lifted, and life will start to return to normal. . . . More people will be out, dumpsters will start to fill, and more trash will be generated at local businesses. . . . This could result in a variety of outcomes, most of which may not end well for the bear."[15] According to Vermont statutes, a bear can legally be killed for damaging property. Such a decision would not be taken lightly, and "a property owner would need to take a reasonable, nonlethal measure to secure the beehives or whatever property has been damaged, before the bear could be killed."[16] Nonetheless, this would be a very unfortunate outcome for a young bear who was doing something as seemingly innocuous and understandable as foraging in a resident's bird feeders—a situation that can be easily remedied with small modifications.

Moreover, when these incidents happen, a bear can be labeled as a "nuisance" or "problem bear," which is again arguably problematic, especially when we consider that humans are, in many ways, responsible for attracting the bear in the first place. These points are not lost on the VFWD and game warden Dave Taddei, who acknowledges: "We all love to see bears. We love Vermont. We love the wildlife. But intentionally feeding bears is never a good thing. It does not end well for the bears because they then think that, oh, every house is a great place to go get food. It's also illegal so you can be criminally charged for intentionally feeding bears."[17] Rather than creating scenarios where bears get into bird feeders and honey hives, and are subsequently pathologized as "problem" or "nuisance" bears, people can make modifications like moving bird feeders to less bear-accessible areas, or taking them down altogether.

Taddei also recommends that people put electric fencing around their beehives, if they keep bees, and to remove bird feeders from yards. Finally, if somebody sees a bear, Taddei recommends, not unlike advice about mountain lion encounters, simply yelling out, but without using violence, to discourage the bear from hanging around. In other words, it is easy enough to foster a culture of respect and to ensure safe coexistence, even during these times of decreased distance between people and black bears. We can reframe our ideas about "nuisance bears" by not encouraging them to come close in the first place. In doing so, we enact an ethical responsibility to create opportunities for successful coexistence.

At the time of this writing, in summer 2020, the VFWD has not yet received any complaints about the bear in question, beyond its foraging into bird feeders and honey hives at local residences.[18] When we consider ways to foster a culture of reciprocity during the Anthropause, during a cultural moment fraught with stay-at-home orders, we see that people need not be on a large-scale research team to make a positive difference in the lives of vulnerable species. People can help prevent such situations from escalating by taking simple measures like removing bird feeders or just moving them away from bear-accessible areas, and by securing trash properly.

And, similar to the case of mountain lions, it is important to remember that black bears prefer to avoid encounters with humans. Moreover, there has never actually been a documented bear attack in Vermont. That said, the VFWD advises that should someone encounter a black bear, they should "remain calm, ensure the bear has an escape route, back away where possible and, if attacked in a building or tent, immediately fight back. The department also strongly advises against running from a bear, climbing trees to escape a bear or feeding bears."[19] Importantly, they also add that black bears should always be treated with respect and their presence should be admired from a distance.[20]

There are different ideas about the broader implications about this seeming trend in increased human/wildlife encounters during the pandemic. For example, some wildlife biologists suggest that the trend is temporary, and that it takes longer for our more-than-human kin to make permanent behavior changes; rather, it's more likely that, being as adaptable as they are, they are just adapting to us once again. For instance, Shannon Schaller, senior wildlife biologist for Colorado Parks and Wildlife, cautions against making any inferences in the short term about the perceived, recent increase in wildlife sightings: "I think you are going to have short-term movements, but you likely will not see anything drastic. . . . It takes a while for wildlife to figure it out. It's an over-time, repeated and learned behavior that generally has to become habitual."[21] That said, it makes logical sense that wildlife will seek out areas that are less populated with humans and will try to avoid confrontations with people: "In principle, if parks, trails or open spaces are crowded with people, wildlife will go to areas with less disturbance. If urban areas, parks or open spaces that provide food, shelter or water are quiet, you could see wildlife utilizing those areas more."[22] To understand the responses of wildlife as reasonable adaptations to shifts in human behavior is an empathetic approach that is grounded in a relational and ecological understanding of the relationships between people and wildlife.

Additionally, as Vermont game warden David Taddei has cautioned, some wildlife specialists are concerned that when the stay-at-home orders are eventually lifted, wildlife will need to readapt. Moreover, young wildlife who were "born while people are scarce" may have internalized certain habits and will need to adapt when people return.[23] Or, some species may have become more accustomed to frequenting certain places and may take longer to shift back to previous habits, potentially putting them in greater danger. As Ryan Koziatek, stewardship field director at the Kalamazoo Nature Center in Michigan, describes, "there might be a little learning phase, where we might see some impacts of the wildlife still trying to use some of those corridors as we pick up our activities again." Nonetheless, he feels that eventually, things will balance out: "The pandemic won't last forever, and animals will retreat when normal human activity resumes. It may take a while, though."[24] In other words, it is still unclear what the longer-term implications of the stay-at-home orders will be for our more-than-human kin. But what is clear, however, "is that humans and wildlife have become more interdependent than ever before," and "now is the time to study this complex relationship."[25] It is also clear that our wild kin are quite attentive to their surroundings and to human behavior, and will readily adapt to people: "Wildlife learns to adapt to what we are doing and as we change. . . . Whether that is being outside more, concentrating in places where we leave trash, or because we avoid an area, then they learn to adapt to that."[26] As Beth Pratt of the National Wildlife Federation reminds us, though, the question is, really, can *we* adapt as well?[27] And if so, how might we adapt to and coexist with our more-than-human kin, in ways that help ensure their well-being during this particularly challenging cultural moment?

The group of researchers who authored the Anthropause study suggest that there will be "unforeseen opportunities" during this time "to reinvent the way we live our lives, and to forge a mutually beneficial coexistence with other species." They are hopeful that research during this period can help identify "innovative ways of reining in our increasingly expansive lifestyles, to rediscover how important a healthy environment is for our own well-being, and to replace a sense of owning with a sense of belonging."[28] I would add that part of forging such a "mutually beneficial coexistence with other species" and replacing a "sense of owning with a sense of belonging" means participating in a culture of reciprocity and learning the language of animacy.

To participate in a culture of reciprocity, even in seemingly minor ways, is easier and more important than we might realize. Participating in a culture of reciprocity and learning a language of animacy during the Anthropause means several things. It means we can likely expect to observe more wildlife than usual when going about our new daily routines, for, "with more people at home looking or being outside, wildlife sightings could go up. This won't be a new phenomenon, the animals have always been there, but they may have previously gone undetected."[29] Participating in a culture of reciprocity also means understanding such encounters, even from a distance, as an opportunity to appreciate the multitude of species with whom we share habitats, even if, and especially if, we each understand, use, and story the same places in distinct and meaningful ways. As Schaller notes: "This is also a time that can be used as an educational opportunity to learn about nature and wildlife."[30] Relatedly, wildlife advocates like Ryan Koziatek recommend starting a nature journal, and "observing some of the animals out there, noting some of those interactions, maybe describing some of the feelings that come up about that, whether it's writing a poem or just some short thoughts about that, and then letting it pique your curiosity."[31] There are indeed many possible ways to participate in a culture of reciprocity during the Anthropause, and writing is but one possible contribution that we might make.

To help foster and sustain a culture of reciprocity during the Anthropause also means taking responsibility for what might otherwise uncritically be perceived as "nuisance" or "problem" creatures. We must reframe the question of how to deal with "nuisance bears," for instance, to one of how to help ensure the well-being of black bears during a time of crisis for this species. It means coming from a place of personal accountability rather than placing blame. Both the scientific community, as well as broader publics and individuals can help foster and perpetuate this necessary shift in mindset and discourse. By first being open and receptive to the languages and behaviors of our more-than-human kin, we may chart a course that more readily engages internatural communication, a language of animacy, and entangled empathy. There are many approaches to such engagement, including but not limited to some of the everyday practices described here: bird-watching, journaling, and reimagining our possible backyards or outdoor areas as ecosystems *shared* with our more-than-human kin who are perhaps just as curious about us as we may be about them. As we expand our willingness to learn from and reciprocate these relationships, we may be pleasantly surprised by the myriad gifts that surround us.

CHAPTER 4

# At Home with Big Kin

We are bound in a covenant of reciprocity, a pact of mutual responsibility to sustain those who sustain us. And so the empty bowl is filled.
—Robin Wall Kimmerer, *Braiding Sweetgrass*

Stark had made his den in a blowdown area in the woodas of southern Vermont's Green Mountain National Forest. "Blowdown" refers to downed trees and tree trunks, and broken trunks and branches, which are often the result of windthrow and windsnap from storms. In this region of the Green Mountains, blowdown is typically composed of northern hardwoods like spruce, yellow birch, sugar maple, American beech, eastern hemlock, and white pine. Stark's den was likewise surrounded by several tree stumps, upturned trees, and much dirt and debris. His den was fairly typical for an adult male black bear, but bears can also create dens along rock ledges, in actual tree hollows, or even within logs or fallen trees that are large enough to provide such accommodation. Most black bears will also create some kind of padding in their dens, using pieces of bark, leaves, grasses, or moss.[1] Stark had likely wandered at least thirty miles or so to find enough food, and to put on enough weight, before hibernating this fall. But he returned here, to his home range in the Green Mountains, for this is his community. This environmental meshwork, home to so many creatures and put to so many uses—his storied place, where he and his kin participate in a culture of reciprocity, and where black bears and beech trees alike can be said to participate in a kind of communal generosity that helps sustain lives and habitats.

Blowdown areas and debris-filled brush piles like Stark's den site are fairly common in the Vermont woods during "mud season," or late winter and early spring, from about March to May. Mud season also tends to overlap with denning season; that is, black bears tend to hibernate from about October until around April, although climate change and the related availability of food supplies greatly determines how early in the fall bears will move into their dens. Nonetheless, the Vermont woods can make for some challenging but satisfying hiking this time of year, while also providing good cover and a safe home for a hibernating black bear like Stark, who was, during this mid-spring, deep in hibernation in the corner of his den.

> There're huge trees upturned, and dirt and detritus everywhere.
> —Vermont Public Radio journalist[2]

A team of biologists from the Vermont Fish and Wildlife Department and the US Forest Service, including biologist and bear specialist Jaclyn Comeau and wildlife biologist Forrest Hammond, along with two journalists from Vermont Public Radio, hiked up into the slightly thawed but still slushy, densely wooded forest of southern Vermont. It was mid-spring, the time of year in the Green Mountains when the sound of earth underfoot alternates between crunch and slosh; a hat and gloves might still be in order, but one's breath does not necessarily condense when exhaling. It was April 2019, and the team looked for Stark, who, according to the GPS data that they followed, should be hibernating in his den. They had current location data for him and had been receiving a GPS signal all winter, which meant that his den was probably not so deep or covered with rocks as to obscure the signal. This group of researchers needed to replace the GPS collar that supplied information about his travels and whereabouts, and they would conduct a physical wellness exam while they were at it. Much like P-22 and other large mammals tracked by biologists with Fish and Wildlife Departments or the National Park Service, these collars periodically need to be replaced, offering an additional opportunity for a wellness checkup in the process.

Black bears with collars must also be monitored because their weight tends to fluctuate during the year. A black bear who was collared in June or July, for instance, will ideally put on weight during the fall before going into hibernation, and so by March or April, they will need to be rechecked for a good collar fit. These were the team's current goals, that is, if they could successfully locate Stark, humanely sedate him, and remove him from his den to carry out these tasks.

Stark was given his nickname based on his home range near the Molly Stark Highway and Route 9 in southern Vermont. Biologists with the VFWD are also leading the Deerfield Wind Black Bear Study, which explores the impact of the ongoing Deerfield Wind Energy Project and wind turbines on black bear populations in this region. The Deerfield Wind Energy Project is a wind farm in the Manchester District of the Green Mountain National Forest. The wind farm is situated along two ridgelines in Searsburg and Readsboro, Vermont, and became operational in 2017.[3] The VFWD is specifically interested in the possible impacts of wind turbines on the bears' beechnut-foraging behaviors, and Stark is one of the local bears in this area who they think could be potentially affected by the project. Of particular interest to the researchers is how the wind project impacts critical black bear habitat—namely, forested areas dense with beech trees.

## BEAR-STORIED BEECH: A RECIPROCAL RELATIONSHIP

The American beech tree is quite common throughout New England; they are a subtle, unassuming tree, known for their smooth, light gray bark that some people compare with the look and texture of elephant skin. Beech is a fairly prevalent tree because it is a shade-tolerant hardwood. This means it can grow easily under dense canopy without as much sunlight as other species require.[4] Beech trees are often responsible for that greenish hue that the sunlight casts through the leaves of trees on to the forest floor.

When I first moved to central California, I tried to put my finger on what it was that I missed about New England hiking. I soon realized that I missed the fragrant cushion of pine needle–covered terrain, and that I longed for that comforting, green glow of shaded tree canopy. In the fall and winter, the light gray bark of the beech tree, coupled with the now-bronzed leaves that the trees still hold, blends with the cool gray of overcast New England skies and gives the forest a stillness and calm born from a palette of muted earth tones. I've come to appreciate the more direct exposure of the southern California sun, but as Bill McKibben conveys when quoting from a conversation with John Davis, the original editor of the *Earth First! Journal,* "I have the Eastern forest in my bones."[5]

In the Vermont and New Hampshire regions, the American beech tree holds special relevance for the storied territories of black bear populations. As wildlife rehabilitator and black bear expert Ben Kilham describes, these bears are highly reliant on unpredictable food sources that vary from year to year, such as "beechnuts, wild apples, raspberries, blackberries, blueberries, winterberries, chokeberries, mountain ash," and others.[6] As Kilham puts it: "Bears live in a world of feast or famine. One summer, they might feast on a huge raspberry crop in a clear-cut; the next summer, there may be none. The trees they live among might produce an enormous nut crop one year, but only a few nuts the next. The amount and reliability of black bears' food supply, then, determines not only their survival, but also the survival of the next generation."[7] Beechnuts in particular play a large role in New England black bears' ability to thrive in their home ranges.

The beechnut, or the "hard mast" produced by these trees, is quite high in fat and protein and an incredibly important food source for black bears, turkeys, deer, and other species. More specifically, beechnuts have about "the same protein content as corn but five times the fat content and they have nearly twice the protein of acorns."[8] In much of the Green Mountain National Forest, beech is the predominant nut-producing species and represents the major fall food source for bears. Beechnuts ripen in the fall, around the time that black bears need to build their fat reserves before hibernating for the winter. Black bears are notoriously good climbers, especially given their size, and will actually climb beech trees to feed on beechnuts, or harvest them, in essence, often shaking them from their branches before the nuts even fall to the ground.

When black bears climb and descend from these trees, they leave claw marks in the bark, thus "scarring" the tree and giving reference to the term "bear-scarred beech." These marks arguably look so much like a part of the tree's natural aesthetic that it is possible to happen across bear-scarred beech without even realizing it.[9] The markings are also a physical, indelible rendering of the bears' close and meaningful relationships with these trees, and it even appears that bears may use these marks to communicate with each other about territories, food availability, and a bear's presence in the general vicinity. Perhaps, then, a more apt descriptor for these marked trees might be "bear-storied beech."

## BEAR-STORIED BEECH AND THE GENEROSITY OF MAST FRUITING

Beechnuts are such an integral food source for black bears that the VFWD "considers concentrations of bear scarred beech trees critical habitat" for these creatures.[10] Moreover, it takes a lot of energy for a tree to produce hard mast, and so, much like other nut-bearing trees, beech trees typically yield nuts about every other year. The reproductive patterns of female black bears are also closely tied to beechnut yields. The close, even reciprocal relationship between beechnut yields and black bear populations is made apparent through research that "has shown that in areas where beech nuts are a major food source most of the female bears give birth in the winter after a good beechnut crop."[11] The reproductive strategies of female black bears are linked to annual food yields, and particularly beechnuts. In good mast years, bears will fill up on beechnuts, and that extra protein helps support the fetal development of black bear cubs. In a less ideal winter, the female bear's body might not have accumulated enough fat stores, and the embryo that she has carried since early summer will not fertilize.[12] As Kimmerer has described, "Nuts are like the pan fish of the forest, full of protein and especially fat. . . . High in calories and vitamins—everything you need to sustain life. After all, that's the whole point of nuts: to provide the embryo with all that is needed to start a new life."[13] Thus, the lives of beechnuts and black bears are inextricably linked—all part of the environmental meshworks that constitute life in the Green Mountain National Forest.

The energy it takes for beech trees to produce a supply of nuts significant enough to sustain bear populations is no small feat, and again, for this reason, nut-bearing trees are unable to muster such a consistently high level of energy every year. The unpredictable boom-bust cycle of beech trees is known as "mast fruiting," and is also related to what biologists would call the "predator-satiation" hypothesis. Kimmerer clearly summarizes the process of mast fruiting: "For mast fruiting to succeed in generating new forests, each tree has to make lots and lots of nuts—so many that it overwhelms the would-be seed predators. If a tree just plodded along making a few nuts every year, they'd all get eaten and there would be no next generation" of nuts. Because nuts are so high in calories, nut-bearing trees "can't afford this outpouring every year— they have to save up for it, as a family saves up for a special event."[14] Beech trees, for instance, "spend years making sugar, and rather than spending it little by little, they stick it under the proverbial mattress, banking calories as starch in their roots."[15] When these trees amass enough of a surplus, they will produce their yield.

Described somewhat differently, from a tree's vantage point, being unpredictable can have its advantages. As the "predator-satiation hypothesis" would have it, these boom-bust cycles help "keep seed predators in check." During a plentiful year, "the woods are flooded with nuts—more than any squirrel or mouse can eat. The next fall, when rodent populations are high thanks to all the easy living, the trees take the year off and the surplus rodents starve. Beech trees and rodents share the strategy of flooding an area with offspring in a way that ensures species survival," even though such scenarios can have what feels like an unfortunate evolutionary downside.[16]

Perhaps even more interesting, nut-bearing trees produce their yields consistently as whole groups, or as entire groves—not as individual trees: "If one tree fruits, they all fruit—there are no soloists. Not one tree in a grove, but the whole grove; not one grove in the forest, but every grove; all across the county and all across the state. The trees act not as individuals, but somehow as a collective."[17] While Kimmerer acknowledges that it is still unknown how exactly these trees act in unison, she sees this collective action as demonstrating the "power of unity": "What happens to one happens to us all. We can starve together or feast together. All flourishing is mutual."[18] And as forester and author Peter Wohlleben similarly describes in *The Hidden Life of Trees*, scientists in Germany have recently discovered that trees can communicate with each other through their root systems: "Most individual trees of the same species growing in the same stand are connected to each other through their root systems. It appears that nutrient exchange and helping neighbors in times of need is the rule, and this leads to the conclusion that forests are superorganisms with interconnections much like ant colonies."[19] Differing somewhat from Kimmerer, Wohlleben seems to understand this interconnection and communication less as a demonstrated act of agency and more as a necessary system of "give and take."[20] While he acknowledges that trees can "create what looks like a social network," he seems to shy away from the idea that they actively support each other with a stronger or more demonstrable sense of agency. Nonetheless, Wohlleben does refer to trees as "social beings," and cites research that shows that trees are "perfectly capable of distinguishing their own roots from the roots of other species and even from the roots of related individuals."[21] Taken together, the ideas of Kimmerer and Wohlleben illuminate how the collective action of mast fruiting has a ripple effect across species that some biologists and ecologists view as strategic on the part of these trees.

If we remain open to the idea that trees indeed have the capacity to communicate in a more purposeful fashion, or, as Wohlleben describes, to help warn or protect each other "using chemical signals sent through the fungal networks around their root tips,"[22] then a culture of reciprocity might also view such processes as a mode of entangled empathy, and, relatedly, what Kimmerer refers to as a kind of "communal generosity" in which we cannot "separate individual well-being from the health of the whole."[23] Within this environmental meshworks, then, black bears and beech trees act upon each other as relationally co-constituted beings that co-emerge together and reciprocally.[24] Again, if we remain open to a language of animacy, then we may work against a hierarchy of species and in the process become privy to worlds previously inaccessible, and from which we may learn a great deal.

When applied to the reciprocal relationship between beech and black bears, for instance, we may consider that the "gift of abundance" provided by beech trees to black bears is also a gift to the trees themselves. By sustaining black bears and other species, beech trees also ensure their own survival: "The genes that translate to mast fruiting flow on evolutionary currents into the next generations, while those that lack the ability to participate will be eaten and reach an evolutionary dead end."[25] And in this way, through the generosity of mast fruiting, both trees and bears alike can also be said to participate in what Kimmerer, drawing on an Indigenous worldview, calls the "Honorable Harvest."

## BEECH, BLACK BEARS, AND THE HONORABLE HARVEST

If we understand beech trees as participating in the generosity of mast fruiting, then it is possible to see how "generously they shower" black bears with food, "literally giving themselves" such that bears can survive.[26] By participating in this cycle, bears' harvesting of beechnuts can also help sustain beech trees, returning the "benefit to them in the circle of life making life, the chain of reciprocity."[27] Thus, it may be argued that black bears participate in the precepts of the Honorable Harvest. To live by the precepts of the Honorable Harvest, Kimmerer tells us, entails taking "only what is given," using it well, and reciprocating the gift.[28] To participate in the Honorable Harvest also entails practicing gratitude for the gift. While we may not know for certain whether black bears experience gratitude in the ways that we may imagine of humans, there is evidence that they indeed form social relationships and share with one another, even if they are not part of the same social group.

As Ben Kilham describes, science thinks of bears as solitary creatures, "but while bears don't live in established groups or obey rigid hierarchies as chimps or wolves do, they have amazingly complex social relationships. Each individual's behavior is controlled by all of the individuals with whom it shares resources, and shifting hierarchies form within families, among males, and among unrelated bears at any place that bears congregate to feed. They communicate through facial expressions, ear movements, body posture, and scent cues."[29] Kilham's description here of the social lives and communication of black bears is quite reminiscent of communication scholar George Kennedy's classic discussion of what he calls "animal rhetoric," when he describes the social hierarchies that exist among packs of lions or wolves, and the "expenditure of physical and emotional energy" that happens when members of the group communicate about "a possible enemy or possible prey."[30] Kennedy stops short of fully acknowledging the individuality of specific creatures— a view that many who study animal communication, including Bekoff, now readily accept—yet agrees "there is no room for doubt that animals communicate among their own species and with other species."[31]

Kilham has also observed that black bears display altruism through sharing: "Black bears are a society of individuals that share surplus food with both kin and strangers with reciprocity. To manage this altruistic type of social behavior they have developed complex verbal and olfactory communication systems that allows them to manage social situations with a high level of emotion and intention."[32] Their cooperation is an outcome of the availability of food sources within their territory. Bears will seek out the highest-quality foods that they can find, and many of these foods are subject to the annual boom-bust cycles that create inconsistent patterns of availability. For this reason, no single bear or group of bears can feasibly remain in a single territory that can provide ample food supply all the time.

Kilham also describes how reciprocal relationships and sharing develop among bears; he writes that female bears have "core home ranges which they share with their offspring in which kinship hierarchies develop to manage the sharing."[33] In addition, when surplus foods "are only available in another bear's home range," then black bears will share with each other.[34] The constantly changing locations of these surplus food supplies also create numerous opportunities for developing reciprocal relationships; finally, because black bears can live for as long as forty years, there is a long-term benefit for them to form reciprocal relationships with other bears.[35] The reciprocal relationships that develop among black bears, even when they are not part of the same social group, show us that other animals besides humans can participate in a culture of reciprocity and implicitly honor the precepts of the Honorable Harvest, and they may in fact do so more adeptly than many humans.

Given the unpredictability of the food sources upon which black bears rely, it then becomes possible to understand how, as foragers, they will search out alternate sources of sustenance, especially during years when beechnuts are in shorter supply. Subsequently, bears may frequent the backyard bird feeders of well-meaning humans who had not realized that in their effort to feed local songbirds, they were also providing an invitation to their resident black bear.

Bears may also wander into corn fields where they will find an ample food source but not an ample welcome from farmers. Based on Stark's GPS data history and his physical exam, for instance, and given that 2019 was not a high-yield year for beechnuts, it would appear that he had indeed found an abundance of either corn or oak prior to denning that winter.

> [The researchers] are underneath the bottom of the tree . . . , and
> the bear is in the very corner of his den. . . . There's a lot of debris,
> and he's way deep in there, so it's very difficult to maneuver.
> —Vermont Public Radio journalist, commenting on Stark[36]

The research team has successfully located Stark at his den site. They communicate with each other in whispers to prevent any unnecessary disturbance. It takes skill and great care to maneuver under the tree enough to be able to sedate this creature and remove him from his den. The biologists administer the drug with a tool that allows them to do so gently and from a distance, and in many cases, bears do not react to being disturbed because they are "deep in their hibernation cycle."[37] At this time, the biologists also administer an eye ointment to protect Stark's eyes, because he loses the ability to blink while sedated.

On the one hand, this field research does constitute an intervention into this bear's life; on the other hand, the team's efforts to minimally disturb Stark during data collection align with the overarching goals of compassionate conservation and the tenet of "do no harm" as it applies in research contexts related to conservation biology. Such interventions are a delicate balance, though, for they involve humans intervening in the lives of other animals, but these individual researchers also do their work with great care, respect, and empathy for this creature, and with the larger concern of ensuring the safety of the lives of other local bears. The goals of the black bear study are also, nonetheless, situated within the larger context of a technocratic framework that seeks to make space for wind energy and the projects of human development. In such larger contexts, we may consider what it means to balance the needs of vulnerable species with the sustainability-related goals of humans. A perfect balance or ideal scenario may not be truly possible in this age of climate crisis, but this does not mean we need to halt such research; rather, it is important to consider these research projects, their broader contexts, and the different macro- and more micro-level contexts that inform them.

From a posthuman vantage point, I suggest that this research team is part of a larger environmental meshwork in which our in/organic entanglements with the material world take shape. Their research is paradoxical, in that it constitutes an intervention into the life of individual creature, but this intervention is also born out of empathy and concern for the well-being of species and ecosystems. It is an intervention that endeavors to help better understand and minimize the potential impacts of the projects of human development on black bears. Thus, when carried out with empathy, compassion, respect, and minimal disturbance, such an intervention also participates in a broader "environmental meshworks" that can help foster more ethical relationships with our worlds. This broader environmental meshworks is, paradoxically, also part of a larger cycle of responses to other, ongoing projects of human development.

As the research team moves the bear from his den, next, they comment on his physical appearance, and what appears to be his good health. On the one hand, from a feminist visual communication perspective, we may see, as described below, the human gaze falling upon and assessing the body of the more-than-human; on the other hand, when contextualized with the knowledge that these individual researchers have great respect for this creature, their gaze becomes perhaps less anthropocentric and more informed by their interest in ensuring the safety of these vulnerable species. For, at the end of the day, as Marc Bekoff has commented, there is, in the Anthropocene, and in conservation biology, no complete way around human intervention in the environment; instead, we must work from informed and critical perspectives that act in the best interests of our more-than-human kin to the best extent possible.[38] In this case, we may see where the goals of conservation biology interconnect with the work of individuals who also have respect for the lives of these creatures.

> "Oh, he's beautiful. . . . You can see him breathing."
> "He smells fantastic too, really."
> "Oh, he's got a great coat—look how thick that is."
> —VFWD research team and Vermont Public Radio
> journalists, commenting on Stark[39]

Stark is currently outside his den; he is larger than the team had anticipated, and so it has taken them a bit longer than usual to move him. They conduct the physical exam and replace his GPS radio collar. These biologists care greatly about the welfare of this bear and are pleasantly surprised by his healthy weight—252 pounds. Here, again, conservation biology intermingles with the work of individuals who seek to ensure a safe future for these creatures, despite the ongoing and seemingly inevitable impacts of human development. As Bekoff describes, many of us would like to develop a more compassionate society, and one that "preserves and sustains the ecosystems and biodiversity upon which we all depend. But it's not easy to change the entrenched practices of industry, business, science, and society," so we must work within them to find a middle ground.[40] While Bekoff's compassionate conservation advocates for as much of a hands-off approach as possible, he also recognizes that humans are still in a position to make these decisions "*on behalf of*" other animals; to this end, he advocates for what he calls "rewilding projects." "Rewilding," says Bekoff, "makes for better and more useful science," and "scientists themselves need rewilding to improve their work. . . . By rewilding, we listen more closely to what animals need; we listen to the land."[41] I suggest here that projects like the Deerfield Wind Black Bear Study constitute and illustrate the complexities of such "rewilding projects" situated in these Anthropocene contexts that have no easy solution.

For Stark to weigh 252 pounds in April means that when he entered his den in November, he likely weighed significantly more than this. Bears will lose weight over the course of hibernation, so the more they weigh when entering their den for the season, the better. Biologist Jaclyn Comeau comments, "Yeah, he really did well this fall—better than we had expected," and the group speculates as to how he managed to put on so much weight before denning, since 2019 was not a strong year for beechnuts.[42]

Comeau also notes that to weigh so much, he must have been eating "a lot of acorns, and maybe a touch of corn."[43] At this elevation in the Green Mountains, though, there are not very many oaks or therefore acorns, which means he must have traveled elsewhere to find adequate sustenance. Indeed, based on Stark's GPS data, the researchers know that Stark "left Vermont and went over into New York, where there are a lot more oaks and acorns."[44] Stark's physical health ought not to be taken for granted, however, because traveling that far in search of food is a risky endeavor for a bear, at best, and that risk is confounded by the fact that bears often seek out food sources that can pose secondary threats to their well-being. As biologist Forrest Hammond describes: "He obviously got in a real good food source. Unfortunately, it may have been a risky food source, where he traveled a lot during the hunting season; he may have been in corn fields where the farmers didn't want him there. And so, it's riskier, but those years, where there's not much for natural food," some of the bears who took on the risk of entering corn fields are actually the heaviest.[45] In Stark's case, he seemed to have trekked the whole distance to New York to find oak, and may have frequented some corn fields as well. This can be a dangerous undertaking, but the payoff is weight gain sufficient for healthy hibernation.

The distance from portions of the Molly Stark Highway and Route 9 in Vermont to the New York State line is a minimum of about fifteen to twenty miles west, one way. This seems to me like quite a trek, even for a larger mammal like a black bear, although I realize that I am likely projecting onto this bear my own feelings of exhaustion at the thought of such a journey. And in fact, in chatting with Jaclyn Comeau, biologist for the Vermont Fish and Wildlife Department and lead biologist for the Deerfield Wind Black Bear Study, I learn that adult black bears with established home ranges will typically move about ten to twenty miles in the fall; however, if their natural food sources are lacking in the areas they typically visit, black bears may travel up to twenty-five or thirty miles in search of food. The cyclical yields of beechnuts play a large role in bears' travel patterns; during years with high beechnut yields, bears generally remain within their summer home range or travel shorter distances of under ten miles. During years with lower beechnut yields, bears like

Stark will travel farther distances of ten to twenty miles to look for oak forests and feed on acorns instead.

Comeau, who was part of the VFWD team that checked on Stark, also makes the more nuanced point that "long distance movements are part of how bears are successful, but *we* [humans] are making it riskier for them" by doing things like creating fragmented habitats and infrastructure that complicates their ability to negotiate what might otherwise be typical travel through their habitats and home ranges.[46] Indeed, as Comeau points out: "We are all members of the same ecosystem—we are the ultimate ecosystem engineers. We need to be aware of our impacts, and do what we can to minimize those impacts."[47] I agree, and I would add to Comeau's points by suggesting that we can help minimize those impacts through conservation practices that understand the lives of more-than-humans, humans, and other species as part of an environmental meshworks, and not as unfolding along separate planes.

A compassionate conservation approach would then maintain that it is part of our ethical obligation to decrease the risk and the harm to affected species when possible. A culture of reciprocity would similarly suggest that it is our obligation to return the gifts that these creatures bestow upon us. As we strive toward peaceful coexistence, it is important to consider whether and how we might reconcile our participation in a culture of reciprocity with the ongoing projects of human development. Bekoff's ideas about rewilding offer a move in this direction; in addition, to support the precepts of the Honorable Harvest, intervene with empathy, and minimize risk to species whenever possible, even in the smallest of ways, are all possibilities that can help offset the impacts of human development. Sustainable energy projects at once aim to reduce our reliance on fossil fuels as they also present unrelenting challenges to ecosystems and the species who reside within them. In the Anthropocene, it seems, there is no easy solution, but that doesn't mean we must resort to despair or hopelessness. As Lori Gruen reminds us, in moments of entangled empathy, the ability to focus on the experiences of other animals in "their communities and environments" can become a source of hope and reveal possibilities for a more equitable world.[48] Projects such as the black bear study, when carried out by those who engage with compassion and empathy, and with the best interests of our more-than-human kin in mind, not only reveal such possibilities but also illuminate the complex entanglements of empathy with conservation biology and related "rewilding projects," as well as the interconnectedness of scientific research with larger-scale projects of human development.

We may, for instance, consider Stark's GPS collar and the data it provides as a posthuman intervention that can illuminate better understandings of how to maintain connectivity. The information gleaned from Stark's GPS collar does more than merely reveal the long distances these bears will travel for sustenance; within that revelation is an important lesson about habitat connectivity and where these bears can successfully travel to locate food. Stark traveled all the way to New York to find food, and then traveled that entire distance back to return home to den in his original home range.[49] On the one hand, a diet of corn might not be ideal, but on the other hand, the travel itself to and from his home range was nonetheless possible. But if food is less available locally, bears must be able to venture farther out and do so safely without being permanently displaced from their home range. It is a delicate balance, to say the least.

When I consider that black bears are actually able to travel longer distances, and that the larger issue at hand is actually our own ethical obligation to make sure that such travel is safe and actually necessary for them in the first place, it makes sense that biologists find usefulness in GPS data that shows how and where Stark was able to travel across habitats to find food. Stark's story and circumstances and the Deerfield Wind Black Bear Study help demonstrate that part of our ethical responsibility to these creatures is to better understand how to maintain habitat connectivity in the face of human development that seems unlikely to cease.[50]

## HABITAT CONNECTIVITY IN THE SHADOW OF WIND TURBINES: LEARNING TO WALK AS IF ALL THINGS MATTERED

Habitat connectivity is indeed part of what is under scrutiny in relation to the Deerfield Wind Energy Project (DWEP). Biologists with the VFWD are interested in Stark's well-being because of the potential for the wind project to influence his and other local black bears' foraging behaviors. Again, of particular interest to the researchers is how the wind project may impact critical habitat like bear-scarred beech stands.

After a decade-long permitting and construction process, the Deerfield Wind Energy Project finally went online in late 2017. Significantly, and not without some public opposition, it was the first industrial wind facility in the United States to be built on national forest land.[51] The DWEP consists of fifteen turbines in the southern Vermont towns of Readsboro and Searsburg, just north of the Massachusetts border.[52] Eight of the turbines are situated along a western ridgeline in Searsburg, and seven turbines sit on a "roughly parallel ridge" in Readsboro."[53] The Searsburg turbines are also "on the same side of the mountain ridge as Green Mountain Power's smaller, 11-turbine facility, which began operating in 1997."[54] The close proximity to the Green Mountain Power facility makes it possible for that facility to expand its existing operation and for the two facilities to collaborate "to produce additional electricity for Vermonters and others."[55] Green Mountain Power, for instance, has also agreed to purchase power from the Deerfield facility as part of these efforts to supply power to about 14,000 homes.[56]

The Deerfield Wind Energy Project was built within one of the largest concentrations of bear-scarred beech trees in southern Vermont. Thus, as part of the approval process to permit the construction and operation of the DWEP, the Vermont Public Service Board required Iberdrola, which operates the wind farm with Avangrid Renewables,[57] to allow and support the Deerfield Wind Black Bear Study, which, as mentioned earlier, is an ongoing study "to evaluate the impacts of an industrial wind facility on black bear habitat use and foraging behaviors."[58] The study itself was designed by the Vermont Fish and Wildlife Department, who are also responsible for data collection and analysis. The VFWD has also had assistance with data collection from local companies and other partners like the US Forest Service, USDA Wildlife Services, and students from the University of Vermont's Rubenstein School of Environment and Natural Resources.[59]

Wind turbines are known to have potentially detrimental impacts on raptors, migratory birds, and bats; however, less is known about the potential impacts of wind power on larger mammals like black bears. Since the DWEP was built within one of the largest areas of bear-scarred beech in Vermont, wildlife officials in Vermont are concerned about "the disturbance to stands of American beech trees on remote ridges that have a history of bear use."[60] The Deerfield Wind Black Bear Study thus looks at whether and how black bears will continue to use these beech trees "in the shadow of these large wind turbines," says Jaclyn Comeau, biologist with the Vermont Fish and Wildlife Department and lead biologist for the study.[61] Bears are considered the "umbrella species" for these beech stands but, as mentioned earlier, beech is also an important food source for deer, turkey, American marten, fisher, and many other birds and mammals.[62]

Local organizations like Vermonters for a Clean Environment have long expressed concern about the potential impacts of the project for black bear populations, and public comment over the years has also been strongly focused on concern for local black bears.[63] As mentioned in the introduction, Melody Walker, a Vermont-based "educator, activist, artist, and citizen of the Elnu Abenaki Band of Ndakinna," reminds us that "'People' in dominant society refers only to humans," and Abenaki culture teaches us "what belonging means, what it means to be a person, and what it means to walk as if all things mattered. Dominant society is largely devoid of these ideas."[64] Walker, who also references Kimmerer's work, says that "for all of us, becoming indigenous to a place means living as if your children's future mattered, to take care of the land as if our lives, both material and spiritual, depended on it."[65] In voicing concern for the projects of human development more broadly, Walker states that the Abenaki "homeland has been drastically altered, and a new set of values has overtaken our own. Reciprocity with us or our non-human kin is rare." To this end, she argues, and rightly so, that the Abenaki voice ought to be included in environmental policy-making: "If our world is to be cared for properly, including us in policy and brainstorming is not politically correct, it is necessary. Our worldview and our spirituality are intricately tied together in place." Walker argues that the voice of the Abenaki people ought to be included in local environmental policy and decision-making not only to help protect and respect the Abenaki culture but also, in doing so, to more fully foster a culture of reciprocity and "to walk as if all things mattered."[66] Indeed, part of being at home in the Anthropocene means walking as if all things mattered, and in doing so, being receptive to the many languages of our more-than-human kin and other earthly species, or the internatural communication inherent in these moments. As Emily Plec reminds us, internatural communication is welcoming of "the possibilities of human and animal communication with other life forms."[67] Being at home in the Anthropocene also requires engaging more fully in environmental policy- and decision-making that accounts for humans as well as other animals and life-forms and the ecosystems we share; it means starting from a compassionate conservation, "gift" mindset and participating in a culture of reciprocity. It means taking the perhaps uncomfortable position of understanding "natural resources" as "earthly gifts," and adjusting our actions based on the implications of such an understanding. Such work is not an all-or-nothing proposition, either. To be at home in the Anthropocene means working iteratively in a positive direction toward these goals. It means acknowledging that these paradigm shifts do not happen overnight; rather, we are in it for the long haul.

Here, it is also worth noting that the Final Environmental Impact Statement (EIS) for the proposed Deerfield wind project responded to many of the public comments received on the earlier, Supplemental Draft Environmental Impact Statement that was released in 2010, and that the Forest Service did consult with and receive feedback from local Abenaki leaders during the permitting processes for the DWEP.[68] Nonetheless, it is clear that such projects must account carefully for a constellation of voices and vantage points, and that to act in integrity with ecosystems is to practice compassionate conservation and a culture of reciprocity. We must consider that projects such as the

DWEP are not only a component of Vermont's sustainable energy future, but that they also pose challenges for the land and ecosystems upon which our more-than-human kin depend. There is clearly no easy solution to these challenges; instead, we must continually consider how to best account for these challenges in a world of competing and sometimes contradicting perspectives. In the process, again, perhaps we may better learn "how to walk as if all things mattered."[69]

The researchers who are carrying out the Deerfield Wind Black Bear Study illustrate one contemporary way that these ideals play out through the practices of technoscience. They arguably participate in a broader environmental meshworks and "rewilding project" that, paradoxically, functions as an ethical and empathetic response to ongoing projects of human development like the DWEP. Again, when working in the positive, research like the black bear study has the potential to illuminate in productive ways the experiences of other animals in "their communities and environments," and can reveal possibilities for a more equitable world.[70] As the VDFW researchers look for ways to decrease risk to local black bears potentially affected by the wind project, they participate in a culture of reciprocity grounded in the need to ensure safe and habitable home ranges for these vulnerable creatures. In short, the VDFW research team works to ensure the gift of abundance by ensuring the gift of sustainable habitat. Through their technoscientific endeavors, they help contribute to a culture of reciprocity in the Anthropocene.

The challenges to maintaining connectivity and accounting for our more-than-human kin are nonetheless ongoing and multifaceted. Again, in the Anthropocene, there seems to be no complete way around human intervention in the environment; instead, as Bekoff helps describe, we must proceed with critical awareness and acknowledge the complex entanglements that inform what are, at the end of the day, human interventions into the lives of more-than-human kin. In this case, we see how the goals of conservation biology are not only interconnected with the work of empathetic researchers who respect the lives of these creatures and want to ensure their safety, but are also paradoxically connected with broader, technocratic efforts to achieve sustainability goals for humans.

## AT HOME WITH WIND POWER: AN ENVIRONMENTAL MESHWORKS REQUIRING COMPASSION AND SENSITIVITY TO CONTEXT

The ethical questions surrounding renewable energy like wind power are not straightforward, and they are made even more complex by the fact that many people consider alternative energy sources, more broadly, as blanket solutions to nonrenewable energy. Alternative energy sources are certainly a move toward a more sustainable energy future, and wind power does have the potential to address many issues of renewable energy needs; however, such resources are not necessarily a panacea. I should also note that it is hardly my intent to critique renewable energy sources or projects like the DWEP; rather, I am suggesting that, like all projects of technoscience, we must proceed with caution in considering the entirety of the environmental meshworks in which these projects unfold. Wind power, like other renewables, poses its own challenges, and it is not feasible to make blanket statements about their impacts, because "the best disposition of each wind project is inevitably contextual."[71] The complexity of and debates about the Deerfield Wind Energy Project illustrate this point.

First, for instance, inland and offshore wind development pose different challenges. Situated within the Green Mountain National Forest, the DWEP is an inland wind farm; while offshore wind development has become more associated with its threats to bird life, "inland wind generation poses special direct and habitat risk to bears, bats, and other mammals."[72] As proponents of compassionate conservation have expressed, the impacts of infrastructure and development projects on birds, mammals, and other animals are often overlooked, subsumed by the human tendency toward anthropocentric thinking. For these reasons, projects like the black bear study seek to prevent bears like Stark from getting lost in the shuffle. As Reed Elizabeth Loder, professor at Vermont Law School, puts it, "the toll on wildlife associated with inland wind power generation" appears to be "an issue ethically less amenable to balancing costs and advantages."[73] To this end, Loder argues for an approach to the DWEP that can safely and ethically account for the well-being of both humans and other animals. In doing so, she advocates for a perspective informed not so much by utilitarian or anthropocentric views but rather by a more relational and ecofeminist approach—one that I would add is also more aligned with compassionate conservation and a posthuman ideal of entangled empathy. We must then consider whether or not a relational approach will ever—can ever—gain enough ground to ensure a sustainable future for both humans and our more-than-human kin; we might ask just how much humans might be willing to give—or, to sacrifice, as some might have it—in order to put such ideas into practice.

Rationales for the benefits of renewable energy sources like wind power tend to be utilitarian because they seek to balance "total benefit over harm."[74] Such a vantage point runs counter to an Indigenous worldview and a compassionate conservation perspective, as utilitarian reasoning "can consider disutilities like wildlife impacts or regional controversy as justified prices of national progress," and utilitarianism is often critiqued for its tendency to sacrifice "minority interests for the aggregate good."[75] In other words, whose interests are being represented, here, in considering "aggregate good"? To put it more bluntly, it becomes hard to imagine Stark as benefiting from wind energy in this formulation. When considered in the context of the DWEP project, for instance, it is also notable that the DWEP is the first wind power facility to be situated on national forest land in the Green Mountains. National forest lands are considered public lands and are federally administered by the Department of Agriculture under the Department of the Interior.

Because federal lands are public, they are sometimes viewed as a more appealing setting for wind farms than private lands, because, in theory, "the land belongs to the public" and, *in theory*, "everyone stands to benefit from independent, non-polluting, and renewable sources of power."[76] In other words, some may assume a utilitarian perspective to apply in the case of the DWEP, because a renewable energy source situated on public land may be perceived as contributing to the aggregate good. In addition, "some public lands are attractive for offering large contiguous acreage," and there are fewer limits than with the "size, scope, and availability of private land."[77] Thus, it is possible to use taller turbines to increase the speed and power of wind energy.[78] The blades on the newer turbines used for the DWEP, for instance, are larger than earlier models, with the tips of the rotor blades reaching "from 400 to 430 feet from the ground at the highest point in their turning radius."[79] Again, the predominant thinking is that more wind energy, at least in theory, contributes to the greater good. At issue here, however, is that, in this case, environmentalists argue that "aggregate good" seems to account mostly for perceived human needs, and not necessarily those of, say, Stark the black bear. Put differently, "aggregate good," in this case, does not necessarily fully understand the lives of our more-than-human kin and life-forms, and the ecosystems we all share, as "intricately tied together in place," to borrow from Walker's words.[80] At the 2016 groundbreaking for the DWEP site, protesters from Vermonters for a Clean Environment and others voiced their opposition to the project, citing similar concerns for "environmental impacts to wildlife" and the "nearby wilderness area" that is the Green Mountain National Forest.[81]

Questions about whether and to what extent black bear populations are impacted by these turbines, and whether potential "detriment to the local population of bears is a justifiable 'downside'" to increased, reliable, renewable energy are some of the ongoing ethical issues being considered by Vermont officials and local publics.[82] Loder notes that utilitarian approaches "can also incorporate mitigation measures that enhance total benefit and commend only those alternatives comparatively least harmful." But even so, if mitigation strategies prove infeasible or prohibitively costly, then they may not be deemed a justifiable sacrifice for the greater good.[83]

Part of the mitigation strategies related to the DWEP have involved what is referred to as "off-site mitigation." Off-site mitigation essentially entails what is referred to as a "trade-off" proposition. In 2016, for instance, the Public Service Board required the energy company Avangrid Renewables to buy land elsewhere to mitigate for the use of the national forest site.[84] According to Catherine Gjessing, general counsel for the VDFW, "36 acres of prime bear habitat were sacrificed to allow the industrial wind project to come to fruition." The VDFW, however, was not a proponent of clearing that much acreage in critical black bear habitat. As Gjessing described, the VFWD

> opposed the project on the basis that it would significantly imperil or destroy wildlife habitat and bear habitat. . . . The Public Utility Commission did not, frankly, rule in the way that the department would have preferred. They issued a decision in which they approved the certificate of public good for the project. They found, based on our testimony, that there were 36 acres of bear scarred beech [trees] that would be removed as part of the project.[85]

According to Gjessing, the commission required that the developer of the DWEP, Avangrid Renewables, would mitigate by identifying "alternative bear habitat to make up for the loss."[86] Identifying such habitat would involve finding and conserving 144 acres of bear-scarred beech. Concerned about the developer's ability to locate such acreage, the VFWD "ultimately decided to take charge of this task to ensure that the bears got proper land and resources," and they have since "closed on two projects within the general area [about thirty to forty miles north] of the turbines, one in Stratton and another in Jamaica. In all, over 800 acres were secured."[87]

As Gjessing described in January 2020, it is still too soon to know the impact of the lost acreage; as she put it: "It's true that 35 acres will always be gone, at least as long as that wind project is in existence, but we think that we did make lemons out of lemonade, if you will, and tried to conserve some really good parcels."[88] This perspective—the idea that habitat trade-off may be likened to making lemonade from lemons—illustrates the trickiness of using a trade-off approach to mitigate potentially lost habitat. First, trade-off approaches are often viewed as controversial because they can be understood as devaluing natural habitats, and as a top-down, artificial way of managing the environment. An additional critique of a trade-off approach is based on concerns related to compassionate conservation.

## COMPASSIONATE CONSERVATION AND
## HABITAT AS CONTEXTUALLY SPECIFIC

A compassionate conservation approach does not view habitat as an abstract entity but rather as highly contextual; as such, "the loss of particular places and things matters even if the overall balance remains stable."[89] From a compassionate conservation perspective, "the particular bears that may starve or suffer from fragmented habitat also matter. The principle of avoiding unnecessary harm also applies to individual animals because they have value and deserve consideration and respect."[90] Thus, as Loder argues, "the particular bears residing in Green Mountain National Forest are neither indispensable nor interchangeable with other bears. Earnest efforts should be made not to displace them."[91] Consistent with this philosophy, the VFWD understands Stark as a specific black bear residing in a specific habitat, and so their efforts are meant to understand, support, and help advocate for his continued engagement with the portion of the Green Mountains that he calls home.

A compassionate conservation approach requires that we be mindful of the impacts of human development and that we proceed with empathy and a contextually specific approach to conservation projects whenever possible. The Deerfield Wind Black Bear Study seeks to provide data that can help inform some of these as-yet unanswered questions about the impacts of the wind project on black bear populations. Data collection for the study has relied on GPS collaring of black bears, along with what are called "camera traps," or installed camera stations that automatically photograph species as they utilize areas of high beech concentrations and surrounding habitats.[92]

Camera traps are an inexpensive and nonintrusive way for the VFWD to gain data about black bear usage of high beech areas. For this reason, camera traps may be used to monitor black bear activity within the DWEP beyond 2021, and the data collected "will help researchers monitor the long-term relationship between the DWEP and wildlife use of the bear scarred beech concentrations."[93] The Deerfield Wind Black Bear Study takes time because it is also necessary to collect data when beechnut production is optimal, as data from a range of years should be collected to help account for different variables. For instance, as Comeau and Hammond describe in their 2018 study update, fewer black bears seemed to utilize beech plots during the construction phase of the DWEP; however, that construction phase also coincided with a low-yield year for beechnuts, so it is necessary to get a broader range of data to tease out these variables.[94]

Between fall 2015 and spring 2017, the VFWD collected 2,714 photographs of black bears, with 1,776 photos collected from bear-scarred beech plots, and 938 from non-bear-scarred beech plots.[95] Of these photos, "during the good beechnut production season of fall 2015/spring 2016 2,470 photographs of bears were collected while only 244 photographs of bears were collected during the poor production season of fall 2016/spring 2017; however, this poor beechnut season overlapped entirely with the construction phase of the DWEP."[96] The VFWD subsequently notes that a wider range of data is needed in order to provide additional insight into the potential role that construction may have played "on wildlife use of these mast production sites."[97] In order to get a fuller picture of the "potential impacts of the DWEP on black bear habitat use," and, for instance, whether any connection may be made between the construction phase of the DWEP and black bear use of that area, "it is key to make these assessments when beechnut production is good," and it is thus possible that data collection may extend through 2021.[98] The VFWD's commitment to this research can help inform future decision-making about the DWEP. Their research also performs an approach to compassionate conservation that is attentive to a complex environmental meshworks in which the projects of technoscience are at work in paradoxical ways. In the Green Mountain National Forest, renewable energy projects like the DWEP help create a sustainable energy future for humans, but their impacts on our more-than-human kin are not fully known. At the same time, projects like the Deerfield Wind Black Bear Study, including its GPS and visualization technologies, may participate in an albeit paradoxical culture of reciprocity by helping to illuminate what is required of the DWEP in order to ensure a more sustainable home range for the black bears whose habitats are impacted by these renewable energy projects.

## AN ECOFEMINIST ENVIRONMENTAL ETHICS AND OUR ENTANGLED RELATIONSHIPS WITH SPECIES AND "EARTH OTHERS"

A culture of reciprocity would then start from a compassionate conservation mindset—one that helps keep anthropocentrism in check and imparts a more relational, ecological, and posthuman perspective. Renewable energy may have benefits for other animals besides humans; however, the trickiness is that the argument for "parallel benefits" of renewables, for both humans and other animals, is still, at the end of the day, "contingent on human interests."[99] Rather than creating and sustaining a false dichotomy, an ecofeminist and, I would argue, posthumanist approach both call for a more relational understanding that is contextual and sensitive to the interrelationships between humans, more-than-humans, and other earthly species. Loder, for instance, advocates for an ecofeminist approach to the Deerfield wind project that "would not disregard bears or other wildlife simply because they are different from humans and thus inferior. Ecofeminists would not view bears, beech trees, or humans in isolation and would treat the entire network of relationships as ethically important."[100] In this case, she says, "the fate of bears would be considered ecologically in relation to the complex environmental and human impacts that various adjustments would create."[101] Such an approach would thus require ongoing adaptations in any approved scenario, leaving little way around some form of human intervention.[102]

On the one hand, it is clear that an ecofeminist approach is very much aligned with compassionate conservation in its acknowledgment that all of our actions happen as part of a larger set of entangled relationships, or the environmental meshworks in which our in/organic entanglements with the material world take shape. On the other hand, when considering more fully an ecofeminist and Indigenous worldview that understands the ecosystem as a vibrant community of beings which may be valued on equal terms, it is also clear that challenges remain when attempting to more fluidly integrate theory with practice.

An ecofeminist approach that considers the "entire network of relationships as ethically important" would implicitly value our ability to empathize with potentially displaced, more-than-human kin. Additionally, however, it would not preclude the possibility of experiencing empathy for what feminist philosopher Val Plumwood calls "earth others,"[103] or the other living elements of the ecosystem, such as, for instance, the beech trees that have been removed as a result of the DWEP. That is, when we consider the ability of trees to communicate through their root systems and act in concert, and when we consider the collective action of mast fruiting, we might question whether clearing the thirty-six acres of bear-scarred beech trees may disrupt their ability to participate in the Honorable Harvest, or whether such clearing may impact their cyclical patterns over time. Moreover, such speculation about the impact of the DWEP on beech trees arguably constitutes a form of empathy for these earth others. In practice, though, we may consider whether environmental policies about sustainable energy need to align more closely with such ideas to more fully engage the philosophies underpinning entangled empathy with other animals and life-forms.

## ENTANGLED EMPATHY AND "EARTH OTHERS"

Gruen's theory of entangled empathy is more explicitly related to our ability to empathize with other animals, and accounts less for the ability of humans to empathize with, say, whole ecosystems or habitats. Gruen says this is because entangled empathy entails understanding "the individual's species-typical behaviors and her individual personality over a period of time. Very often this is not easy to do without expertise and observation," and it is easier to empathize with "sentient beings who have experiences."[104] On the one hand, Gruen argues that "humans and animals are sentient beings to whom we can ascribe consciousness, choice, emotion, imagination, and the like; we are beings for whom life can go better or worse. Given these similarities, we can more readily empathize with other sentient beings."[105] On the other hand, she expresses openness to our ability to connect more empathetically with "earth others," and feels that "once we figure out a way to empathize beyond sentience, we may be able to connect more directly with the rest of the natural world."[106] Implicitly drawing on feminist geography and ideas about sense of place, Gruen acknowledges that many people are in "caring relationships with particular natural spaces."[107] We may feel grief or mourn the loss of ecosystems, although she feels that it "isn't possible to be in empathetic relation to ecosystems or organisms that exist" in ways that we can't imagine "beyond metaphor or projection."[108] That said, she specifically points to Plumwood's work as a starting point for empathizing with and better understanding our entanglements with ecosystems and the natural world.

Like many feminist philosophers, Plumwood rejected the Cartesian, dualistic thinking that perpetuates a mind/body distinction, and much of her thinking and writing was informed by Indigenous knowledges and the value of storytelling for conveying knowledge about places; as such, she called on us "to attend to earth others in non-dualistic ways."[109] Plumwood has acknowledged that it is easy enough for humans to relate to nature or picture ourselves in nature "when it has been colonised, commodified and domesticated," and made into something that reflects our own needs and desires; however, she writes, we need, more importantly, to "recognise in the myriad forms of nature other beings—earth others—whose needs, goals and purposes must, like our own, be acknowledged and respected."[110] Plumwood writes that part of attending to earth others in a nonhierarchical, nonanthropocentric mode involves taking on an "intentional stance" in which "we can encounter the earth other as a potential intentional subject, as one who can alter us as well as we it, and thus can begin to conceive a potential for a mutual and sustained interchange with nature."[111] In other words, if we consider more tangibly an environmental meshwork in which beech trees, black bears, and humans are all ecologically entangled, then beech trees can, in a variety of ways, affect the lives of bears and people. Likewise, black bears, humans, and the projects of technoscience can all affect the lives of beech trees. These entangled relationships can then open up possibilities for more conscious, reciprocal, ongoing interchanges with earth others. Such understanding thus requires an openness to a language of animacy, for "the recognition of difference is especially critical in mutual relationships with earth others."[112]

Plumwood accounts for our ability to empathize with the natural world in part through her definition of "philosophical animism," which, similar to a language of animacy, as Deborah Bird Rose describes, "opens the door to a world in which we can begin to negotiate life membership of an ecological community of kindred beings."[113] Thus, Plumwood's "animism, like indigenous animisms, was not a doctrine or orthodoxy, but rather a path, a way of life, a mode of encounter."[114] I would add that if philosophical animism, similar to a language of animacy, can accommodate a "gift mindset" that acknowledges a communal generosity beyond the lives of humans and more-than-humans, then it becomes easier to understand how we might also view our encounters with earth others as gifts to be returned—as exchanges rooted in a culture of reciprocity that can be of benefit to all creatures: humans, more-than-humans, and earth others alike.

> Listening in wild places, we are audience to
> conversations in a language not our own.
> —Robin Wall Kimmerer[115]

There is much left to be told of the story of the Deerfield Wind Energy Project, the Deerfield Wind Black Bear Study, the ongoing work of the Vermont Fish and Wildlife Department, and the future of Stark and his home range in the Green Mountain National Forest. Like the other narrative accounts in this book, this story may wind down here, but ideas about what counts as "home" and the responsibilities that come with human interventions into the habitats we share with other animals and earth others are open and ongoing. Nonetheless, the story of Stark and the Deerfield Wind Energy Project does help reveal and reiterate certain themes and tensions as we chart a course that attempts to walk the fine line between trying to meet the perceived needs of humans while also accounting for the lives of our vulnerable, more-than-human kin.

The chapter has used the story of the Deerfield Wind Energy Project in particular to consider how we may coexist with these big kin and earth others in an age of human development and climate change, and the most compassionate path forward in this entangled coexistence. Humans have an ethical obligation to help ensure safe passage and to maintain habitat connectivity for these black bears, particularly as our Anthropocene undertakings find us leveraging that habitat to help ensure a sustainable energy future for ourselves.

With this, I take the more ecofeminist stance that if humans create wind farms, then it is also our ethical obligation to try to ensure that our more-than-human kin remain out of harm's way in the process. Moreover, in this extended cultural moment of ongoing deforestation, it seems understandable that some may wonder if such dual outcomes are fully possible. I do not suggest here that this chapter resolves such questions in a tidy package, for that has not been my aim; rather, my goal has been to highlight the contours of these conversations and their inherent tensions with the hope of moving the needle in a productive direction that continues the dialogue while avoiding a discursive impasse. For, as we try to forge a path that ensures the best possible outcomes for all creatures, it is clear that acknowledging and engaging these concomitant discursive tensions remains a necessary part of the equation.

This chapter reiterates that "home" is again about storied place and storied land. Bear-storied beech also tells a unique story about home—one that helps reveal the possibilities for communal generosity and a culture of reciprocity; if we do not help foster such approaches to coexistence, we run the risk of displacing species through habitat fragmentation and putting our kin like Stark in harm's way. To be "at home in the Anthropocene" is thus, in part, about fostering sustainable habitat and ensuring a safe and habitable future for the more-than-human kin with whom we share our ecosystems. In this way, part of a culture of reciprocity involves, as Plec puts it, moving "from complicity to implication," and acting with "a critical awareness and effort to understand and make our role as humans in communicative relationships and interactions with other animals more just and responsible."[116] To achieve these more responsible relationships might mean asking tough questions about what kinds of compromises or sacrifices we are willing to make to achieve a sustainable future that also avoids harm to our more-than-human kin. Along similar lines, a culture of reciprocity means understanding our own ethical responsibility to these vulnerable kin as they seek safe passage through their home ranges and the habitats that we seek to leverage for their provisioning of natural resources—natural resources, which, following Kimmerer, and from an ecofeminist standpoint, might better be understood as earthly gifts.

The complex entanglements created by attempts to preserve habitat connectivity are but one manifestation of posthuman interventions into the lives and storied places of these vulnerable, more-than-human kin. In particular, this chapter has considered the challenges faced by black bears as they must unwittingly negotiate human-induced changes to their foraging and migration patterns, bringing them ever closer to regular encounters with humans and the projects of human development. Subsequently, this chapter has explored the tensions inherent in environmental discourses about these issues, and has illuminated the various perspectives about what it means to act in the best interests of our more-than-human kin as we simultaneously try to develop their home ranges for human use and try to shelter vulnerable species from the impacts of that development. Again, whether both outcomes are possible to achieve remains an open issue and one that in many ways defines the contours of life in the Anthropocene.

Moreover, this chapter argues for an Indigenous worldview that accounts for the kind of reciprocal, integrated understanding that Melody Walker articulates—one that more fully acknowledges a "cultural lens" in which "we not only see creation looming before us in the majesty of a mountain, but we can also see it in the petals of the flower at its base."[117] In this way, belonging is "not only created by people in places, or more-than-humans in places, but actively co-constitutes people and things and processes and places."[118] As we seek to fulfill these ideals, we must remember that part of fostering sustainability grounded in entangled empathy means participating in a culture of reciprocity, and that this is iterative, ongoing work.

The environmental meshworks that is the Green Mountain National Forest is home to myriad creatures and earth others. It is a storied place where black bears and beech trees alike can be said to participate in a kind of communal generosity that helps sustain lives and habitats. Humans can learn from this culture of reciprocity. We may practice and help support the Honorable Harvest in part through exploring and enacting a non-anthropocentric vantage point in the projects of human development.

We also see a culture of reciprocity practiced through the ongoing efforts of the VFWD, who, with compassion and empathy, work to understand and apply knowledge gained through their black bear study and the related efforts of compassionate conservation biology, with the hope of ensuring a safe future for the lives of black bears in the Green Mountain National Forest. There is likely not a perfect solution to these challenges; however, an ecofeminist approach that values entangled empathy and a culture of reciprocity are necessary elements to ensuring a sustainable home for our more-than-human kin and earth others in the Anthropocene. In addition, as Lori Gruen reminds us, in moments of entangled empathy, the ability to focus on the experiences of other animals in their communities and habitats can become a source of hope and reveal possibilities for a more balanced world.

The story of Stark, bear-storied beech, and the Deerfield Wind Energy Project also reveals that in the Anthropocene, helping to foster sustainable food sources for other animals is part of participating in an Honorable Harvest and a culture of reciprocity. Other animals and species besides humans can and do participate in the Honorable Harvest, and they may unwittingly do so more skillfully than us.

For Vermont's black bears, survival in a home range requires sharing, reciprocal altruism, and social and emotional communication. We humans may learn from such a model by being mindful to take only what we need, to share freely, and to communicate more clearly and with greater empathy for one another. An ecofeminist approach implicitly values our ability to empathize with other animals and earth others. In doing so, it does not preclude the possibility of experiencing empathy for other animals and life-forms with which we share our ecosystems. Entangled empathy, however, requires an openness toward acknowledging these complex relationships—only then can we consider possibilities for more conscious, reciprocal, ongoing exchanges with our more-than-human kin and earth others. Where might we look for examples of such open-mindedness? Interestingly, Gruen addresses such questions when she describes what she calls "storied empathy."

Storied empathy, or "the ability that we have as children to empathize with fictional beings, suggests that we have the capacity to engage with very different others through narrative, literature, art and story-telling."[119] Moreover, she says, "this capacity, if honed, may help us to empathetically engage with the more than human world."[120] Here, Gruen sees storied empathy and narrative as points of entry for understanding earth others and our "relationships beyond sensate animals."[121] In contemplating the open-mindedness that is associated with storied empathy, I wonder about how we might return to such an inclusive mindset. Perhaps if we pay attention to the abilities of our younger generations to embrace difference, we, too, might relearn some of these more inclusive and relational ideals. As I consider next, perhaps paying attention to the generous perspectives of our younger generations is indeed another fruitful starting point for engaging empathetically with earth others and our more-than-human kin.

CHAPTER 5

# Gratitude for the Trail and the Gift of Roadside Geology

*Auntie Amy, do you think there's a fossil hidden inside this rock?*
—Curious seven-year-old

It is late September 2020, and I am in northern Illinois visiting my brother and his family. Like most of my travels during these past several months, this trip was not the result of advance planning, exactly, but rather came to fruition as a result of some other travel plans that shifted slightly along the way.

Travel has become a lesson in combining caution with flexibility, in coupling preparation with nonattachment. At this point in early fall, the combination of planning and flexibility has yielded an extended trip to the Midwest, where my partner's home town of Omaha, Nebraska, has become my home base. A relatively short drive from there has allowed for a quick trip to see my brother and his family in Illinois.

I'm traveling by van these days, not by plane. Like others who have opted out of air travel for the time being, I have discovered that van life can allow for unanticipated spontaneity around travel, and has thus changed my experience of place in unexpected ways. I am also aware that just having the option to choose this mode of travel is a form of privilege in itself. Paradoxically, though, this exercise of privilege is born out of fear and concern—out of the need to avoid indoor spaces and especially, sadly, the homes of those friends and family who I haven't seen recently, who are not in my "pod," as we have collectively come to say. That is, if not for the need to exercise caution and avoid close contact with loved ones, opting instead for distanced interactions, the idea of camping in my brother's driveway would likely never have occurred to me as a viable arrangement. Again, preparation combined with an openness to these until-now-unlikely scenarios has yielded a form of being *there*, of being *in place*, that informs how we *story our places* and coexist with one another in ways previously unforeseen.

In this case, while my original plans may have changed, I couldn't be happier to see my brother and his wife and three children—my two nieces and nephew. My brother and I are about ten years apart in age, but people often mistake us for fraternal twins. We are clearly related at first glance, and I have also been told that we have similar, more subtle mannerisms and that our general demeanors are somewhat alike. We briefly lament our temporarily postponed through-hike along Vermont's Long Trail, which would have taken place earlier in the summer, but we are quite happy to plan a more local, Midwest hike and to catch up in person for the first time in almost a year.

When I first arrive that afternoon, I am greeted by a big welcome sign on the front lawn, created by my nieces and nephew, with the assistance of my sister-in-law. A bright green and yellow arrangement of letters spells out my name followed by an exclamation mark—this impossible-to-miss signage blends nicely with the yard and also looks like something out of one of my brother's comic book drawings. This welcome sign serves as the backdrop for an outdoor pop-up canopy tent, arranged with socially distanced seating: two seats, one for my brother and one for me, to be precise, and a small table equipped with hand sanitizer; this has apparently been designated a kid-free area. A family visit during Covid times indeed! I could not feel more welcome and more relieved to be here. My excitement, however, seems unmatched by the combined energy of three young children.

Una is two, and still on the shy side; no interaction is lost on this curious toddler, though, and she watches intently as my school-aged niece and nephew move from activity to activity with unwavering resolve. Lori is five, and Bryce is seven years of age—a combined handful, to say the least.[1] Lori, a reserved but high-energy, fashion-forward five-year-old, wants to show me her latest bike-riding accomplishments. As my brother and I meander along the sidewalk with Lori on bike and Bryce on foot, we follow a path of endearing, multicolored, heart-shaped chalk drawings created by the two of them.

Once back at the house, Bryce, full of a dauntingly unlimited storehouse of energy, wants to show me how fast he can run laps around the backyard: "Auntie Amy, count how many seconds it takes me to run around the yard *really* fast!" This lightning-speed lap around the yard is followed by a demonstration of how high he can swing on the swing set; the finale, of course, is an attempt to nimbly climb the largest tree in the backyard: "Do you want to see how fast I can climb this tree?!" This last feat piques my brother's attention, as it turns out that Bryce should not necessarily be climbing said tree, and so the attempt is gently thwarted and the activity redirected.

The unwavering curiosity of children about the world around them, and the energy that accompanies that curiosity, is both inspiring and humbling; during this short visit, my own faith in humanity is renewed as I realize that perhaps I myself have been sliding too much from hope toward despair. Kids have a unique ability to provide these subtle reminders without even trying; their ability to explore the world without preconceived judgment helps open the door to entangled empathy, and the stories they create to contextualize their environment provide necessary reminders that there are earthly gifts all around us, if we remain curious and open to a language of animacy—one that values and is attentive to the lives and experiences of our fellow kin and earth others and their own storied places. Likewise, we may return the gift of children's open-mindedness by modeling empathetic engagement with our environment for these future generations.

It is now late afternoon after what has been a long drive for me and a very full day of activities with the kids for my brother and sister-in-law. I am grateful for the relative warmth of a September evening in northern Illinois. By "relative" warmth, I mean to say that a temperature in the high 60s is considered a warm fall evening in northern Illinois, but coming from California, this is considered to be on the cooler side. Given the recent fires and heat waves in the West, however, I could not be happier with this climate reprieve—one that makes beer and pizza in my brother's backyard appealing and feasible for both of us, after the kids had gone to bed for the night.

Eventually, I retire to the driveway and settle into the van that I've prepared for an overnight stay. We plan to be up early for coffee and to get ready for our hike with the kids in the morning. I sleep remarkably well, which is not surprising given the fullness of the day.

It's around 8:00 a.m. on Sunday morning. It is about 53 degrees Fahrenheit and steadily warming. Dave and I have been outside drinking coffee for about an hour; we sit in lawn chairs in the front yard under the auspices of the welcome canopy, still catching up and trying to make a realistic plan for the morning. How much could we feasibly do with three kids, have a relaxing hike, and still get me on the road with enough daylight left for the drive back to Nebraska? This might sound like a tall order, but put differently, our goals for the morning are really not that ambitious: Get in a good hike of reasonable time and distance, don't lose the kids, and better yet, try to return them in one piece to my sister-in-law, who has the morning off from mom duties.

We settle on a nearby nature center that is remote enough not to draw crowds on an early Sunday morning, yet local enough not to require too much extra gear. This plan proves successful, as we seem to have the entire trail system to ourselves—well, free of other humans, that is.

After some analysis of the trail map, Bryce, our de facto trail guide, insists that we hike the "Red Trail," which is the longest of the four loops within this trail system. This decision seems appropriate enough, considering that Dave and I had originally planned a through-hike along a section of Vermont's Long Trail. Why not at least challenge ourselves this morning to the "Longest Trail" with three kids in tow?

This "Longest Trail" seems doable, in part because there are no other humans around, which in these times, reduces our stress level considerably. To feel relief at the thought of not encountering fellow humans on a hiking trail also makes me uneasy, though. These are the strange times we find ourselves in; that is, I would normally *hope* to happen across other people on the trail—knowing that there are other hikers around can provide a sense of comfort in secluded woods. Today, though, I am grateful that we have the woods to ourselves, for unfamiliar humans have become yet another variable to negotiate, even in more defined, outdoor spaces like trails or sidewalks. We also still wear masks around each other, because we haven't seen each other for some time, and technically speaking, even though we are family, we are not in the same human "pod." The woods and more-than-humans and earth others that we hike among, however, are perhaps also our family—our broader pod. Our broader earthly, and more-than-human pod, however, poses no risk in the way that most concerns us now. In fact, these surroundings and fresh air provide solace and comfort now in a way that I would not have anticipated six months ago. For Lori and Bryce, who are on foot, and for Una, who travels in Dave's camo-print, kid-carrier backpack, this setting also provides an opportunity to explore their surroundings and to engage their curiosity in ways that my brother and I find both refreshing and humbling.

As we begin our hike (Una in Dave's kid-carrier backpack, and Lori and Bryce alongside us), Lori soon slows down and looks pensive; it turns out she is chilly, which Bryce attentively discerns before either of us. Bryce offers to give Lori one of his extra layers: "Here, do you want my fleece jacket? For some reason, I'm wearing an extra layer." Lori accepts the fleece and quickly warms up. Dave furtively glances over at me with a look of pleasant surprise. He is heartened by this empathetic act of kindness and thanks Bryce for his generosity—a big brother looking out for his little sister—and we keep going.

Lori and Bryce start out hiking in sync with us, but they quickly each become immersed in their own curiosities, and their pace diverges from ours and from each other. Una is not yet as talkative as Lori and Bryce, but is quite attentive, it seems to me, to both her siblings and her environment. My brother and I soon realize that we are each mindful of and curious about vastly different aspects of our surroundings.

Dave and I marvel at the cattails along the trail, and I am grateful for elements of this ecosystem that I haven't encountered for some time: the dense tree canopy above our heads, the humid breeze that seems in sync with and guides our movements, the way the sun filters through the trees. I realize that I can still feel the breeze through the mask I'm wearing. And in this 50-degree weather that, at least for me, calls for gloves, I notice that my mask actually keeps me warm. As we chat and appreciate these elemental moments, we pause to take a fuller look around. It seems that one member of our crew has forged ahead while the other has stopped a few paces behind. We remember my sister-in-law's request to bring everyone back with us.

Lori enjoys collecting rocks and minerals, and she has stopped a few yards behind us. There, she kneels on the ground, picking up and inspecting small pieces of granite, gneiss, quartzite, and sandstone, among others. When she finds a piece that intrigues her, she quietly places it in the pocket of the fleece jacket. We beckon her to come along, but she motions for us to keep going— she is clearly absorbed with this task, and her pockets will soon be filled with small rocks and minerals, each with their own "specific histories attached."[2] Literary scholar Jeffrey Jerome Cohen was not specifically referencing children's fascination with digging for rocks along a hiking trail, but he puts it well when he writes that "through abiding alliance humans become stone's time travelling companions, with the lithic offering multiple, noncoincidental modes of worldly inhabitance, a dizzying multiplication of prospect. Because of its density, extensiveness, tempo, and force, there is something in a rock that is actively unknowable."[3] This "Longest Trail" is alive with the actively unknowable; these small pieces of stone, which have perhaps been privy to the movements of glaciers, now travel along the trail in Lori's pockets. At the same time, these actively unknowable rocks and minerals make our connection with the earth more tangible.

Lori and Bryce continue to explore the narrative possibilities of the elemental—stone being the current point of entry for their storied place: "Stone is a catalyst for relation, a generative substantiality through which story tenaciously emerges. This elemental agency is likely shared with all materiality, but its plots, structures, tempo, and denouements are its own."[4] Bryce continues to guide our way, his own navigational choices catalyzed in part by the presence of intriguing stones along these pathways. Up ahead he stops at a trail marker to ponder which direction would be best—or rather, he considers which route would extend our hike for the longest amount of time. I imagine him a future Outward Bound instructor, always encouraging his group to press on. While he waits for us, he has begun an archaeological dig of his own.

In the midst of her siblings' excavations, Una remains quiet, but is highly attentive to her surroundings, surveying the environment from Dave's kid-carrier backpack. She smiles when Dave asks her hypothetical questions about which direction we should take. She is, in fact, a bit more patient than us at this point. As we wait for Lori to collect her last mineral sample, and simultaneously instruct Bryce to wait for us up ahead, Dave and I speculate about the glacial history of northern Illinois and the geologic time scale that has brought us to the point of this lithic moment.

•

*"About 85 percent of what is now Illinois was covered by glaciers at least once during the Pleistocene Epoch (1.6 million to 10,000 years ago) of the Cenozoic Era. The glacial periods affecting Illinois are known as the pre-Illinoian, Illinoian and Wisconsinian. Only the extreme northwestern and extreme southern parts of the state . . . were not glaciated. No one is sure what caused this ice age. It could have been due to a cyclic pattern of factors relating to the earth's orbit and tilt on its axis; shifts in the Gulf Stream in the Atlantic Ocean; reversals in the earth's magnetic field; volcanic activity; galactic dust clouds; or other reasons. The evidence does show that the glaciation occurred as the result of abrupt climatic changes, not gradual ones. Ice sheets began to grow from regions near the North Pole at this time when the summers were about 7 to 13 degrees Fahrenheit cooler than those of today, and the winter snows did not completely melt."*[5]

•

As we debate the geomorphology of the region, and the somewhat unsettling fact that this September morning in Illinois is warm enough to hike comfortably, Bryce comes bounding over to us, holding what appears to be a small chunk of sandstone or maybe limestone.

Bryce asks with an out-of-breath curiosity that makes us all hopeful on his behalf: "Auntie Amy, do you think there's a fossil hidden inside this rock?" At this moment, I scan my memory for my undergraduate geology courses; I consider that he appears to be holding a type of sedimentary rock, which makes plausible the possibility that this rock may contain some kind of fossil remains.

So, yes—the answer is yes! "Well, I think it is definitely *possible* that the rock contains some kind of fossil. We would need to do some more research to learn the details . . ." I try to marshal the enthusiasm of someone who is not exactly sure and doesn't want to overpromise, but I certainly don't want to squelch his curiosity, either. In fact, maybe I am the one who needs to be more curious.

•

*"Most of the rocks native to Illinois are sedimentary rocks. Some are made of small pieces of shells, plant and animal remains, and weathered fragments of other rocks (sediments) that have been moved by rivers, waves, winds, or ice (glaciers). These sediments have been deposited and compacted or cemented by mineral matter that precipitated out of water moving through the voids between sediment particles."*[6]

•

Bryce is heartened by the possibility of his fossil find, and he and Lori study this small piece of gritty beige stone flecked with bits of quartz or maybe feldspar. This moment prompts me to recall the archaeological artifact that I found when I was about his age.

When I was in grade school, I tell them, I also conducted a "curiosity-dig" in my parents' front yard in southern Connecticut. There, in the middle of the sloped, grassy field in front of their house, I unearthed a small, one-inch piece of white quartz that had an unusual but specific shape to it. The artifact had a somewhat blunted but clear triangular shape—it had a pointed but slightly dulled tip at one end, and was notched inward at each side of the base, to create a sort of stem. The sides and edges had a notched or scalloped pattern, which made it clear that somebody had, at one point, created this projectile point by hand or with the use of other tools. The scalloped sides had little bits of dirt embedded in them, which helped show the relief of the piece and give dimension to the otherwise shiny, translucent, white quartz surface.

My mother had brought the piece to our local natural history museum at the time, where it was deemed to be an approximately 3,000-year-old (~1,000 BC) quartzite arrowhead. If this estimate is accurate, then the arrowhead would date back to the Middle to Late Archaic Period in this region near the Lower Connecticut River Valley.

Indeed, in further researching the artifact, now from memory as an adult, I learn that quartz was the dominant choice of stone for these kinds of spear tips and projectile points during this time period. Only certain types of stone with "certain predictable fracture properties and hardness" can be effectively made into a tool; quartz meets these requirements and is abundant in New England.[7] These early projectile point tools are also commonly found in Connecticut and typically date back to this time period. It was during the Middle Archaic period that ground stone tools began to appear in Connecticut's archaeological record.[8] The Early and Middle Archaic periods follow the Paleo-Indian period, and the Paleo-Indians were the first known settlers in this area of southern Connecticut; during this time, the environment in southern New England was rapidly changing.

•

"The Early and Middle Archaic is a dry and very warm period, which caused environmental changes that affected both the human and animal populations in the area. Water sources shrunk and some dried up as temperatures rose. Human population was still very small worldwide and Connecticut was no exception. People were still mobile hunters and gatherers, who were very skilled at use of their environment."[9]

•

I consider that my childhood memory of unearthing this quartzite arrowhead is a memory and experience intimately my own; at the same time, that arrowhead had a full and storied history before it appeared in my life. I storied that arrowhead with my own perspective and ideas about its value as a utilitarian tool and an elemental, earthly artifact. Cohen writes that, on the one hand, the "stories we know of stone will always be human stories."[10] On the other hand, however, stone allows us to consider the "inhuman" in ways that "emphasize both difference ('in-' as negative prefix) and intimacy ('in-' as indicator of estranged interiority)."[11] When we tell a story with stone, for instance, when we "examine a quarry from the eyes of a miner, a marble block as a mason or a sculptor," or a piece of sedimentary rock through the eyes of a curious child, we tell a story in ways that "intensely inhabit the preposition *with*, to move from solitary individuation to ecosystems environments, shared agencies, and companionate properties."[12] As Bryce and Lori listen intently to my story of the found arrowhead, and as Una's attention focuses on our conversation, I can already see the wheels turning, and I suspect that the next time my brother and his family visit my parents in Connecticut, they may find their yard excavated by school-aged children once again.

Gruen writes that "the ability that we have as children to empathize with fictional beings, suggests that we have the capacity to engage with very different others through narrative, literature, art and story-telling and this capacity, if honed, may help us to empathetically engage with the more than human world."[13] While fossils and arrowheads are not exactly "fictional beings," per se, they are artifacts that spark curiosity and speculation, and that invite possibilities for narrative engagement. Gruen calls this potential for engagement "storied empathy," and sees storytelling as a point of entry for understanding earth others and our "relationships beyond sensate animals."[14] In that kinetic space between child and found piece of rock, "mineral life emerges"—a shared moment between human and environment that is alive with possibility.[15] Cohen captures this moment well when he writes that "when stones are examined as something more than fixed and immobile things, as partners in errantry, then facts likewise begin to ambulate," and curiosity begins to drive myriad possibilities for how we story our places and for relational exchanges with the world around us.[16]

I consider the different stories and the different places that we remember from when we were young. How, like the story of the found arrowhead, might they relate to the stories we may share with younger generations? If memory serves, that arrowhead is still somewhere in a drawer in my parents' house. Bryce and Lori's curiosity makes me wonder why I haven't looked at that piece more recently. And I wonder when it was that I stopped digging for fossils. Why don't we all dig for fossils more?

The ability we have as children to empathize with fictional beings, and relatedly with more-than-humans and earthly others, raises the question of whether and how we as adults might regain some of that lost curiosity and return to earlier moments of open-mindedness. Perhaps if we are attentive to children's willingness to embrace difference, then we, too, might relearn some of these more inclusive and relational ideals. The natural curiosity of children is a gift that we arguably have a responsibility to encourage rather than close down. Moreover, in an era of climate crisis, it becomes all the more important that we return the gift of children's open-mindedness by modeling empathetic engagement with our environment for these future generations.

We are now about a half hour into our hike, and we have entered a more densely wooded portion of the Red/Longest Trail. The trail is covered with pine needles—my favorite type of terrain for walking and hiking, and we have the treat of hiking among tall pines. My brother is scanning the landscape more closely now, since visibility is somewhat reduced in this section of pine forest. Una is still content in Dave's kid-pack and readily takes in the stimuli of this natural environment. Lori and Bryce are equally content with their environment, but less eager to stay within our sight.

Soon enough, though, we happen across what appears to be an owl pellet. While I'm not sure for certain, my first guess based on size and shape would be that it's a great-horned owl pellet, and our current habitat would certainly be suitable for a great-horned owl.

•

*"Look for this widespread owl in woods, particularly young woods interspersed with fields or other open areas. The broad range of habitats they use includes deciduous and evergreen forests, swamps, desert, tundra edges, and tropical rainforest, as well as cities, orchards, suburbs, and parks."[7]*

•

Dave and I point out the owl pellet, and Dave asks Una, Lori, and Bryce if they know what it is, or who it might belong to. Lori and Bryce are familiar with owls but they are not exactly sure what an owl *pellet* is. I realize that I have never tried to explain an owl pellet to a child before, and I wonder how much detail my sister-in-law would want me to provide. My brother is amused at this prospect and eager to hear my impromptu definition.

I must first explain that owls often eat small animals like mice or rodents. (I leave out the part about how owls will typically swallow small mammals whole.) Much to my relief, the kids seem to accept that the owl must eat small rodents to survive; this was the part of the story I was most concerned about. Next, I tell them, after an owl eats its meal, the owl's body separates out the parts of the animal that it can't digest, like bones and fur. Now I have their attention. The owl's digestive system separates those undigestible parts into a small ball, or pellet, which the owl then spits back out. When the owl spits out the owl pellet, it usually winds up on the ground, which is where hikers like us might then happen across it. I also mention that owl pellets provide interesting clues about the environment and help us solve mysteries about what exactly the owl might have eaten. If we look closely, for instance, we can see little bits of what is likely rodent fur mixed into this pellet.

Bryce and Lori inspect the pellet closely, but without touching it, at our request. "Where does the owl live?" Lori asks. She wants to picture the owl in its habitat. I explain that this owl probably lives in a nearby tree—that the owl may have found an older nest that another hawk or large bird used to live in, or that maybe the owl lives in a large hole up in one of these pine trees.

•

*"Like other owls, Great-horned Owls don't build their own nests, but use the abandoned nests of other large birds such as ravens or Red-tailed Hawks. They may also nest in tree cavities, on the ground, on platforms, rocky outcroppings, cliff ledges, artificial nests or tree snags."*[18]

•

Lori gazes up at the large pines around her. "Where is the owl now?" she asks, clearly considering the prospect that our owl friend is in our midst. I explain that most owls rest during the day, and that this one is most likely sleeping in a nearby tree and will come out to search for food when it starts to get dark out. "And then the owl will make more pellets?" she asks me.

"Yes," I tell her, "after the owl eats dinner, it will make more owl pellets and leave them nearby." *Owl pellets,* I consider—*small gifts within our midst.*

Dave is growing mindful of the time and gently tries to move us along. "Let's keep going," he says, "and see what we find next."

As we continue on our hike, I am grateful for the opportunity to explain owl pellets to my nieces and nephew. I'm also grateful that great-horned owls are not currently considered threatened species; however, much like mountain lions and other predators who hunt rodents and small mammals, these raptors are vulnerable to ingesting rodenticide and to other harm born out of human action or intervention. I think about how vulnerable these species are to the decisions that humans make, and I wonder how much longer we'll have access to the gifts that they provide. Would we have happened across even more owl pellets on this same walk five years ago? Ten years ago? For Una, Lori, and Bryce, the experience of encountering this single owl pellet on our hike may set their own baseline norm for who and what they expect to encounter in this place. But to have a more fully accurate picture of this or any area's biodiversity, and to be able to help preserve that biodiversity, we must consistently maintain our connections with such places over time, as well as gain knowledge of their history more broadly.

Again, while great-horned owls are not threatened, per se, the idea that we set our expectations of an ecosystem's biodiversity based on what we personally see, encounter, or experience in a specific place is related to the ecological concept of "shifting baseline syndrome," which describes "a new basal state which has significantly diverged from the original system state. Shifting Baseline Syndrome (SBS) however, describes a social and psychological phenomenon by which individuals, communities or generations compare change in the ecological system against a single point of reference or 'baseline,' often set at the beginning of their life or career."[19] The main caution with this mode of thinking or observation is that if we base our understanding of the environment solely on discrete or individual experiences of it, then our frame of reference could become too narrow, and "valuable historical information is therefore lost and individuals are unable to accurately perceive long-term change beyond their own biographical experience."[20] In other words, if we lose perspective about shifts or losses in species abundance, then we may come to view those losses as the norm for what we expect to encounter.

The concept of shifting baseline syndrome, or "the problem of forgetting past natural abundance, or of new generations not knowing about it," was first devised in 1995 by Daniel Pauly at the University of British Columbia and is just now gaining traction. Famous photographs of "fishermen in Florida, who, over generations, pose equally proudly with ever-shrinking catches," help illustrate the idea.[21] As naturalist Chris Packham notes: "'We all think the world was perfect when we first encountered it, i.e. when we were young.' He recalls turtle doves nesting in the grounds of his Hampshire school in 1970, a species that has long since vanished from the county. But he says good records are important so that we aren't reliant on such subjective anecdotes."[22] In addition to good record-keeping, there is another easy solution to shifting baseline syndrome: the sharing of stories across generations. And as ecologist Lizzie Jones describes, addressing the issue is simple: "Get older generations to describe how things were. 'All we need to do is get grandparents to talk to grandchildren about environmental things,' she says."[23] The alternative, says Jones, is that "we risk losing connections to wildlife and the will to care about stopping its loss."[24] Moreover, "if we don't learn about nature from an early age, and we don't go and experience it and recognise species, then [our collective amnesia] could just get worse and worse."[25] With this hike, then, perhaps Bryce, Lori, and even Una at her young age have just set their own baseline standards for the biodiversity of this place. And in learning about the natural world at such early ages, they not only set their own baseline for knowledge about this place, but they may also eventually share that knowledge with their own future generations.

## THE GIFT OF ENTANGLED EMPATHY

The potential solutions to building, sharing, and maintaining knowledge about biodiversity are thus multifaceted and multigenerational. Moreover, as adults, we have an ethical responsibility to future generations to model empathy for our more-than-human kin and earth others. By providing such experiences and frames of reference, younger generations can then follow suit; they may experience the gift of diverse ecosystems at a young age and continue to share those experiences and similarly model entangled empathy. I like to think that Dave and I just helped Una, Lori, and Bryce experience the gift of an encounter with our more-than-human kin and earth others. I consider Kimmerer's thoughts on how she understands her own acts of reciprocity—she wants to help people understand, see, and value earth others for the gifts that they provide. As she puts it: "I want to help them become visible to people. People can't understand the world as a gift unless someone shows them how it's a gift."[26]

Further yet, by embracing and encouraging the gift of children's curiosity about the natural world and their openness to difference, perhaps adults, too, can regain potential losses of our own. Una, Lori, and Bryce's various experiences of the environment, as young children, are different from Dave's and mine as adults—their perceptions and engagements are informed by different curiosities, fewer fears and inhibitions, and fewer preconceived notions of what is or is not possible here and now. As Dave and I become increasingly mindful of the time, for instance, we realize that time has no bearing on the kids' experiences of this moment. They are each busy storying their place through their engagement with environmental stimuli, rocks, minerals, owl pellets, and trail markers. Yet Dave and I combine an appreciation of our visit, our elemental surroundings, and our interactions with the kids with an awareness of the time and the plan for the rest of the day, as well as our larger concerns about current events. Our appreciation for the elemental is set against the backdrop of our anxieties; Una, Lori, and Bryce's appreciation for the elemental is set against the backdrop of their innate curiosity.

In real time, these different worldviews play out as we must move toward concluding our hike. Dave and I are on the same page, but we realize that the kids would be perfectly happy to remain on the trail, seemingly with or without us. Moving back toward the trailhead is thus an artful negotiation. Enticements of what more we might encounter as we hike out is one way that we keep the whole crew moving along; the promise of ice cream later in the day is another.

As we return to the trailhead, Bryce pauses to dig for more fossils. This is fine with me, as I am taken with a gorgeous flock of cedar waxwings feasting on berries at the top of a now-leafless tree adjacent to Bryce's new excavation site. The high-pitched, melodic, collective burbling of the waxwing flock provides a celebratory coda to our hike. Their visual boisterousness gives them a look that is both formal and rebellious. Their formality is in the conservative look of their small beige bodies and pale yellow bellies; their rebelliousness may be attributed to the bandit-like, narrow black mask around their eyes, their narrow head crest, and the bright red wingtips that are occasionally visible with a flash of their wings. This whole visual package is complemented by a bright yellow bar at the base of their tails. The waxwings are migrating through this part of the Midwest right now and it is a gift to encounter them here, at this moment. I attempt to direct the kids' attention to the waxwing flock, but they are busy digging for fossils.

There is much to celebrate in this elemental moment, and just as we have an immediate obligation to keep track of the kids' well-being on the trail, we have a broader ethical obligation to share this knowledge and these experiences with them—to model empathetic engagement with our kin, our earth others, and our environment. The sharing of knowledge through narrative, and the elemental experiences of these storied places are small steps in this direction. At the same time, children's engagement with the environment is something we can then learn from ourselves. We have much to learn, or perhaps relearn, from younger generations. Children's innate curiosity, lack of preconceived judgment, and ability to engage with new ideas are ways of being that we can return to—these are gifts to behold and to reciprocate.

In this moment, we are each attentive to the different gifts of this place, but we are all part of this environmental meshworks. We do our best to rethink our assumptions of boundaried places and our ideas about who belongs where. In doing so, we recognize that we are co-constituted beings who co-emerge together in these elemental moments of understanding. Entangled and empathetic, we do our best to learn a language of animacy. We do our best to return the gifts of these encounters through acts of compassion and respect. Adults and young humans, cedar waxwings, earth others. We each story this place uniquely. We are each at home here in different ways, at different times, for different reasons. We are at home because we are nearby our kin. We are at home because our habitats rejuvenate and sustain us. We are at home in these places that provide shelter and connectivity. We are at home in places both material and imaginative. We are at home in the Anthropocene.

# NOTES

## NOTES TO INTRODUCTION

1. I would later edit this chapter while under Governor Newsom's shelter-in-place order, and later yet again from the Midwest, while seeking reprieve from wildfire smoke that pervaded much of California during the summer of 2020. In returning to edit this chapter later on, I marvel at the fact that I was not yet wearing a mask on this walk, in early March 2020.

2. On this theme, readers might also appreciate the earlier work of James G. Cantrill and Christine L. Oravec, who remarked in their introduction to *The Symbolic Earth*: "Of our environment, what we say is what we see" (1).

3. The phrase "more-than-human" was first coined by philosopher David Abram, who used the term in his now-famous work, *The Spell of the Sensuous: Perception and Language in a More-than-Human World*, which was first published in 1996. My first interaction with the term was through reading feminist geographers Leila Harris and Helen Hazen's 2009 essay, "Rethinking Maps from a More-than-Human Perspective," in *Rethinking Maps*. Harris and Hazen link the term to work in animal geographies that seeks to rethink human relationships with nonhuman or more-than-human natures in more inclusive ways that move beyond what they feel to be the less recuperative framing of *non*human; the term "more-than-human," they say, "suggests the need for our interest, attention, and commitment to reach beyond an exclusive focus on the human world" (51). In some of my previous work (*Locating Visual-Material Rhetorics, Visualizing Posthuman Conservation*), I referred largely to "human/nonhuman animal relationships," which has also been a common frame of reference within animal studies. With this work, however, I have come to feel that "more-than-human" has a greater ability to work against the anthropocentric ideas of human mastery over other animals in particular. I suggest that the phrasing *more-than*-human further helps deprivilege the realm of the human by inviting the idea that we humans just might not be first in a hierarchy of species. Additionally, I feel the term

better accounts for a multitude of species and life-forms beyond animals and thus represents a more ecological perspective. To this end, I also do not use the term "nonhuman" to refer to plant life or other elements of ecosystems. Instead, when specifically seeking to distinguish more-than-human animals from other life-forms or, say, plant or tree species in some of the analyses in this book, I use phrasing like "other animals and earthly species," or, following Plec, "other animals and life forms" ("Perspectives"). In chapter 4, I also explore Val Plumwood's use of "earth others" to account for our relationships with other living elements of the ecosystems that we share with our more-than-human animal kin. So, then, while I do understand "more-than-human" as encompassing a range of species beyond animals, I also use the term to help work against human anthropocentrism and our tendency to privilege humans over other animals in particular.

4. Kimmerer, *Braiding Sweetgrass*, 31.

5. Kimmerer, *Braiding Sweetgrass*, 31.

6. At this point, the pandemic has no immediate, discernable bearing on the mating habits of songbirds, but as I edit this chapter almost a year into the pandemic, I also wonder about the environmental impacts of the unprecedented production of cold-storage systems designed to transport vaccines across the globe, and I shudder to think where all those freezers will eventually wind up. What are our ethical responsibilities to account for this inevitable environmental impact? I include this thought as a note and not as body text, because I was not yet thinking about this in March 2020.

7. Creswell, *Place*, 18.

8. Creswell, *Place*, 18.

9. Boyle and Rice, "Introduction," 2.

10. Boyle and Rice, "Introduction," 3.

11. Boyle and Rice, "Introduction," 3.

12. Rush, *Rising*, 199.

13. Plec, "Perspectives," 5–6.

14. Kimmerer, *Braiding Sweetgrass*, 58.

15. Wright, "More-than-Human," 393.

16. Kimmerer, *Braiding Sweetgrass*, 31.

17. Kimmerer, *Braiding Sweetgrass*, 56.

18. Tonino, "Two Ways of Knowing." The Potawatomi people are originally from the Great Lakes region and today have a reservation in Oklahoma.

19. Kimmerer, *Braiding Sweetgrass*, 55–56.

20. Kimmerer, *Braiding Sweetgrass*, 57–58.

21. Gruen, *Entangled Empathy*, 3.

22. Cohen, *Stone*, 12.

23. Cohen, *Stone*, 12.

24. Cohen, *Stone*, 12.

25. Plumwood, *Feminism and the Mastery of Nature*, 164.

26. Lorimer, *Wildlife in the Anthropocene*, 7.

27. Lorimer, *Wildlife in the Anthropocene*, 7.

28. See Barad, *Meeting the Universe Halfway*; Bekoff, *The Animal Manifesto* and *Rewilding Our Hearts*; Braidotti, *The Posthuman*; Propen, *Visualizing Posthuman Conservation*. It is also worth noting that posthumanism has not always smoothly aligned with a relational or ecological view, especially in areas related to early conceptions of informatics and theories of the cyborg; more recently, however, posthumanism has become more readily accepted as bearing ecological and relational connotations and allowances.

29. See Braidotti, *The Posthuman*; Wolfe, *What Is Posthumanism?*; Propen, *Visualizing Posthuman Conservation*.

30. For a longer discussion of Derrida's essay, "The Animal That Therefore I Am (More to Follow)," see Propen, *Visualizing Posthuman Conservation*, especially the preface and pages 160–61.

31. Bruns, "Derrida's Cat," 404.

32. Haraway, *When Species Meet*, 20.
33. Haraway, *When Species Meet*, 20.
34. Haraway, *When Species Meet*, 20.
35. Haraway, *When Species Meet*, 21.
36. Kimmerer, *Braiding Sweetgrass*, 331.
37. Clary-Lemon, "Gifts, Ancestors, and Relations." See chapter 2 for some further discussion of these points.
38. Ingold, *Being Alive*, 63. In this book, I align with Ingold's concept of meshworks specifically, although it bears noting that his concept is also based on the biologist and animal behaviorist Jakob von Uexküll's earlier theory of the *Umwelt*. I discuss these ideas in more detail in chapter 1. Finally, in using the formulation "in/organic," I am referring to the perhaps uneasy interconnections of human-made and organic matter, and in a sense attempting to perform and acknowledge the difficulty of ever truly being able to separate them.
39. McDowell and Sharp, *A Feminist Glossary*, 201; see also Massey, *Space, Place, and Gender*.
40. Massey, *Space, Place, and Gender*, 5.
41. Van Dooren, *Flight Ways*, 66.
42. Days, "Histories of Individual Parks." The Pacific Horticultural Society says the property was purchased in 1903.
43. Days, "Histories of Individual Parks." Franceschi and his wife returned to Italy in 1913, and the property was purchased a few years after his passing. The city of Santa Barbara initially declined the donation based on financial concerns related to its upkeep, but later accepted the property in 1931, "on condition that the land is used for park and recreation purposes for the benefit of residents of the city, and any revenue to be used for maintenance and improvement."
44. Molina, "Santa Barbara Decides." The city has been unable to successfully fund a restoration project and has almost torn down the structure several times over the years. At this writing, the house still exists on that site, although it has arguably become more of an eerie fascination among locals and interested tourists than a thriving horticultural hub.
45. Wapotich, "Trail Quest." While I have not done so myself, the curious and determined visitor can apparently find "examples of rare palms, two specimens of grass tree from Australia, as well as pines from around the world including a chir pine from the Himalayas."
46. Chamberlin, "The Life of Dr. Francesco Franceschi and His Park."
47. Chamberlin, "The Life of Dr. Francesco Franceschi and His Park."
48. Ritvo, "Going Forth and Multiplying."
49. Ritvo, "Going Forth and Multiplying."
50. Ritvo, "Going Forth and Multiplying."
51. Hynes, "Why Is the World So Beautiful?"
52. Days, "Histories of Individual Parks." This part of the park was reportedly given to the city by a builder in 1976, after some apparent complaints that two houses that he had constructed nearby had blocked a scenic vista in the area.
53. Salazar, "Who Are the Chumash?" As I describe also in chapter 3, Alan Salazar, referenced in this source citation, is a descendent of the Chumash and Tataviam people and an elder in the Ferdandiño Tataviam Band of Mission Indians. Salazar has worked to protect Native American cultural sites for twenty years, and has also served as a consultant or "monitor" for sites throughout southern and central California; he is also a traditional storyteller, and in chapter 3, I draw upon his telling of the story of the Rainbow Bridge, in the context of describing the work of a planned wildlife corridor in southern California. I am grateful for his permission to quote from and summarize his telling of the Rainbow Bridge story, as I do later in this book. Finally, for further detail about the fate of the Chumash under European settler colonialism, readers may also refer to "Little Choice for the Chumash," which describes the ways in which Spanish colonialism caused "wrenching cultural changes that afflicted the Chumash between about ad 1542 and ad 1834" (Dartt-Newton and Erlandson, "Little Choice," 417).

54. Bratta and Powell, "Introduction to the Special Issue."
55. Bratta and Powell, "Introduction to the Special Issue."
56. Chamberlin, "The Life of Dr. Francesco Franceschi and His Park."
57. The Santa Barbara Botanic Garden, "Mission Dam and Aqueduct."
58. Perazzo and Perazzo, "Santa Barbara Mission."
59. McCall and Perry, *California's Chumash Indians*, 15.
60. McCall and Perry, *California's Chumash Indians*, 14.
61. Wright, "More-than-Human," 396.
62. Wright, "More-than-Human," 396.
63. McCall and Perry, *California's Chumash Indians*, 16–17.
64. McCall and Perry, *California's Chumash Indians*, 12.
65. John Johnson, curator of anthropology, Santa Barbara Museum of Natural History, email message to author, December 2, 2020.
66. John Johnson, curator of anthropology, Santa Barbara Museum of Natural History, email message to author, December 2, 2020.
67. Wright, "More-than-Human," 402.
68. McCall and Perry, *California's Chumash Indians*, 20.
69. McCall and Perry, *California's Chumash Indians*, 47.
70. I am confident with birds and other mammals, but my knowledge of plants and trees is an ongoing and welcome learning process.
71. See Just, *Women in Athenian Law and Life*; Lehmann, "Feeling Home"; Macdowell, "The Oikos."
72. E360 Digest, "Dozens of U.K. Species."
73. Rush, *Rising*, 197.
74. M. Taylor and Murray, "Overwhelming and Terrifying."
75. The Cornell Lab, "Lesser Goldfinch Range Map."
76. Rush, *Rising*, 197.
77. I am grateful to Tim Jensen for his insights and good conversation during a trip to Oregon State University in April 2019.
78. Wright, "More-than-Human," 395.
79. Walker, "The Mountains."
80. Walker, "The Mountains."
81. Seegert, "Play of Sniffication," 159.
82. Seegert, "Play of Sniffication," 160.
83. Pratt, "How a Lonely Cougar in Los Angeles Inspired the World."
84. Van Dooren, *Flight Ways*, 68.
85. McHugh, *Animal Stories*, 7.

## NOTES TO CHAPTER 1

1. It is worth noting that practices and approaches to wildlife rehabilitation are always shifting in response to new contexts, new technologies and materials, and new ideas and approaches. At the time of this writing, these are the approaches that were in use, but approaches to wildlife care, including enclosure design, do change. I always welcome the learning and experience that comes from such changes.
2. See Bekoff, *The Animal Manifesto*.
3. Haraway, *Staying with the Trouble*, 4. In her recent work, feminist philosopher Donna Haraway argues that neither hope nor despair is a "sensible attitude" in coexisting with our more-than-human kin; that "we require each other in unexpected collaborations and combinations," and that when we are "alone, in our separate kinds of expertise and experience, we know both too much and too little, and so we succumb to despair or to hope, and

neither is a sensible attitude." Rather, as we make our way through Anthropocene times and the challenges of negotiating climate change, we must be co-present with other species, make "oddkin," and "stay with the trouble."

4. Cohen, "Elemental Relations."

5. Ingold, *Being Alive*, 63.

6. Kimmerer, *Braiding Sweetgrass*, 381.

7. Wright, "More-than-Human," 404.

8. Animal Medical Center, "Ruptured Air Sac."

9. Drew, "First Aid and Your Pet Bird."

10. Animal Medical Center, "Ruptured Air Sac."

11. Drew, "First Aid and Your Pet Bird."

12. Gruen, *Entangled Empathy*, 44–45.

13. Gruen, *Entangled Empathy*, 45.

14. Gruen, *Entangled Empathy*, 50.

15. Gruen, *Entangled Empathy*, 51.

16. Propen, *Visualizing Posthuman Conservation*.

17. Alaimo, *Exposed*, 10.

18. Alaimo, *Exposed*, 130.

19. Wright, "More-than-Human," 395.

20. Hancock, "How Albatrosses Taught Photographer Chris Jordan How to Grieve."

21. Hancock, "How Albatrosses Taught Photographer Chris Jordan How to Grieve."

22. Plastic also allows for easy cleaning and sterilization and does not conduct heat like other materials such as metal. Young birds are often brought outside for periods of time during the day so that they may begin acclimating to outdoor temperatures and such. In the summer especially, it would not be prudent to house these birds in any sort of enclosure that more readily retains heat.

23. Hayles, *How We Became Posthuman*, 196.

24. Gruen, *Entangled Empathy*, 64.

25. Gruen, *Entangled Empathy*, 64.

26. Gruen, *Entangled Empathy*, 64.

27. Here, Gruen also invokes the work of feminist philosopher and physicist Karen Barad (*Meeting the Universe Halfway*), whose theory of "posthuman intra-actions" is not incompatible with how Gruen understands the contexts in which entanglements take shape. In some ways, Barad's description of the "intra-actions" of all matter help Gruen account for the stuff of entangled empathy; however, Gruen focuses more on human relationships with other animals specifically, whereas Barad, coming from a physics background, is interested in the "intra-actions" of all matter. Gruen provides an accessible description of Barad's understanding of the "intra-actions" of all bodies and matter. As Gruen describes: "Intra-actions differ from interactions in that interactions occur when there are two or more separate things that come into contact. Intra-actions are what makes those separate things possible in the first place" (65). Gruen goes on to note the connections between entanglements and intra-actions more specifically when she says that "there can be no individuals that exist prior to and separate from the entangled intra-actions that constitute them. But, importantly, the individual that emerges from her entanglements is distinctly constituted by particular intra-actions" (65). Finally, Gruen acknowledges that "understanding and reflecting on our entanglements are part of what it takes to constitute our selves because there is no self or other prior to our intra-actions" (65). While Gruen clearly appreciates Barad's theory of intra-actions, she seems to find it most suitable for material feminist scholars who more readily focus on entanglements beyond those with more-than-humans, and more so on entire ecosystems or other organisms and life-forms; thus, while she acknowledges the value of intra-actions, she seems to favor "entanglements" more explicitly. In addition, Gruen's other work (see "Attending to Nature") does begin to align with

and account for the ideas of feminist philosopher Val Plumwood, whose theory of "earth others" accounts more readily for our relationships with nonhuman species. I discuss these ideas more in subsequent chapters.

Finally, while I also appreciate and have worked with Barad's theories of the intra-activities of matter, I find Gruen's entangled empathy to align more easily with Ingold's notion of "environmental meshworks" and Cohen's "elemental relationships," and so I use "meshworks" rather than intra-action, here and throughout, when thinking about the contexts, environments, and ever-changing habitats in which entangled empathetic relationships take shape and are constituted. Moreover, in acknowledging these two terms, "intra-actions" and "environmental meshworks," I am not suggesting them to be synonymous. Rather, while they are each nuanced in their differences, I see environmental meshworks as more aligned with geography and anthropology, for instance, and thus more in sync with how I'm thinking of the contexts and elemental environments in which the entangled, empathetic relationships of humans and other animals take place. Thus, in this chapter and throughout the book, I use "meshworks" because I think it works more fluidly with Cohen's concept of the elemental, Ingold's environmental meshworks, and ideas about compassionate conservation. That said, I do appreciate Barad's work with posthuman intra-action, and interested readers may look to portions of *Visualizing Posthuman Conservation* for my further discussion and explication of these concepts.

28. Cohen, "Elemental Relations," 55.
29. Cohen, "Elemental Relations," 55.
30. Cohen, "Elemental Relations," 55.
31. Cohen, *Stone*, 12.
32. Ingold, *Being Alive*, 63.
33. As Ingold describes in *Being Alive*, *Umwelt* theory refers to "the world as it is constituted within [an] animal's circuit of perception and action" (80). (Here, readers may note that I substituted "*an* animal's" for "*the* animal's" to allude to my added argument that there is no singular "*Animal*"; rather, as compassionate conservation would also have it, I understand every animal life as unique and particular.) *Umwelt* theory subsequently suggests that "meaning is bestowed by the organism on its environment" in an always open and unfolding manner (64). In this way, there is meaning in an animal's world because every animal's actions in the world are so closely tied to their perception of their environment (79). Thus, every organism perceives its own subjective world. It is on the finer points of *Umwelt* theory that my perspective diverges somewhat, which is why I prefer Ingold's more nuanced and contemporary notion of meshworks. Of *Umwelt* theory, Ingold further conveys that no animal "is in a position to observe the environment from such a standpoint of neutrality. To live, it must already be immersed in its surroundings and committed to the relationships this entails. And in these relationships, the neutrality of objects is inevitably compromised" (80). Moreover, as Ingold conveys, a thrush, for instance, "does not first perceive the stone as a stone, and then wonder what to do with it. . . . Rather, using both stone and beak, it smashes shells" (80). He then suggests that humans, unlike more-than-human animals, are "capable of making their own life activity the object of their attention, and thus of seeing things *as they are*, as a condition for deliberating about the alternative uses to which [things] might be put" (80). On this point, I might respectfully push back, pointing to the growing number of studies that document, for instance, the creative and selective tool-using capacities of crows and other animals. Boeckle et al., for instance, demonstrate that crows can plan for future events, and may even plan for specific future tool use, thus suggesting crows' potential for deliberation ("New Caledonian Crows"). Again, the points above are in reference to *Umwelt* theory and not the concept of meshworks, per se. Regarding meshworks, I do appreciate how Ingold has adapted an earlier theory to account more fluidly for the nuanced and integrated lives of humans and more-than-human animals; he does so also with his "dwelling perspective," which similarly seeks to erase the divides between human and animal when conceptualizing the ways that we move together in shared environments (Ingold, *Being Alive*, 11).

34. Ingold, *Being Alive,* 63.
35. Ingold, *Being Alive,* 63.
36. Ingold, *Being Alive,* 63.
37. Ingold, *Being Alive,* 64.
38. Ingold, *Being Alive,* 64.
39. Wright, "More-than-Human," 404.
40. National Wildlife Rehabilitators Association, "What Is Wildlife Rehabilitation?"
41. See Bekoff, *The Animal Manifesto* and *Rewilding Our Hearts.*
42. See Bekoff, *The Animal Manifesto*; Propen, *Visualizing Posthuman Conservation.*
43. Propen, *Visualizing Posthuman Conservation.*
44. Bekoff, *The Animal Manifesto,* 209.
45. Gruen, *Entangled Empathy,* 57.
46. Gruen, *Entangled Empathy,* 57.
47. Seegert, "Play of Sniffication," 164.
48. Gruen, *Entangled Empathy,* 60.
49. Gruen, *Entangled Empathy,* 60.
50. Bennett, *Vibrant Matter,* 98.
51. Bennett, *Vibrant Matter,* 99.
52. Gruen, *Entangled Empathy,* 60.
53. Evidence about animal communication continues to mount, suggesting that they can and do communicate with each other and with humans. Interested readers might look to Frans de Waal's recent *Are We Smart Enough to Know How Smart Animals Are?* for intricate accounts of animal communication, as well as Marc Bekoff's *Emotional Lives of Animals.*
54. Kilham, *In the Company of Bears.*
55. Ingold draws on Heidegger's essay, "Building, Dwelling, Thinking" (see Heidegger, *Poetry*), in which Heidegger also opposes built structures to the notion of "dwelling" in order to recover what he feels is the more fundamental meaning of dwelling, which he says refers to "being, encompassing the entire way in which one lives one's life on earth" (Ingold, *Being Alive,* 10). As Heidegger writes, which Ingold also recounts, the German verb *bauen,* "to build, is really to dwell; it also gives us a clue as to how we think about the dwelling it signifies. . . . I dwell, you dwell. The way in which you *are* and I am, the manner in which we humans are on the earth, is *Buan,* dwelling. To be a human being means to be on the earth as a mortal. It means to dwell" (Heidegger, *Poetry,* 145). Thus, building is not logically prior to dwelling, nor does dwelling determine the designs implemented through building (Ingold, *Being Alive,* 10). Rather, they are co-constituted, or, as Heidegger writes, "dwelling and building are related as end and means" (Heidegger, *Poetry,* 144). These ideas then inform what Ingold calls the "dwelling perspective" (*Being Alive,* 10).
56. Ingold, *Being Alive,* 9.
57. Ingold, *Being Alive,* 10.
58. Ingold, *Being Alive,* 10.
59. Cohen, "Elemental Relations," 54.
60. Cohen, "Elemental Relations," 58 (emphasis added).

## NOTES TO CHAPTER 2

1. Aldous, "Merged 120,000-Acre Wildfire"; Staff Writer, "Klondike and Taylor Creek Fire."
2. Urness, "Klondike Fire Grows."
3. Mann, "Fires Make History."
4. Anderson and Jenkins, *Applying Nature's Design,* 143.
5. US Department of the Interior, Bureau of Land Management, "Cascade-Siskiyou National Monument" (emphasis added).
6. Hynes, "Why Is the World So Beautiful?"
7. Urness, "Klondike and Taylor Creek Fires Grow Together."

8. Urness, "Klondike Fire Grows."

9. Kimmerer, *Braiding Sweetgrass,* 58.

10. Zielinski, "What Do Wild Animals Do in a Wildfire?"

11. Zielinski, "What Do Wild Animals Do in a Wildfire?"

12. Mountain Lion Foundation, "When There's a Fire, Where Do the Wild Things Go?"

13. Zielinski, "What Do Wild Animals Do in a Wildfire?"

14. Mountain Lion Foundation, "When There's a Fire, Where Do the Wild Things Go?"

15. Mountain Lion Foundation, "When There's a Fire, Where Do the Wild Things Go?"

16. This term can also apply to domesticated animals. Following the Thomas Fire in central California in 2017, for example, many local animal shelters were seeing an influx of domesticated cats who had fled their homes during the fire; they were turning up in nearby or remote neighborhoods, thinner and sometimes with burned paws or skin, and shelters were listing them as possibly "fire-lost" domesticated cats.

17. Here, I am consciously alternating between references to the "Oregon woman," "the resident," and "the homeowner" based on the references used in the news media, and as a gesture toward protecting privacy. While several published media articles about this wildlife encounter did refer to the homeowner using more specific details, I have chosen not to do so, because I did not find it necessary and preferred to maintain privacy. I am using the pronoun "she" in this chapter to describe the homeowner, as the media articles also did, but even so, this anecdote does not focus on gender per se. I did reach out to the homeowner via social media, just to thank her for sharing her story and to let her know that I planned to describe it in the context of this chapter, and she wrote back to thank me for reaching out, and to express her support for the book. Finally, I am using "she" when referring to the mountain lion to maintain narrative consistency with the homeowner's description of the creature.

18. KHQ.com, "Cat Nap."

19. Plec, "Perspectives on Human-Animal Communication," 6.

20. Ingold, *Being Alive,* 64.

21. Kimmerer, *Braiding Sweetgrass,* 57–58.

22. Kimmerer, *Braiding Sweetgrass,* 331.

23. Clary-Lemon, "Gifts, Ancestors, and Relations."

24. Clary-Lemon, "Gifts, Ancestors, and Relations."

25. KHQ.com, "Cat Nap"; Padgett, "Oregon Woman Discovers."

26. KHQ.com, "Cat Nap"; Padgett, "Oregon Woman Discovers."

27. KHQ.com, "Cat Nap"; Padgett, "Oregon Woman Discovers."

28. "The slow blink involves relaxed eyes; it shows your cat is not worried," says Mikel Delgado, PhD, and certified cat behavior consultant at Feline Minds. "He is not avoiding any stressors or wincing." See LeBeau, "The Cat Slow Blink." In addition, "the eye blink is another way that non-aggressive cats signal that their intentions are not hostile. Cats blink at each other, as well as at the humans they trust, with a slow eye blink." See Shojai, "Why Cats Blink Their Eyes at You."

29. Seegert, "Play of Sniffication," 164.

30. Seegert, "Play of Sniffication," 164.

31. Gruen, *Entangled Empathy,* 50.

32. Gruen, *Entangled Empathy,* 51.

33. Wright, "More-than-Human," 395, 402–3.

34. Blunt and Dowling, *Home,* 22.

35. Kimmerer, *Braiding Sweetgrass,* 58.

36. Warfield, "Woman Comes Home."

37. KHQ.com, "Cat Nap." Here, I am relaying this story as conveyed by the homeowner to media outlets. While an approach that involves this sort of creative visualizing or picturing may be considered less traditional to some readers, I want to be careful here in respect-

ing this individual's attempts at peaceful, nonviolent intervention. It is not my goal in this discussion to delve more deeply into the merits of creative visualization, per se, except to acknowledge that there are a range of possible modes of communication about which we arguably know less. In making this point, I do not mean to state uncritically that all communicative approaches or styles are to be viewed as similar or as on par with one another; rather, my goal with relaying this example is to describe an instance of what is arguably a more relational interaction that achieved the intended goal of getting the lion to exit the home without a harsher kind of intervention. We might not know precisely which approach or approaches aided in the successful outcome of this situation, which is also to acknowledge that there may be many facets of nonlinguistic communication among more-than-human animals, or to which they are receptive, that we know relatively less about.

38. Warfield, "Woman Comes Home."
39. KHQ.com, "Cat Nap."
40. KHQ.com, "Cat Nap."
41. Hawk, *Resounding the Rhetorical*, 7.
42. Hawk, *Resounding the Rhetorical*, 9. The quote is from David Byrne's *How Music Works* (San Francisco: McSweeney's, 2012).
43. Hawk, *Resounding the Rhetorical*, 7–8.
44. Hawk, *Resounding the Rhetorical*, 8.
45. Yin, "Drumming."
46. Yin, "Drumming."
47. Beauty of Birds, "Palm Cockatoos."
48. Yin, "Drumming."
49. Van Dooren, *Flight Ways*, 66.
50. McHugh, *Animal Stories*, 5.
51. Van Dooren, *Flight Ways*, 22.
52. Warfield, "Woman Comes Home."
53. Warfield, "Woman Comes Home" (emphasis added).
54. Kimmerer, *Braiding Sweetgrass*, 23.
55. Kimmerer, *Braiding Sweetgrass*, 22.
56. Kimmerer, *Braiding Sweetgrass*, 23–24.
57. Clary-Lemon, "Gifts, Ancestors, and Relations."
58. Gruen, *Entangled Empathy*, 44–45.
59. UC Santa Barbara Department of Recreation, "UCSB and Isla Vista Walking Tour."
60. UC Santa Barbara Cheadle Center for Biodiversity and Ecological Restoration, "Lagoon Island & Campus Point."
61. Edhat Santa Barbara, "State Commission Grants Temporary Protection to Mountain Lions."
62. California Department of Fish and Wildlife, "Keep Me Wild."
63. Kimmerer, *Braiding Sweetgrass*, 205.
64. California Department of Fish and Wildlife, "Keep Me Wild."
65. California Department of Fish and Wildlife, "Keep Me Wild."
66. California Department of Fish and Wildlife, "Keep Me Wild."
67. California Department of Fish and Wildlife, "Keep Me Wild."
68. University of California Natural Reserve System, UCSB, "Welcome to Coal Oil Point Reserve."
69. UC Santa Barbara Department of Recreation, "UCSB and Isla Vista Walking Tour."
70. UC Santa Barbara Department of Recreation, "UCSB and Isla Vista Walking Tour."
71. Chambers, "UCSB's Wandering Mountain Lion."
72. Chambers, "UCSB's Wandering Mountain Lion."
73. Chambers, "UCSB's Wandering Mountain Lion."
74. UC Santa Barbara, text message to the UCSB community, 3:16 p.m., Sept. 20, 2019.

75. Kimmerer, *Braiding Sweetgrass*, 30.
76. UC Santa Barbara, text message to the UCSB community, 9:22 p.m., Oct. 7, 2019.
77. UC Santa Barbara, text message to the UCSB community, 2:22 p.m., Oct. 8, 2019.
78. See Just, *Women in Athenian Law and Life*; Lehmann, "Feeling Home"; Macdowell, "The Oikos."
79. KHQ.com, "Cat Nap."
80. Wright, "More-than-Human," 405.
81. Kimmerer, *Braiding Sweetgrass*, 58.
82. California Department of Fish and Wildlife, "Keep Me Wild."
83. Readers may reference one news article in particular, which included video of this moment and the drumming. Readers may infer here, as did I, that the drumming was rhythmic and intentional—not erratic or random in its approach. See IE Staff, "Woman Comes Home."
84. Rush, *Rising*, 197.
85. Although in some cases, if mountain lions show what appears to be aggressive behavior, authorities will kill them. Such an incident took place in Salem, Oregon, in September 2019, when a mountain lion had apparently chased a jogger. See Associated Press, "Wildlife Officials Kill Cougar."
86. Gruen, *Entangled Empathy*, 44–45.
87. Readers empathetic to the challenges of these vulnerable mountain lions may be encouraged to know that in April 2020, the California Fish and Game Commission voted unanimously "to consider the candidacy of Southern California and Central Coast mountain lions for the state's Endangered Species Act" (Osgood, "California Takes Steps"). This means for that one year, the protections of the Endangered Species Act will apply to California's mountain lion population. During this time, mountain lions will also be "considered for permanent protection under the law," and the Department of Fish and Wildlife will conduct its own peer-reviewed study of specific mountain lion populations in the state (Edhat Santa Barbara, "State Commission Grants Temporary Protection to Mountain Lions"). Several studies have predicted that without certain protections, mountain lions could face extinction within fifty years. While it has been illegal to hunt mountain lions in California for over thirty years, these species still face threats not only from drought and fires but also from a host of other types of human intervention.

## NOTES TO INTERLUDE I

1. CalFire. "2020 Incident Archive."
2. Air Pollution Control District, Santa Barbara County, "Air Quality Summary by Date."
3. Albrecht, *Earth Emotions*, 38.
4. Plec, "Presence and Absence in the Watershed," 36.
5. Rush, *Rising*, 255.
6. Rush, *Rising*, 255–56.
7. Rush, *Rising*, 256.
8. Rush, *Rising*, 256.
9. Rush, *Rising*, 256–57.
10. Shain, "Got Climate Anxiety?"
11. M. Taylor and Murray, "Overwhelming and Terrifying."
12. M. Harris, "Indigenous Knowledge Has Been Warning Us."
13. Weiss, "Who Gets to Have Ecoanxiety?"
14. Weiss, "Who Gets to Have Ecoanxiety?"
15. Haraway, *Staying with the Trouble*, 35.
16. Haraway, *Staying with the Trouble*, 35.
17. Haraway, *Staying with the Trouble*, 35.

18. Haraway, *Staying with the Trouble*, 35–36.
19. Graham-McLay, "New Zealand Schools."
20. Graham-McLay, "New Zealand Schools."
21. P. Taylor, "Ardern Disputes Greta Thunberg's Criticism."
22. Shain, "Got Climate Anxiety?"
23. Shain, "Got Climate Anxiety?"
24. Lertzman, *Environmental Melancholia*, 4. Lertzman takes a psychoanalytic approach in addressing climate anxiety. While it is beyond the scope of this work to delve deeply into the workings of psychoanalytic theory, I appreciate some of what I think are applicable ideas and recommendations related to the need for active listening and clear communication with one another, and relatedly how to more productively channel and express our care for the environments that we share with our kin.
25. Lertzman, *Environmental Melancholia*, 4.
26. Rush, *Rising*, 197. See also Barnett, "Vigilant Mourning."
27. I would have also liked to have been able to travel even farther east, but timing and other factors made this less feasible at this time, and I was very grateful to visit areas of the Midwest during these travels.
28. Boyle and Rice, "Introduction," 3.
29. The "Given-New Strategy" is an older cognitive theory of learning based in linguistics, which essentially suggests that sentences contain both "Given information (what the listener is expected to know already) and New information (what the listener is not expected to know already). According to a proposed Given-New Strategy, the listener, in comprehending a sentence, first searches his memory for antecedent information that matches the sentence's Given information; he then revises memory by attaching the New information to that antecedent" (Haviland and Clark, "What's New?," 512). In the field of writing studies, this is also referred to as the "Given/New Contract," or the "Known/New Contract," and is often invoked in reference to strategies for clear paragraph construction (George Mason University Writing Center, "Improving Cohesion"). I am extrapolating from this idea, somewhat speculatively, to suggest that when we experience a new place, we might first search our memory for earlier, existing ideas about places we know and that we may liken to the new place, and then integrate that new place into our already existing schema of places.
30. Wright, "More-than-Human," 404.
31. Rush, *Rising*, 196.
32. Wood, "Jay's Whisper Song."
33. The Cornell Lab, "Blue Jay: Sounds."
34. Wright, "More-than-Human," 395.
35. Boyle and Rice, "Introduction," 4.
36. Creswell draws on political geographer John Agnew, who refers to a "locale" as one of the "fundamental aspects of a place as a 'meaningful location.'" As such, a locale is a "material setting for social relations—the actual shape of a place within which people conduct their lives" (Creswell, *Place*, 13–14).
37. A. Taylor, "In Photos."
38. Deaton, "What Is a Bomb Cyclone?"
39. Nebraska Department of Natural Resources, "Nebraska Flooding: March 2019."
40. Nebraska Department of Natural Resources, "Nebraska Flooding: March 2019."
41. Nebraska Department of Natural Resources, "Nebraska Flooding: March 2019."
42. Plourde, "Haworth Park Plans."
43. Ortega, "Haworth Park Might Need $3 Million."
44. Plourde, "Haworth Park Plans."
45. Rush, *Rising*, 249.
46. Rush, *Rising*, 249.

47. NASA Earth Observatory, "Deadly Debris Flows in Montecito."
48. Stewart, "Bellevue to Rebuild Haworth Park Campground."

## NOTES TO CHAPTER 3

1. "P" stands for "puma"; "22" means that P-22 is the twenty-second lion collared in the ongoing study of mountain lions in the Santa Monica Mountains.
2. Pratt-Bergstrom, *When Mountain Lions Are Neighbors*, 6.
3. Pratt-Bergstrom, *When Mountain Lions Are Neighbors*, 7.
4. Salahieh, "Wildlife Officials."
5. According to the National Park Service, "The connection between exposure to anticoagulant rodenticide and mange, a parasitic disease of the hair and skin, is still not fully understood. Mange in wild cats is rare and only two other mountain lions in the 12-year study have developed mange, with both ultimately dying of rodenticide poisoning. More is known about mange in bobcats, with previous NPS research finding that bobcats who have ingested rodenticide are much more likely to suffer from severe mange." See Kuykendall, "Griffith Park Mountain Lion."
6. As of 2014, the California Department of Pesticide Regulation restricted public use of several rodenticide products known to be harmful to wildlife, pets, and children. See California Department of Fish and Wildlife, "Rodenticides Can Harm Wildlife." However, in 2019, a bill that would have banned additional second-generation rodenticides was pulled from the Senate Appropriations Committee, effectively squelching it for the foreseeable future. See Harbison, "California Rodenticide Ban."
7. Kuykendall, "Griffith Park Mountain Lion."
8. Pratt, "How a Lonely Cougar in Los Angeles Inspired the World."
9. Pratt, "How a Lonely Cougar in Los Angeles Inspired the World."
10. National Wildlife Federation, #SaveLACougars, home page.
11. National Wildlife Federation, #SaveLACougars, home page. Around April 2022, the Liberty Canyon wildlife crossing became publicly known as the Wallis Annenberg Wildlife Crossing.
12. *Los Angeles Daily News*, "Mountain Lion P-22's Journey."
13. *Los Angeles Daily News*, "Mountain Lion P-22's Journey."
14. Kirksey, Schuetze, and Helmreich, "Introduction," 1–2.
15. Bennett, *Vibrant Matter*, 98.
16. See Zertuche, "Animal Representations in Visual Culture."
17. Bennett, *Vibrant Matter*, 99.
18. Bennett, *Vibrant Matter*, 99.
19. Kimmerer, *Braiding Sweetgrass*, 331.
20. Pratt, "How a Lonely Cougar in Los Angeles Inspired the World."
21. Lorimer, *Wildlife in the Anthropocene*, 7.
22. Lorimer, *Wildlife in the Anthropocene*, 182.
23. Beth Pratt, personal interview with the author, May 19, 2020.
24. Pratt, "How a Lonely Cougar in Los Angeles Inspired the World."
25. Pratt, "How a Lonely Cougar in Los Angeles Inspired the World."
26. Pratt, "How a Lonely Cougar in Los Angeles Inspired the World."
27. Pratt, "How a Lonely Cougar in Los Angeles Inspired the World."
28. Pratt, "How a Lonely Cougar in Los Angeles Inspired the World."
29. Pratt, "How a Lonely Cougar in Los Angeles Inspired the World."
30. Lorimer, *Wildlife in the Anthropocene*, 161–62.
31. Lorimer, *Wildlife in the Anthropocene*, 161–62.
32. Lorimer, *Wildlife in the Anthropocene*, 163.

33. Lorimer, *Wildlife in the Anthropocene,* 164.
34. Pratt, "How a Lonely Cougar in Los Angeles Inspired the World."
35. Pratt, "How a Lonely Cougar in Los Angeles Inspired the World."
36. Pratt, "How a Lonely Cougar in Los Angeles Inspired the World."
37. Cronon, "A Place for Stories."
38. Van Dooren, *Flight Ways,* 17.
39. Van Dooren, *Flight Ways,* 17.
40. Van Dooren, *Flight Ways,* 17.
41. Lorimer, *Wildlife in the Anthropocene,* 176.
42. Lorimer, *Wildlife in the Anthropocene,* 177.
43. Van Dooren, *Flight Ways,* 78.
44. Anderson and Jenkins, *Applying Nature's Design,* 4.
45. Lorimer, *Wildlife in the Anthropocene,* 31.
46. Lorimer, *Wildlife in the Anthropocene,* 31.
47. As the CDFW notes: "Relocation is illegal in California and is biologically unsound. Studies have shown that relocated mountain lions have poor rates of survival and rarely stay at release sites," and behaviors that are considered by humans to be "undesirable" are "unaffected by the relocation." See California Department of Fish and Wildlife, "CDFW's Wildlife Forensics Lab."
48. Stowe Land Trust, "Putting the Shutesville Hill Wildlife Corridor on the Map."
49. Kimmerer, *Braiding Sweetgrass,* 331.
50. Kimmerer, *Braiding Sweetgrass,* 358–59.
51. National Park Service, "Lions in the Santa Monica Mountains?"
52. Bloom, "P-65 Becomes 2nd Female Mountain Lion to Cross 101 Freeway."
53. Solly, "California Will Build the Largest Wildlife Crossing in the World."
54. Pratt, "A Bridge to the Future."
55. Artsy, "Here's What You Need to Know."
56. Stevens, "The New West."
57. Stevens, "The New West."
58. California Coastal Conservancy, "Liberty Canyon Wildlife Crossing."
59. Groves, "Mountain Lion Killed on 101 Freeway."
60. *Agoura Hills Tomorrow,* "Wildlife Board Approves Funding."
61. Kim, "Liberty Canyon Puma Crossing."
62. California Association of Resource Conservation Districts, "Bringing the Wildlife Crossing at Liberty Canyon to Life."
63. Pratt, "A Bridge to the Future."
64. Associated Press, "New Calif. Freeway Bridge to Carry Wildlife."
65. Artsy, "Here's What You Need to Know."
66. Artsy, "Here's What You Need to Know."
67. Artsy, "Here's What You Need to Know."
68. Goldman, "Here's How to Design a Wildlife Crossing."
69. Goldman, "Here's How to Design a Wildlife Crossing."
70. Pratt, "A Bridge to the Future."
71. Goldman, "Here's How to Design a Wildlife Crossing."
72. Goldman, "Here's How to Design a Wildlife Crossing."
73. Goldman, "Here's How to Design a Wildlife Crossing."
74. Goldman, "Here's How to Design a Wildlife Crossing."
75. Stevens, "The New West."
76. To take a fascinating and slightly eerie virtual tour of the Santa Susana Field Lab, visit https://www.nps.gov/hdp/exhibits/ssfl/tour/index.html.
77. Boeing, "Santa Susana Field Laboratory."
78. Boeing, "Boeing Santa Susana Restoration."

79. Shatkin, "What Happened at the Santa Susana Nuclear Site."
80. Solis, "Residents Blast Plan."
81. National Aeronautics and Space Administration, "A Look Back."
82. National Aeronautics and Space Administration, "A Look Back."
83. Save Open Space, Santa Monica Mountains (SOS), "NASA Announces Decision."
84. Save Open Space, Santa Monica Mountains (SOS), "NASA Announces Decision."
85. Save Open Space, Santa Monica Mountains (SOS), "NASA Announces Decision."
86. OhRanger.com, "Burro Flats Painted Cave."
87. OhRanger.com, "Burro Flats Painted Cave."
88. OhRanger.com, "Burro Flats Painted Cave."
89. Krupp, *Echoes of the Ancient Skies*, 129.
90. Krupp, *Echoes of the Ancient Skies*, 129; Chatsworth Historical Society, "The History of Burro Flats."
91. Boeing, "Santa Susana Field Laboratory."
92. Haraway, *Staying with the Trouble*, 35.
93. P22 Mountain Lion of Hollywood, "Chumash Stories."
94. Salazar, "About Alan Salazar."
95. P22 Mountain Lion of Hollywood, "Chumash Stories."
96. P22 Mountain Lion of Hollywood, "Chumash Stories."
97. P22 Mountain Lion of Hollywood, "Chumash Stories."
98. See Salazar, *Tata the Tataviam Towhee*.
99. P22 Mountain Lion of Hollywood, "Chumash Stories."
100. P22 Mountain Lion of Hollywood, "Chumash Stories."
101. P22 Mountain Lion of Hollywood, "Chumash Stories." Again, I gratefully acknowledge permission from Alan Salazar to quote from and summarize his telling of the Rainbow Bridge story in this chapter. While this video segment is publicly available, I also reached out to Alan Salazar to thank him for sharing this story, and to ask, out of respect for the story and its connections with Chumash culture, if it was okay with him that I quoted from and summarized it here. For the full version of this story, visit https://www.facebook.com/p22mountainlionofhollywood/videos/564149154236146/. I should also note that this Chumash story of the Rainbow Bridge is different from the contemporary story that relates to the loss of a beloved companion animal.
102. P22 Mountain Lion of Hollywood, "Chumash Stories."
103. P22 Mountain Lion of Hollywood, "Chumash Stories."
104. P22 Mountain Lion of Hollywood, "Chumash Stories."
105. P22 Mountain Lion of Hollywood, "Chumash Stories."
106. P22 Mountain Lion of Hollywood, "Chumash Stories."
107. P22 Mountain Lion of Hollywood, "Chumash Stories."
108. Planet Forward Staff, "2017 Summit."
109. P22 Mountain Lion of Hollywood, "Chumash Stories." Here, I should also note that I find this analogy apt and wonderfully suited to help contextualize the Liberty Canyon corridor as participating in a culture of reciprocity; however, I would not have necessarily felt comfortable articulating this analogy or adapting it in this way myself. I thus convey these ideas here with great respect, and only because they have been articulated by someone with deeper and long-standing knowledge of the cultural contexts within which these ideas are situated.
110. P22 Mountain Lion of Hollywood, "Chumash Stories."
111. Kimmerer, *Braiding Sweetgrass*, 328.
112. Kimmerer, *Braiding Sweetgrass*, 384.
113. Van Dooren, *Flight Ways*, 78.
114. Kimmerer, *Braiding Sweetgrass*, 336.
115. Kimmerer, *Braiding Sweetgrass*, 336.
116. McNaughton, "UDOT."
117. Pierce, "New $5 Million, Animals-Only Overpass."

118. McNaughton, "UDOT."
119. McNaughton, "UDOT."
120. McNaughton, "UDOT."
121. @UtahDWR, "We're excited!"
122. Kimmerer, *Braiding Sweetgrass*, 331. Here, readers might appreciate the website Animals and Media: A Style Guide for Giving Voice to the Voiceless, at http://www.animalsandmedia.org/main/, which was created by Carrie P. Freeman and Debra Merskin, with the goal of "offer[ing] concrete guidance for how to cover and represent nonhuman animals in a fair, honest, and respectful manner in accordance with professional ethical principles."
123. Kimmerer, *Braiding Sweetgrass*, 58.
124. Kimmerer, *Braiding Sweetgrass*, 328.
125. Kimmerer, *Braiding Sweetgrass*, 31.
126. Kimmerer, *Braiding Sweetgrass*, 31.
127. Kimmerer, *Braiding Sweetgrass*, 337.
128. Wright, "More-than-Human," 395, 402–3.
129. Kimmerer, *Braiding Sweetgrass*, 58.
130. Ingold, *Being Alive*, 63.

## NOTES TO INTERLUDE II

1. See Garcia, "When Humans Are Sheltered in Place"; Lampariello, "Animals Emerge."
2. McGreevy, "Scientists Propose a New Name for Nature."
3. To further clarify their use of this term, these scientists say they are "aware that the correct prefix is 'anthropo-' (for 'human') but opted for the shortened form, which is easier to remember and use, and where the missing 'po' is still echoed in the pronunciation of 'pause' (pɔːz)."
4. Rutz et al., "COVID-19 Lockdown."
5. Rutz et al., "COVID-19 Lockdown."
6. McGreevy, "Scientists Propose a New Name for Nature."
7. Fortin, "The Birds Are Not on Lockdown."
8. Rutz et al., "COVID-19 Lockdown."
9. Rutz et al., "COVID-19 Lockdown."
10. Rutz et al., "COVID-19 Lockdown."
11. Lindholm and Smith, "Vermont Bears."
12. State of Vermont, "Steeped in History, Embracing Change."
13. Frett, "'Stay Home' Order Brings Bear to Bellows Falls."
14. Frett, "'Stay Home' Order Brings Bear to Bellows Falls."
15. Frett, "'Stay Home' Order Brings Bear to Bellows Falls."
16. Lindholm and Smith, "Vermont Bears."
17. Lindholm and Smith, "Vermont Bears."
18. Frett, "'Stay Home' Order Brings Bear to Bellows Falls."
19. Frett, "'Stay Home' Order Brings Bear to Bellows Falls."
20. Frett, "'Stay Home' Order Brings Bear to Bellows Falls."
21. Colorado Parks and Wildlife News Release, "Wildlife Activity During Stay-at-Home Order."
22. Colorado Parks and Wildlife News Release, "Wildlife Activity During Stay-at-Home Order."
23. Robins, "Wildlife Comes Out as People Stay Indoors."
24. Robins, "Wildlife Comes Out as People Stay Indoors."
25. McGreevy, "Scientists Propose a New Name for Nature."
26. Colorado Parks and Wildlife News Release, "Wildlife Activity During Stay-at-Home Order."
27. Pratt, "How a Lonely Cougar in Los Angeles Inspired the World."

28. Rutz et al., "COVID-19 Lockdown."
29. Colorado Parks and Wildlife News Release, "Wildlife Activity During Stay-at-Home Order."
30. Colorado Parks and Wildlife News Release, "Wildlife Activity During Stay-at-Home Order."
31. Robins, "Wildlife Comes Out as People Stay Indoors."

## NOTES TO CHAPTER 4

1. Vermont Fish and Wildlife Department, "Black Bears."
2. Albertine, "Outdoor Radio."
3. Vermont Fish and Wildlife Department, "Deerfield Wind Black Bear Study."
4. Tapper, "Into the Woods."
5. McKibben, *Wandering Home,* 79.
6. Kilham, *In the Company of Bears,* 2.
7. Kilham, *In the Company of Bears,* 31–32.
8. Comeau and Hammond, "Deerfield Wind Black Bear Study."
9. Bears are also thought to scratch or tear beech bark for other reasons, such as to mark territory or communicate with other black bears, but less is known about this practice.
10. Vermont Fish and Wildlife Department, "Deerfield Wind Black Bear Study."
11. Vermont Fish and Wildlife Department, "Deerfield Wind Black Bear Study."
12. Mance, "Mast Mysteries."
13. Kimmerer, *Braiding Sweetgrass,* 13.
14. Kimmerer, *Braiding Sweetgrass,* 15.
15. Kimmerer, *Braiding Sweetgrass,* 15.
16. Mance, "Mast Mysteries."
17. Kimmerer, *Braiding Sweetgrass,* 15.
18. Kimmerer, *Braiding Sweetgrass,* 15.
19. Wohlleben, *The Hidden Life of Trees,* 3.
20. Wohlleben, *The Hidden Life of Trees,* 3.
21. Wohlleben, *The Hidden Life of Trees,* 3.
22. Wohlleben, *The Hidden Life of Trees,* 10.
23. Kimmerer, *Braiding Sweetgrass,* 15–16.
24. Wright, "More-than-Human," 395, 402–3.
25. Kimmerer, *Braiding Sweetgrass,* 16.
26. Kimmerer, *Braiding Sweetgrass,* 20.
27. Kimmerer, *Braiding Sweetgrass,* 20.
28. Kimmerer, *Braiding Sweetgrass,* 20–21.
29. Kilham, *In the Company of Bears,* 34.
30. Kennedy, "A Hoot in the Dark," 4.
31. Kennedy, "A Hoot in the Dark," 6.
32. Kilham, "Black Bear Social Behavior."
33. Kilham, "Black Bear Social Behavior."
34. Kilham, "Black Bear Social Behavior."
35. Kilham, "Black Bear Social Behavior."
36. Albertine, "Outdoor Radio."
37. Albertine, "Outdoor Radio."
38. Bekoff, *Rewilding Our Hearts.*
39. Albertine, "Outdoor Radio."
40. Bekoff, *Rewilding Our Hearts,* 2.
41. Bekoff, *Rewilding Our Hearts,* 59.
42. Albertine, "Outdoor Radio."

43. Albertine, "Outdoor Radio."
44. Albertine, "Outdoor Radio."
45. Albertine, "Outdoor Radio."
46. Jaclyn Comeau, personal interview with the author, July 28, 2020.
47. Jaclyn Comeau, personal interview with the author, July 28, 2020.
48. Gruen, *Entangled Empathy,* 95.
49. Albertine, "Outdoor Radio."
50. Albertine, "Outdoor Radio."
51. Comeau and Hammond, "Deerfield Wind Black Bear Study."
52. Therrien, "Long-Awaited Deerfield Wind Turbines Go Online."
53. Comeau and Hammond, "Deerfield Wind Black Bear Study."
54. Therrien, "Long-Awaited Deerfield Wind Turbines Go Online."
55. Loder, "Breath of Life," 509.
56. Therrien, "Long-Awaited Deerfield Wind Turbines Go Online."
57. See Weiss-Tisman, "After Agreement over Bear Habitat"; Avangrid Renewables, "Avangrid Renewables Commissions Deerfield Wind."
58. Comeau and Hammond, "Deerfield Wind Black Bear Study."
59. Vermont Fish and Wildlife Department, "Deerfield Wind Black Bear Study."
60. Comeau and Hammond, "Deerfield Wind Black Bear Study."
61. Vermont Fish and Wildlife Department, "Bear Den Visit."
62. Vermont Fish and Wildlife Department, "Deerfield Wind Black Bear Study."
63. Therrien, "Long-Awaited Deerfield Wind Turbines Go Online"; Weiss-Tisman, "After Agreement over Bear Habitat."
64. Walker, "The Mountains."
65. Walker, "The Mountains."
66. Walker, "The Mountains."
67. Plec, "Perspectives on Human-Animal Communication," 6.
68. It is beyond the scope of this chapter to undertake a full analysis of the Final EIS for the Deerfield Wind Energy Project. However, it is worth noting that the Final EIS, cited in the bibliography of this book and available online, does in fact acknowledge and respond to many past public comments. For instance, the Final EIS uses language that directly addresses prior comments, such as: "The proposal in the DEIS to close the area immediately surrounding the turbines and access roads received considerable public comment. To address the issues raised by the public, that closure is not proposed to be implemented in the SEDIS" (USDA-Forest Service, Final EIS, 19).

    It is also worth noting that throughout the permitting process, Forest Service officials asked Abenaki leaders "to identify any areas of concern in the project area." More specifically: "As the first step to comply with the Forest Plan and Section 106 regarding heritage resources, a Phase IA Archaeological Survey and Historic Resource Screening Study was conducted. Part of this study included 'Consultation with the Tribal Historic Preservation Offices (THPOs) of the Stockbridge-Munsee Community Band of Mohican Indians and the Mississquoi Band of the Abenaki Nation, to inform them of the Project and request comments'" (166). According to the Final EIS, "Correspondence dated December 22, 2005 from the Stockbridge-Munsee Tribal Historic Preservation Office stated '. . . the proposed ground disturbing activity of this project does not appear to be in a region of archaeological interest to the Stockbridge-Munsee Tribe.' (White, 2005). . . . Concerns about potential human remains and associated funerary objects were raised in the letter. None have been identified to date during surveys in the Project's construction footprint. No correspondence was received from the Abenaki Nation at that time. Additional (email) contacts with both Tribes were made by the GMNF's archaeologist in November 2007 (Lacy, 2007a, 2007b), to inform them of the changes made to the Proposed Action. Both tribes responded that they had no further concerns with these changes" (172–73).
69. Walker, "The Mountains."

70. Gruen, *Entangled Empathy,* 95.
71. Loder, "Breath of Life," 508.
72. Loder, "Breath of Life," 508.
73. Loder, "Breath of Life," 508.
74. Loder, "Breath of Life," 513.
75. Loder, "Breath of Life," 513.
76. Loder, "Breath of Life," 512.
77. Loder, "Breath of Life," 512.
78. Loder, "Breath of Life," 512.
79. Therrien, "Long-Awaited Deerfield Wind Turbines Go Online."
80. Walker, "The Mountains."
81. Therrien, "Long-Awaited Deerfield Wind Turbines Go Online."
82. Loder, "Breath of Life," 514.
83. Loder, "Breath of Life," 513.
84. Weiss-Tisman, "After Agreement over Bear Habitat."
85. Bielawski, "Years Later."
86. Bielawski, "Years Later."
87. Bielawski, "Years Later."
88. Bielawski, "Years Later."
89. Loder, "Breath of Life," 521.
90. Loder, "Breath of Life," 521–22.
91. Loder, "Breath of Life," 521–22.
92. I have argued elsewhere that when we make species more visible through the practices of visualization, we may run the risk of making them more vulnerable in the process. I would also suggest that in this context, the use of nonintrusive camera traps that are not necessarily meant for public viewing performs an approach to compassionate conservation that is attentive to and respectful of the vulnerability of these species. When it comes to the practices of visualization, then, the surrounding context matters greatly. See Propen, *Visualizing Posthuman Conservation,* 2018.
93. Comeau and Hammond, "Deerfield Wind Black Bear Study," 9.
94. Comeau and Hammond, "Deerfield Wind Black Bear Study," 9.
95. Comeau and Hammond, "Deerfield Wind Black Bear Study," 9.
96. Comeau and Hammond, "Deerfield Wind Black Bear Study."
97. Comeau and Hammond, "Deerfield Wind Black Bear Study."
98. Comeau and Hammond, "Deerfield Wind Black Bear Study."
99. Loder, "Breath of Life," 522.
100. Loder, "Breath of Life," 525.
101. Loder, "Breath of Life," 525.
102. Loder, "Breath of Life," 525–26.
103. Plumwood, *Feminism and the Mastery of Nature,* 137.
104. Gruen, *Entangled Empathy,* 67.
105. Gruen, *Entangled Empathy,* 71.
106. Gruen, *Entangled Empathy,* 71.
107. Gruen, *Entangled Empathy,* 74.
108. Gruen, *Entangled Empathy,* 70–71.
109. Gruen, "Attending to Nature," 23.
110. Plumwood, *Feminism and the Mastery of Nature,* 137.
111. Plumwood, *Feminism and the Mastery of Nature,* 137.
112. Plumwood, *Feminism and the Mastery of Nature,* 156.
113. Rose, "Val Plumwood's Philosophical Animism," 93.
114. Rose, "Val Plumwood's Philosophical Animism," 93.
115. Kimmerer, *Braiding Sweetgrass,* 48.

116. Plec, "Perspectives on Human-Animal Communication," 7.
117. Walker, "The Mountains."
118. Wright, "More-than-Human," 393.
119. Gruen, "Attending to Nature," 32.
120. Gruen, "Attending to Nature," 32.
121. Gruen, *Entangled Empathy,* 68.

## NOTES TO CHAPTER 5

1. I use pseudonyms for my nieces and nephew out of respect for their privacy.
2. Cohen, *Stone,* 7.
3. Cohen, *Stone,* 8.
4. Cohen, *Stone,* 33.
5. Illinois Department of Natural Resources, "Illinois' Natural Divisions—Glaciers."
6. Illinois Department of Natural Resources, *Illinois Rocks and Minerals.*
7. Cape Cod Museum Trail, "The Discovery of a Young Boy's Lifetime."
8. Institute for American Indian Studies Museum and Research Center, "Connecticut's Archaeological Record."
9. Institute for American Indian Studies Museum and Research Center, "Connecticut's Archaeological Record."
10. Cohen, *Stone,* 9.
11. Cohen, *Stone,* 10.
12. Cohen, *Stone,* 11–12.
13. Gruen, "Attending to Nature," 32.
14. Gruen, *Entangled Empathy,* 68.
15. Cohen, *Stone,* 12.
16. Cohen, *Stone,* 12.
17. The Cornell Lab, "Great Horned Owl."
18. The Peregrine Fund, "Great Horned Owl."
19. ZSL Institute of Zoology, "Lizzie Jones."
20. ZSL Institute of Zoology, "Lizzie Jones."
21. Vaughan, "Young People Can't Remember."
22. Vaughan, "Young People Can't Remember."
23. Vaughan, "Young People Can't Remember."
24. Vaughan, "Young People Can't Remember."
25. Vaughan, "Young People Can't Remember."
26. Yeh, "Robin Wall Kimmerer."

# BIBLIOGRAPHY

Abram, David. *The Spell of the Sensuous: Perception and Language in a More-than-Human World.* New York: Vintage, 1996.

*Agoura Hills Tomorrow.* "Wildlife Board Approves Funding for Phase 1 of Liberty Canyon Wildlife Crossing." December 1, 2014. http://www.agourahillstomorrow.org/2014/.

Air Pollution Control District, Santa Barbara County. "Air Quality Summary by Date." September 13, 2020. https://www.ourair.org/air-quality-summary-by-date/.

Alaimo, Stacy. *Exposed: Environmental Politics and Pleasures in Posthuman Times.* Minneapolis: University of Minnesota Press, 2016.

Albertine, Chris. "Outdoor Radio: Meet Stark the Bear, a Thriving Resident of the Green Mountain National Forest." *Vermont Public Radio,* April 24, 2019. https://www.vpr.org/post/outdoor-radio-meet-stark-bear-thriving-resident-green-mountain-national-forest?fbclid=IwAR0eQ8hddEDpGom_sMfPnUXl36F2RRTBUTSsarFW25-pzLHu6nFn3ILraUY.

Albrecht, Glenn A. *Earth Emotions: New Words for a New World.* New York: Cornell University Press, 2019.

Aldous, Vickie. "Merged 120,000-Acre Wildfire Splits Battle into Two Fronts." *Mail Tribune,* August 19, 2018. https://mailtribune.com/news/top-stories/fires-make-history.

Anderson, Anthony B., and Clinton N. Jenkins. *Applying Nature's Design: Corridors as a Strategy for Biodiversity Conservation.* New York: Columbia University Press, 2006.

Animal Medical Center. "Ruptured Air Sac: A Unique Bird Disease." Animal Medical Center blog, March 28, 2012. https://www.amcny.org/blog/2012/03/28/ruptured-air-sac-a-unique-bird-disease.

Artsy, Avishay. "Here's What You Need to Know about the Liberty Canyon Wildlife Crossing." *KCRW,* February 20, 2018. https://www.kcrw.com/culture/shows/design-and-architecture/heres-what-you-need-to-know-about-the-liberty-canyon-wildlife-crossing.

Associated Press. "New Calif. Freeway Bridge to Carry Wildlife." *USA Today,* August 20, 2019. https://www.usatoday.com/videos/news/nation/2019/08/20/new-calif-freeway-bridge-carry-wildlife/2059568001/?fbclid=IwAR2eySFkvyt8hnSCP00gKMxkLj0ShxdH7A1k8yNGRjKMZcY20dMzwFN68Q0.

———. "Wildlife Officials Kill Cougar That Had Threatened Jogger." *Q13 Fox All Local,* September 5, 2019. https://q13fox.com/2019/09/05/wildlife-officials-kill-cougar-that-had-threatened-jogger/.

Avangrid Renewables. "Avangrid Renewables Commissions Deerfield Wind, the Company's First Project in Vermont." December 29, 2017. https://www.avangridrenewables.com/wps/portal/aren/aboutus/!ut/p/z0/fY7NCsIwEIRfZS89J7Wi9VhEEEVR8FBzkbVddbVNajao-vbGs-BthvnhUoaVyljs-YqBncUm-qOZnLJos1iO53qbF1mh9-vsMMu3-6XeTdRKmf-F-MD359MUylTOBn0FVaIne-08iXjn2kT_SGoIhSTRI51OE4092qvnGuKOBjw3JFC5tmWRi-ClQE_kLU1PDwLaGcKNv3KF9C1zYS4DOuztVAdhCT76NIKp7mOMHjMSLJg!!/.

Barad, Karen. *Meeting the Universe Halfway: Quantum Physics and the Entanglement of Matter and Meaning.* Durham: Duke University Press, 2007.

Barnett, Joshua Trey. "Vigilant Mourning and the Future of Earthly Coexistence." In *Communicating in the Anthropocene: Intimate Relations,* edited by Alexa M. Dare and C. Vail Fletcher, 13–33. New York: Lexington Books, 2021.

Beauty of Birds. "Palm Cockatoos aka Black Palm Cockatoos." 2011. Accessed January 21, 2021. https://www.beautyofbirds.com/palmcockatoos.html.

Bekoff, Marc. *The Animal Manifesto: Six Reasons for Expanding Our Compassion Footprint.* Novato: New World Library, 2010.

———. *The Emotional Lives of Animals: A Leading Scientist Explores Animal Joy, Sorrow, and Empathy—and Why They Matter.* Novato: New World Library, 2008.

———. *Rewilding Our Hearts: Building Pathways of Compassion and Coexistence.* Novato: New World Library, 2014.

Bennett, Jane. *Vibrant Matter: A Political Ecology of Things.* Durham: Duke University Press, 2010.

Bielawski, Michael. "Years Later, Deerfield Wind Impact on Bear Habitat in Question." *True North Reports: The Other Side of Vermont News,* January 31, 2020. http://www.truenorthreports.com/years-later-dearfield-wind-impact-on-bear-habitat-in-question.

Bloom, Tracy. "P-65 Becomes 2nd Female Mountain Lion to Cross 101 Freeway during Santa Monica Mountains Study." *KTLA5,* September 4, 2019. Accessed November 30, 2019. https://ktla.com/2019/09/04/p-65-becomes-2nd-female-mountain-lion-to-cross-101-freeway-in-santa-monica-mountains-study/?fbclid=IwARoLsPBbQtDr94J98YqU9hY5Go153HtqJ-Q-bHryhq1-CjKr5sISk5vnAFk.

Blunt, Alison, and Robyn Dowling. *Home.* New York: Routledge, 2006.

Boeckle, Markus, M. Schiestl, A. Frohnwieser, R. Gruber, R. Miller, T. Suddendorf, R. D. Gray, A. H. Taylor, and N. S. Clayton. "New Caledonian Crows Plan for Specific Future Tool Use." *Proceedings of the Royal Society B* 287 (2020): 1–7. http://doi.org/10.1098/rspb.2020.1490.

Boeing. "Boeing Santa Susana Restoration." 2020. Accessed June 10, 2020. http://www.boeing.com/principles/environment/santa-susana/index.page.

———. "Santa Susana Field Laboratory." 2019. Accessed June 10, 2020. http://www.boeing.com/resources/boeingdotcom/principles/environment/pdf/Santa_Susana_backgrounder.pdf.

Boyle, Casey, and Jenny Rice. "Introduction: Bodies, Place, and Poiesis." In *Inventing Place: Writing Lone Star Rhetorics,* edited by Casey Boyle and Jenny Rice, 1–16. Carbondale: Southern Illinois University Press, 2018.

Braidotti, Rosi. *The Posthuman.* Malden: Polity Press, 2013.

Bratta, Phil, and Malea Powell. "Introduction to the Special Issue: Entering the Cultural Rhetorics Conversations." *Enculturation: A Journal of Rhetoric, Writing, and Culture* (April 20, 2016). http://enculturation.net/entering-the-cultural-rhetorics-conversations.

Bruns, Gerald L. "Derrida's Cat (Who Am I)?" *Research in Phenomenology* 38 (2008): 404–23.

CalFire. "2020 Incident Archive." February 8, 2021. https://www.fire.ca.gov/incidents/2020/.

California Association of Resource Conservation Districts. "Bringing the Wildlife Crossing at Liberty Canyon to Life." July 15, 2019. https://carcd.org/rcds/impact-stories/bringing-the-wildlife-crossing-at-liberty-canyon-to-life/.

California Coastal Conservancy. "Liberty Canyon Wildlife Crossing: Environmental Assessment and Project Design." January 29, 2015. https://scc.ca.gov/webmaster/ftp/pdf/sccbb/2015/1501/20150129Board06_Liberty_Canyon_Wildlfe_Crossing.pdf.

California Department of Fish and Wildlife. "CDFW's Wildlife Forensics Lab Confirms Identify of Cupertino Mountain Lion." September 12, 2014. https://cdfgnews.wordpress.com/tag/mountain-lions-2/.

———. "Keep Me Wild: Mountain Lion." March 4, 2020. https://wildlife.ca.gov/Keep-Me-Wild/Lion.

———. "Rodenticides Can Harm Wildlife." Accessed January 23, 2021. https://wildlife.ca.gov/Living-with-Wildlife/Rodenticides.

Cantrill, James G., and Christine L. Oravec. Introduction to *The Symbolic Earth: Discourse and Our Creation of the Environment*, edited by James G. Cantrill and Christine L. Oravec, 1–5. Lexington: University Press of Kentucky, 1996.

Cape Cod Museum Trail. "The Discovery of a Young Boy's Lifetime." 2020. Accessed February 3, 2021. https://www.capecodmuseumtrail.com/discovery-young-boys-lifetime/.

Chamberlin, Susan. "The Life of Dr. Francesco Franceschi and His Park." Pacific Horticultural Society, July 2002. https://www.pacifichorticulture.org/articles/dr-francesco-franceschi-and-his-park/.

Chambers, Terene. "UCSB's Wandering Mountain Lion." *The Bottom Line,* October 17, 2019. https://thebottomline.as.ucsb.edu/2019/10/uc-santa-barbaras-wandering-mountain-lion.

Chatsworth Historical Society. "The History of Burro Flats, Rocketdyne and the SSFL." June 30, 2020. http://www.chatsworthhistory.com/Program%20Downloads/Burro%20Flats%20Rocketdyne%20SSFL%20History.pdf.

Clary-Lemon, Jennifer. "Gifts, Ancestors, and Relations: Notes toward an Indigenous New Materialism." *Enculturation: A Journal of Rhetoric, Writing, and Culture* (November 12, 2019). http://enculturation.net/gifts_ancestors_and_relations.

Cohen, Jeffrey Jerome. "Elemental Relations." *O-Zone: A Journal of Object-Oriented Studies* 1 (2014): 54–61.

———. *Stone: An Ecology of the Inhuman.* Minneapolis: University of Minnesota Press, 2015.

Colorado Parks and Wildlife News Release. "Wildlife Activity during Stay-at-Home Order: What to Expect." *The Fort Morgan Times,* April 6, 2020. https://www.fortmorgantimes.com/2020/04/06/wildlife-activity-during-stay-at-home-order-what-to-expect/.

Comeau, Jaclyn, and Forrest Hammond. "Deerfield Wind Black Bear Study, Progress Update: Fall 2018." Vermont Fish and Wildlife Department, 2018. Accessed October 7, 2020. https://vtfishandwildlife.com/sites/fishandwildlife/files/documents/Learn%20More/Library/REPORTS%20AND%20DOCUMENTS/WILDLIFE%20MANAGEMENT/BLACK%20BEAR/Deerfield-Wind-Black-Bear-Study-Update-2018.pdf.

The Cornell Lab: All About Birds. "Blue Jay: Sounds." 2019. Accessed February 18, 2021. https://www.allaboutbirds.org/guide/Blue_Jay/sounds.

———. "Great Horned Owl." 2019. Accessed November 16, 2020. https://www.allaboutbirds.org/guide/Great_Horned_Owl/id.

———. "Lesser Goldfinch Range Map." 2019. Accessed December 4, 2020. https://www.allaboutbirds.org/guide/Lesser_Goldfinch/maps-range.

Creswell, Tim. *Place: An Introduction.* Malden, MA: John Wiley & Sons, 2015.

Cronon, William. "A Place for Stories: Nature, History, and Narrative." *The Journal of American History* 78, no. 4 (1992): 1347–76.

Dartt-Newton, Deana, and Jon Erlandson. "Little Choice for the Chumash: Colonialism, Cattle, and Coercion in Mission Period California." *The American Indian Quarterly* 30 (2006): 416–30.

Days, Mary Louise. "Histories of Individual Parks." City of Santa Barbara, California, City Planning Division, Community Development Department. 1977. Accessed December 17, 2020. https://www.santabarbaraca.gov/civicax/filebank/blobdload.aspx?blobid=165941.

Deaton, Jeremy. "What Is a Bomb Cyclone?" *Mach: NBC News,* October 18, 2019. https://www.nbcnews.com/mach/science/what-bomb-cyclone-ncna1067731.

Derrida, Jacques. *The Animal That Therefore I Am.* Edited by Marie-Louise Mallet. Translated by David Wills. New York: Fordham University Press, 2008.

de Waal, Frans. *Are We Smart Enough to Know How Smart Animals Are?* New York: W. W. Norton & Company, 2017.

Drew, Lori A. "First Aid and Your Pet Bird." Center for Animal Rehab and Education, 2019. https://www.centerforanimalrehab.org/first-aid-and-your-pet-bird/.

E360 Digest. "Dozens of U.K. Species Have Been Displaced by Climate Change in Last 10 Years." Yale School of Forestry and Environmental Studies, July 19, 2019. https://e360.yale.edu/digest/dozens-of-uk-species-have-been-displaced-by-climate-change-in-last-10-years.

Edhat Santa Barbara. "State Commission Grants Temporary Protection to Mountain Lions." April 19, 2020. https://www.edhat.com/news/state-commission-grants-temporary-protection-to-mountain-lions.

Fortin, Jacey. "The Birds Are Not on Lockdown, and More People Are Watching Them." *The New York Times,* May 29, 2020. https://www.nytimes.com/2020/05/29/science/bird-watching-coronavirus.html.

Freeman, Carrie P., and Debra Merskin. Animals and Media: A Style Guide for Giving Voice to the Voiceless [website]. Accessed September 18, 2021. http://www.animalsandmedia.org/main/.

Frett, Michael. "'Stay Home' Order Brings Bear to Bellows Falls." *Saint Albans Messenger,* April 22, 2020. https://www.samessenger.com/news/stay-home-order-brings-bear-to-bellows-falls/article_c0228394-84e4-11ea-a1da-cf80b0e82473.html.

Garcia, Sandra E. "When Humans Are Sheltered in Place, Wildlife Will Play." *The New York Times,* April 1, 2020. https://www.nytimes.com/2020/04/01/science/coronavirus-animals-wildlife-goats.html.

George Mason University Writing Center. "Improving Cohesion: The 'Known/New Contract.'" Accessed February 13, 2021. https://writingcenter.gmu.edu/guides/improving-cohesion-the-known-new-contract.

Goldman, Jason. "Here's How to Design a Wildlife Crossing That Wildlife Will Actually Use." *KCET.org,* October 7, 2016. https://www.kcet.org/redefine/heres-how-to-design-a-wildlife-crossing-that-wildlife-will-actually-use.

Graham-McLay, Charlotte. "New Zealand Schools to Teach Students about Climate Crisis, Activism and 'Eco Anxiety.'" *The Guardian,* January 12, 2020. https://www.theguardian.com/world/2020/jan/13/new-zealand-schools-to-teach-students-about-climate-crisis-activism-and-eco-anxiety.

Groves, Martha. "Mountain Lion Killed on 101 Freeway Was from North, Officials Say." *Los Angeles Times,* November 6, 2013. https://www.latimes.com/local/la-xpm-2013-nov-06-la-me-1105-mountain-lion-dna-20131106-story.html.

Gruen, Lori. "Attending to Nature: Empathetic Engagement with the More than Human World." *Ethics and the Environment, Special Issue on Ecofeminism in Honor of Val Plumwood* 14, no. 2 (2009): 23–38.

———. *Entangled Empathy: An Alternative Ethic for Our Relationships with Animals.* New York: Lantern Books, 2015.

Hancock, Travis. "How Albatrosses Taught Photographer Chris Jordan How to Grieve." *HONOLULU,* July 22, 2016. http://www.honolulumagazine.com/Honolulu-Magazine/July-2016/How-Albatrosses-Taught-Photographer-Chris-Jordan-How-to-Grieve/.

Haraway, Donna J. *Staying with the Trouble: Making Kin in the Chthulucene.* Durham: Duke University Press, 2016.

———. *When Species Meet.* Minneapolis: University of Minnesota Press, 2008.

Harbison, Brad. "California Rodenticide Ban Dies in State Senate." *Pest Control Technology (PCT),* August 26, 2019. https://www.pctonline.com/article/rodenticide-ban-bill-california-ab1788/.

Harris, Leila, and Helen Hazen. "Rethinking Maps from a More-than-Human Perspective: Nature-Society, Mapping and Conservation Territories." In *Rethinking Maps: New Frontiers in Cartographic Theory,* edited by Martin Dodge, Rob Kitchin, and Chris Perkins, 50–67. New York: Routledge Studies in Human Geography, 2009.

Harris, Malcolm. "Indigenous Knowledge Has Been Warning Us about Climate Change for Centuries." *Pacific Standard,* March 4, 2019. https://psmag.com/ideas/indigenous-knowledge-has-been-warning-us-about-climate-change-for-centuries?fbclid=IwAR2RQ1OD6bumfjtoh Ky3hDAF6eMhqtXfVTlpgs3TimEgF-h6gjATusq3Cz8.

Haviland, Susan E., and Herbert H. Clark. "What's New? Acquiring New Information as a Process in Comprehension." *Journal of Verbal Learning and Verbal Behavior* 13 (1974): 512–21.

Hawk, Byron. *Resounding the Rhetorical: Composition as a Quasi-Object.* Pittsburgh: University of Pittsburgh Press, 2018.

Hayles, Katherine N. *How We Became Posthuman: Virtual Bodies in Cybernetics, Literature, and Informatics.* Chicago: University of Chicago Press, 1999.

Heidegger, Martin. *Poetry, Language, Thought.* Translated by Albert Hofstadter. New York: HarperCollins Publishers, 1971.

Hynes, Mary. "Why Is the World So Beautiful? An Indigenous Botanist on the Spirit of Life in Everything." Produced by Arman Aghbali and Rosie Fernandez. *CBC Radio,* November 27, 2020. https://www.cbc.ca/radio/tapestry/why-is-the-world-so-beautiful-an-indigenous-botanist-on-the-spirit-of-life-in-everything-1.5817787.

Illinois Department of Natural Resources. "Illinois' Natural Divisions—Glaciers." 2020. Accessed November 14, 2020. https://www2.illinois.gov/dnr/education/Pages/SchwegmanGlacier.aspx.

———. *Illinois Rocks and Minerals* [poster]. 2017. Accessed November 14, 2020. https://www2.illinois.gov/dnr/publications/Documents/00000673.pdf.

Ingold, Tim. *Being Alive: Essays on Movement, Knowledge, and Description.* New York: Routledge, 2011.

IE Staff. "Woman Comes Home to Find Mountain Lion Sleeping behind Her Sofa." *Inside Edition,* July 26, 2018. https://www.insideedition.com/woman-comes-home-find-mountain-lion-sleeping-behind-her-sofa-45421.

Institute for American Indian Studies Museum and Research Center. "Connecticut's Archaeological Record." Accessed November 28, 2020. https://diggingintothepast.org/connecticuts-archaeological-record/.

Just, Robert. *Women in Athenian Law and Life*. New York: Routledge, 1991.

Kennedy, George. "A Hoot in the Dark: The Evolution of General Rhetoric." *Philosophy & Rhetoric* 25, no. 1 (1992): 1–21.

KHQ.com. "Cat Nap: Woman Finds Mountain Lion Sleeping behind Couch." July 25, 2018. https://www.khq.com/news/cat-nap-woman-finds-mountain-lion-sleeping-behind-couch/article_3f706d43-4bc8-599a-abb8-ab4d7fb1a5c3.html.

Kilham, Benjamin. "Black Bear Social Behavior." 2020. Accessed July 29, 2020. http://www.benkilham.com/BLACK_BEAR_BEHAVIOR.html.

———. *In the Company of Bears: What Black Bears Have Taught Me about Intelligence and Intuition*. White River Junction, VT: Chelsea Green Publishing, 2013.

Kim, Jed. "Liberty Canyon Puma Crossing Gets $1 Million from State." *89.3KPCC,* January 29, 2015. https://www.scpr.org/news/2015/01/29/49550/liberty-canyon-puma-crossing-gets-1-million-from-s/.

Kimmerer, Robin Wall. *Braiding Sweetgrass*. Minneapolis: Milkweed Editions, 2013.

Kirksey, Eben, Craig Schuetze, and Stefan Helmreich. "Introduction: Tactics of Multispecies Ethnography." In *The Multispecies Salon,* edited by Eben Kirksey, 1–24. Durham: Duke University Press, 2014.

Krupp, Edwin. *Echoes of the Ancient Skies: The Astronomy of Lost Civilizations*. Mineola, NY: Dover Publications, 2003.

Kuykendall, Kate. "Griffith Park Mountain Lion Exposed to Poison, Suffering from Mange." National Park Service, April 17, 2014. https://www.nps.gov/samo/learn/news/gp-lion-exposed-to-poison.htm.

Lampariello, Dan. "Animals Emerge in Cities as Humans Stay Home during COVID-19." *Baltimore, WBFF,* April 10, 2020. https://foxbaltimore.com/news/coronavirus/animals-emerge-in-cities-as-humans-stay-home-during-covid-19.

LeBeau, Denise. "The Cat Slow Blink—What It Means." *Catster,* March 19, 2019. https://www.catster.com/cat-behavior/cat-slow-blink-meaning.

Lehmann, Hilary. "Feeling Home: House and Ideology in the Attic Orators." PhD diss., University of California Los Angeles, 2016. UCLA Electronic Theses and Dissertations: https://escholarship.org/uc/item/99n9k56z.

Lertzman, Renee. *Environmental Melancholia: Psychoanalytic Dimensions of Engagement*. New York: Routledge, 2015.

Lindholm, Jane, and Matthew F. Smith. "Vermont Bears Emboldened by 'Stay Home, Stay Safe.'" *Vermont Public Radio,* April 29, 2020. https://www.vpr.org/post/vermont-bears-emboldened-stay-home-stay-safe.

Loder, Reed Elizabeth. "Breath of Life: Ethical Wind Power and Wildlife." *Vermont Journal of Environmental Law* 10 (2009): 507–31.

Lorimer, Jamie. *Wildlife in the Anthropocene: Conservation after Nature*. Minneapolis: University of Minnesota Press, 2015.

*Los Angeles Daily News*. "Mountain Lion P-22's Journey from Santa Monica Mountains Retraced in Hike." October 19, 2016. https://www.dailynews.com/2016/10/19/mountain-lion-p-22s-journey-from-santa-monica-mountains-retraced-in-hike/.

Macdowell, Douglas M. "The *Oikos* in Athenian Law." *Classical Quarterly* 39 (1989): 10–21.

Mance, Dave. "Mast Mysteries." Northern Woodlands, November 18, 2013. https://northernwoodlands.org/outside_story/article/mysteries.

Mann, Damian. "Fires Make History." *Mail Tribune,* September 17, 2018. https://mailtribune.com/news/top-stories/fires-make-history.

Massey, Doreen. *Space, Place, and Gender.* Minneapolis: University of Minnesota Press, 1994.

McCall, Lynne, and Rosalind Perry. *California's Chumash Indians: A Project of the Santa Barbara Museum of Natural History Education Center.* San Luis Obispo: EZ Nature Books, 1986.

McDowell, Linda, and Joanne P. Sharp. *A Feminist Glossary of Human Geography.* New York: Oxford University Press, 1999.

McGreevy, Nora. "Scientists Propose a New Name for Nature in the Time of COVID-19: The 'Anthropause.'" *Smithsonian Magazine,* July 1, 2020. https://www.smithsonianmag.com/smart-news/scientists-have-name-nature-time-covid-19-anthropause-180975224/.

McHugh, Susan. *Animal Stories: Narrating across Species Lines.* Minneapolis: University of Minnesota Press, 2011.

McKibben, Bill. *Wandering Home: A Long Walk across America's Most Hopeful Landscape.* New York: St. Martin's Griffin, 2014.

McNaughton, Angelique. "UDOT Completes Utah's Largest Wildlife Crossing at Parleys Summit." *Park Record,* December 14, 2018. https://www.parkrecord.com/news/udot-completes-utahs-largest-wildlife-crossing-at-parleys-summit/.

Molina, Joshua. "Santa Barbara Decides to Demolish Franceschi House, Build Interpretive Pavilion." *Noozhawk,* February 14, 2018. https://www.noozhawk.com/article/santa_barbara_demolish_franceschi_house_build_interpretive_pavilion.

Mountain Lion Foundation. "When There's a Fire, Where Do the Wild Things Go?" *Mountain Lion Foundation News,* October 10, 2017. https://mountainlion.org/newsstory.php?news_id=1781.

NASA Earth Observatory. "Deadly Debris Flows in Montecito." January 10, 2018. https://earthobservatory.nasa.gov/images/91573/deadly-debris-flows-in-montecito.

National Aeronautics and Space Administration. "A Look Back at Space Mission Engine Testing at the Santa Susana Field Laboratory." 2010. Accessed June 6, 2020. https://ssfl.msfc.nasa.gov/files/documents/factsheets/Space_History_at_SSFL_2010-04-28.pdf.

National Park Service. "Lions in the Santa Monica Mountains?" February 18, 2020. https://www.nps.gov/samo/learn/nature/pumapage.htm.

National Wildlife Federation, #SaveLACougars. Home page. Accessed May 28, 2020. https://savelacougars.org/.

National Wildlife Rehabilitators Association. "What Is Wildlife Rehabilitation?" 2015. https://www.nwrawildlife.org/page/What_Is_WLRehab.

Nebraska Department of Natural Resources. "Nebraska Flooding: March 2019." Accessed February 17, 2021. https://storymaps.arcgis.com/stories/9ce70c78f5a44813a326d20035cab95a.

OhRanger.com. "Burro Flats Painted Cave." APN Media, 2013. Accessed June 11, 2020. http://www.ohranger.com/ca/chumash-painted-cave/poi/burro-flats-painted-cave.

Ortega, Jennifer. "Haworth Park Might Need $3 Million in Flood Repair." *WOWT 6News,* June 13, 2019. https://www.wowt.com/content/news/Haworth-Park-might-need-3-million-in-flood-repair-511253991.html.

Osgood, Brian. "California Takes Steps to Protect Mountain Lions." *Santa Barbara Independent,* April 20, 2020. https://www.independent.com/2020/04/20/california-takes-steps-to-protect-mountain-lions/.

P22 Mountain Lion of Hollywood. "Chumash Stories." Facebook, April 27, 2020. https://www.facebook.com/p22mountainlionofhollywood/videos/564149154236146/.

Padgett, Lauren. "Oregon Woman Discovers Mountain Lion Napping on Her Couch." *Fox 23 News,* July 24, 2018. https://www.fox23.com/news/trending-now/oregon-woman-discovers-mountain-lion-napping-on-her-couch/797403131.

Perazzo, Peggy B., and George (Pat) Perazzo. "Santa Barbara Mission, Santa Barbara, California Uses of Locally Quarried Stone: Santa Barbara Mission & Lavanderia." Stone Quarries and Beyond, 2020. Accessed December 18, 2020. https://quarriesandbeyond.org/states/ca/structures/ca-santa_barbara_mission_2_a.html#top.

The Peregrine Fund. "Great Horned Owl." 2020. Accessed November 16, 2020. https://peregrinefund.org/explore-raptors-species/owls/great-horned-owl.

Pierce, Scott D. "New $5 Million, Animals-Only Overpass at Parleys Summit Is Saving Wildlife (and Drivers) Already." The Salt Lake Tribune, June 20, 2019. https://www.sltrib.com/news/2019/06/20/new-million-animals-only/.

Planet Forward Staff. "2017 Summit: Stories That Last: Native American Traditions of Storytelling with Dr. Robin Kimmerer." Planet Forward, April 18, 2017. https://www.planetforward.org/idea/2017-summit-stories-that-last-native-american-traditions-of-storytelling-with-dr-robin-kimmerer.

Plec, Emily. "Perspectives on Human-Animal Communication: An Introduction." In Perspectives on Human-Animal Communication: Internatural Communication, edited by Emily Plec, 1–13. New York: Routledge, 2013.

———. "Presence and Absence in the Watershed: Storytelling for the Symbiocene." In Communicating in the Anthropocene: Intimate Relations, edited by Alexa M. Dare and C. Vail Fletcher, 35–52. Lanham, MD: Lexington Books, 2021.

Plourde, Austin. "Haworth Park Plans." Omaha World-Herald, May 16, 2019. https://omaha.com/sarpy/haworth-park-plans/article_caccd6bc-046d-5d06-bbb7-9e060ee56bd2.html.

Plumwood, Val. Feminism and the Mastery of Nature. New York: Routledge, 1993.

Pratt, Beth. "A Bridge to the Future: Building California's First Freeway Wildlife Crossing." National Wildlife Federation, #SaveLACougars. Accessed June 4, 2020. https://savelacougars.org/wp-content/uploads/2019/10/SaveLACougars-Overview-2019-Final.pdf.

———. "How a Lonely Cougar in Los Angeles Inspired the World." TEDx Talks, February 22, 2016. https://www.youtube.com/watch?v=pMO8-f7onFY.

Pratt-Bergstrom, Beth. When Mountain Lions Are Neighbors. Berkeley: The National Wildlife Federation, 2016.

Propen, Amy D. Locating Visual-Material Rhetorics: The Map, the Mill, and the GPS. Anderson: Parlor Press, 2012.

———. Visualizing Posthuman Conservation in the Age of the Anthropocene. Columbus: The Ohio State University Press, 2018.

Ritvo, Harriet. "Going Forth and Multiplying: Animal Acclimatization and Invasion." On the Human: A Project of the National Humanities Center. Accessed December 18, 2020. https://nationalhumanitiescenter.org/on-the-human/2011/11/going-forth-and-multiplying/.

Robins, Andrews. "Wildlife Comes Out as People Stay Indoors." Public Radio from Western Michigan University, April 12, 2020. https://www.wmuk.org/post/wildlife-comes-out-people-stay-indoors.

Rose, Deborah Bird. "Val Plumwood's Philosophical Animism: Attentive Inter-Actions in the Sentient World." Environmental Humanities 3, no. 1 (2013): 93–109.

Rush, Elizabeth. Rising: Dispatches from the New American Shore. Minneapolis: Milkweed Editions, 2019.

Rutz, Christian, Matthias-Claudio Loretto, Amanda E. Bates, Sarah C. Davidson, Carlos M. Duarte, Walter Jetz, Mark Johnson, Akiko Kato, Roland Kays, Thomas Mueller, Richard B. Primack, Yan Ropert-Coudert, Marlee A. Tucker, Martin Wikelski, and Francesca Cagnacci. "COVID-19 Lockdown Allows Researchers to Quantify the Effects of Human Activity on

Wildlife." *Nature Ecology & Evolution* 2020 (4): 1156–59. https://doi.org/10.1038/s41559-020-1237-z.

Salahieh, Nouran. "Wildlife Officials Say Griffith Park's Lone Mountain Lion, P-22, Is 'Doing Well' after Health Check." *KTLA5*, May 2, 2019. https://ktla.com/news/local-news/wildlife-officials-say-griffith-parks-lone-mountain-lion-p-22-is-doing-well-after-health-check/.

Salazar, Alan. "About Alan Salazar." *My Native Stories*. Accessed June 11, 2020. https://www.mynativestories.com/bio.html.

———. *Tata the Tataviam Towhee: A Tribal Story*. Ventura, CA: Sunsprite Publishing, 2020.

———. "Who Are the Chumash?" Accessed January 27, 2021. https://alansalazar.tripod.com/.

The Santa Barbara Botanic Garden. "Mission Dam and Aqueduct." 2020. Accessed December 18, 2020. https://www.sbbg.org/explore-garden/garden-features/mission-waterworks.

Save Open Space, Santa Monica Mountains (SOS). "NASA Announces Decision to Demolish the Coca Test Stands." 2020. Accessed June 6, 2020. http://saveopenspace.com/current-projects/santa-susana-field-laboratory/.

Seegert, Natasha. "Play of Sniffication: Coyotes Sing in the Margins." *Philosophy & Rhetoric* 47, no. 2 (2014): 158–78.

Shain, Susan. "Got Climate Anxiety? These People Are Doing Something about It." *The New York Times*, February 4, 2021. https://www.nytimes.com/2021/02/04/climate/climate-anxiety-stress.html?.

Shatkin, Elina. "What Happened at the Santa Susana Nuclear Site during the Woolsey Fire?" *LAist*, November 13, 2018. https://laist.com/2018/11/13/santa_susana_nuclear_site_woolsey_fire.php.

Shojai, Amy. "Why Cats Blink Their Eyes at You." *The Spruce Pets*, November 6, 2019. https://www.thesprucepets.com/cat-eye-blinks-553911.

Solis, Nathan. "Residents Blast Plan to Clean Up Cold War-Era Testing Site near LA." *Courthouse News Service*, December 18, 2018. https://www.courthousenews.com/residents-blast-plan-to-clean-up-cold-war-era-testing-site-near-la/.

Solly, Meilan. "California Will Build the Largest Wildlife Crossing in the World." *Smithsonian.com*, August 21, 2019. https://www.smithsonianmag.com/smart-news/california-will-build-largest-wildlife-crossing-world-180972947/?utm_source=facebook.com&utm_medium=socialmedia&fbclid=IwAR33rOdutsS3-vG2xSn5bErMsYirW3froJhp1dJ2HF_BtclY6ACEf__mkNg.

Staff Writer. "Klondike and Taylor Creek Fire Miles from Agness." *The Wild Coast Compass*, August 20, 2018. https://www.wildcoastcompass.com/klondike-and-taylor-creek-fire-miles-from-agness/.

State of Vermont. "Steeped in History, Embracing Change." Accessed July 2, 2020. https://www.vermontvacation.com/towns-and-regions/historic-downtowns/bellows-falls.

Stevens, Clark. "The New West: Re-Engagement with the Land, Cultural and Ecological Conservation at the Urban Interface." *Clark Stevens / Architect: New West Land Company: Writings*. Accessed June 9, 2020. https://www.clarkstevens.com/writing-by-clark.

Stewart, Scott. "Bellevue to Rebuild Haworth Park Campground." *The Daily Record*, September 10, 2020. https://omahadailyrecord.com/content/bellevue-rebuild-haworth-park-campground.

Stowe Land Trust. "Putting the Shutesville Hill Wildlife Corridor on the Map." *Stowe Land Trust*, December 22, 2017. https://www.stowelandtrust.org/news/detail/news/putting-the-shutesville-hill-wildlife-corridor-on-the-map/.

Tapper, Ethan. "Into the Woods: American Beech Profile." *The Charlotte News: Vermont's Oldest Nonprofit Newspaper since 1958,* February 7, 2018. https://www.charlottenewsvt.org/2018/02/07/woods-american-beech-profile/.

Taylor, Alan. "In Photos: Deadly Floods Sweep the Midwest." *The Atlantic,* March 18, 2019. https://www.theatlantic.com/photo/2019/03/nebraska-flood-photos/585169/.

Taylor, Matthew, and Jessica Murray. "'Overwhelming and Terrifying': The Rise of Climate Anxiety." *The Guardian,* February 10, 2020. https://www.theguardian.com/environment/2020/feb/10/overwhelming-and-terrifying-impact-of-climate-crisis-on-mental-health.

Taylor, Phil. "Ardern Disputes Greta Thunberg's Criticism of New Zealand Climate Policy." *The Guardian,* December 14, 2020. https://www.theguardian.com/world/2020/dec/14/ardern-disputes-greta-thunbergs-criticism-new-zealand-climate-policy.

Therrien, Jim. "Long-Awaited Deerfield Wind Turbines Go Online." *VTDigger,* December 30, 2017. https://vtdigger.org/2017/12/30/long-awaited-deerfield-wind-turbines-go-online/.

Tonino, Leath. "Two Ways of Knowing: Robin Wall Kimmerer on Scientific and Native American Views of the Natural World." *The Sun,* April 2016. https://www.thesunmagazine.org/issues/484/two-ways-of-knowing.

UC Santa Barbara Cheadle Center for Biodiversity and Ecological Restoration. "Lagoon Island & Campus Point." Accessed May 3, 2020. https://www.ccber.ucsb.edu/ecosystem/management-areas-campus-lagoon/lagoon-island-campus-point.

UC Santa Barbara Department of Recreation. "UCSB and Isla Vista Walking Tour." Accessed May 2, 2020. https://web.archive.org/web/20131221213110/http://recreation.sa.ucsb.edu/walk/pdf/walkucsb.pdf.

University of California Natural Reserve System, UCSB. "Welcome to Coal Oil Point Reserve." Accessed May 3, 2020. https://copr.nrs.ucsb.edu/welcome-coal-oil-point-reserve.

Urness, Zach. "Klondike and Taylor Creek Fires Grow Together, but Progress Allows Improved Rogue River Access." *Statesman Journal,* August 21, 2018. https://www.statesmanjournal.com/story/news/2018/08/21/klondike-fire-taylor-creek-fire-southern-oregon-grants-pass-selma-rogue-river-illinois-valley/1050197002/.

———. "Klondike Fire Grows to 100,000 Acres, Becomes Oregon's Second Megafire in Two Years." *Statesman Journal,* August 30, 2018. https://www.statesmanjournal.com/story/news/2018/08/30/oregon-wildfires-klondike-fire-southern-oregon-taylor-creek-fire-grants-pass/1144228002/.

USDA-Forest Service, Green Mountain National Forest. Final Environmental Impact Statement: Proposed Deerfield Wind Project. Manchester, Vermont, 2011. Accessed January 2, 2021. http://a123.g.akamai.net/7/123/11558/abc123/forestservic.download.akamai.com/11558/www/nepa/9046_FSPLT2_071032.pdf.

US Department of the Interior, Bureau of Land Management. "Cascade-Siskiyou National Monument." Accessed March 5, 2020. https://www.blm.gov/programs/national-conservation-lands/national-monuments/oregon-washington/cascade-siskiyou.

@UtahDWR. "We're excited to see #wildlife using the new Parleys Summit overpass!" Twitter, June 20, 2019. https://twitter.com/UtahDWR/status/1141716080206868480.

Van Dooren, Thom. *Flight Ways: Life and Loss at the Edge of Extinction.* New York: Columbia University Press, 2014.

Vaughan, Adam. "Young People Can't Remember How Much More Wildlife There Used to Be." *NewScientist,* December 11, 2019. https://www.newscientist.com/article/2226898-young-people-cant-remember-how-much-more-wildlife-there-used-to-be/#ixzz6ed6p2Abr.

Vermont Fish and Wildlife Department. "Bear Den Visit: March 16, 2020." YouTube video, March 30, 2020. https://www.youtube.com/watch?time_continue=11&v=dazwiv5NwGE&feature=emb_title.

————. "Black Bears." Accessed July 15, 2020. https://vtfishandwildlife.com/learn-more/vermont-critters/mammals/black-bear.

————. "Deerfield Wind Black Bear Study." Accessed August 26, 2020. https://vtfishandwildlife.com/conserve/deerfield-wind-bear-study.

Walker, Melody. "The Mountains through a Different Cultural Lens: An Abenaki Perspective." *Long Trail News,* October 10, 2019. https://www.greenmountainclub.org/the-mountains-through-a-different-cultural-lens-an-abenaki-perspective/.

Wapotich, James. "Trail Quest: Orpet and Franceschi Parks." *Songs of the Wilderness,* July 21, 2014. https://songsofthewilderness.com/2014/07/21/trail-quest-orpet-and-franceschi-parks/.

Warfield, Kristen. "Woman Comes Home and Finds Stranger Getting Cozy on Her Couch: She Couldn't Believe Who It Was." *The Dodo,* July 17, 2018. https://www.thedodo.com/in-the-wild/mountain-lion-home-intruder.

Weiss, Joseph. "Who Gets to Have Ecoanxiety?" Edge Effects: Center for Culture, History, and Environment: University of Wisconsin, Madison, October 12, 2019. https://edgeeffects.net/who-gets-to-have-ecoanxiety/.

Weiss-Tisman, Howard. "After Agreement over Bear Habitat, Deerfield Wind Project Will Move Forward." *Vermont Public Radio,* August 11, 2016. https://www.vpr.org/post/after-agreement-over-bear-habitat-deerfield-wind-project-will-move-forward#stream/0.

Wohlleben, Peter. *The Hidden Life of Trees: What They Feel, How They Communicate—Discoveries from a Secret World.* Vancouver: Greystone Books, 2016.

Wolfe, Cary. *What Is Posthumanism?* Minneapolis: University of Minnesota Press, 2010.

Wood, Frances. "Jay's Whisper Song." BirdNote, 2021. https://www.birdnote.org/listen/shows/jays-whisper-song.

Wright, Sarah. "More-than-Human, Emergent Belongings: A Weak Theory Approach." *Progress in Human Geography* 39 (2015): 391–411.

Yeh, James. "Robin Wall Kimmerer: 'People Can't Understand the World as a Gift unless Someone Shows Them How.'" *The Guardian,* May 23, 2020. https://www.theguardian.com/books/2020/may/23/robin-wall-kimmerer-people-cant-understand-the-world-as-a-gift-unless-someone-shows-them-how.

Yin, Steph. "Drumming Cockatoos and the Rhythms of Love." *The New York Times,* June 28, 2017. https://www.nytimes.com/2017/06/28/science/drumming-palm-cockatoos.html?hpw&rref=science&action=click&pgtype=Homepage&module=well-region&region=bottom-well&WT.nav=bottom-well.

Zertuche, Hayley. "Animal Representations in Visual Culture: An Overview and a Haunting." *Trace: Journal of Writing, Media, and Ecology* 1 (April 17, 2017). http://tracejournal.net/trace-issues/issue1/06-zertuche.html.

Zielinski, Sarah. "What Do Wild Animals Do in a Wildfire?" *National Geographic,* July 22, 2014. https://www.nationalgeographic.com/news/2014/7/140721-animals-wildlife-wildfires-nation-forests-science/#close.

ZSL Institute of Zoology. "Lizzie Jones." Zoological Society of London, 2020. Accessed November 23, 2020. https://www.zsl.org/science/users/lizzie-jones.

# INDEX

Abenaki people, 19–20, 133–34, 177n68

Abram, David, 161n3

abundance, gift of, 108–10, 125–26, 135, 158–59

acclimatization, 11–12, 14. *See also* human infrastructure and development

aggregate good, 137

Agnew, John, 171n36

Agoura Hills region (California), 97

Alaimo, Stacy, 33–34

albatrosses, 33–35

Albrecht, Glenn, 75–76

altruism, 42, 127

American beech trees: about, 122–23; bear-storied, 122–26, 144; in environmental meshworks, 142–43; ethical considerations, 131–32, 136–41, 143–46; Honorable Harvest of, 126–32, 141, 145–46

American Psychiatric Association, 79

animacy. *See* language of animacy

Animal Medical Center of New York, 31

animal rhetorics, 21

"Animal That Therefore I Am, The" (Derrida), 8–9

animic ontology, 37

Anishinaabe story of Original Man, 65

Anthropause animal behavior, 111–19; adaptations and readaptations during, 114–18; defined, 112; and gift mindset, 118–19, 160; and human mobility reduction, 111–15

Anthropocene, defined, 7–8

anthropocentric mindset: and acclimatization, 11–12; alternative approaches, 5–6, 24, 39, 76 (*see also* culture of reciprocity; entangled empathy; gift mindset; language of animacy; posthumanism); defined, 22; on environmental projects, 135–38; and fear mindset, 60–61, 67–69; on human development, 133–34; on wildlife and wilderness, 7–8

anthropomorphization (projections): of bear home range sizes, 130–31; of companion animals, 9, 40–41; in wildlife campaigns, 88–90, 109–10; in wildlife rehabilitation, 40–42

arrowhead, 153–54

Ashland (Oregon), 48

Avangrid Renewables, 133, 138

Barad, Karen, 165n27

basin metate (millingstone), 15–16

bears. *See* black bears

beech trees and beechnuts. *See* American beech trees

*Being Alive* (Ingold), 166n33

Bekoff, Marc, 40, 126, 129, 131, 135

Bellows Falls (Vermont), 114–15

belonging: and body in place, 80–81; defined, 5, 19–20; and entangled empathy, 37, 54–55, 145; expressions of belonging, 14–16, 133–34; and language of animacy, 109, 118; lost sites of, 98–102; and wildlife rehabilitation, 30, 37–38

Bennett, Jane, 89, 109–10

Berry, Thomas, 4

big kin. *See* black bear habitat; black bears

biodiversity conservation, 21, 94, 110, 158

bird air sacs, 31–32, 35

bird migration, 18–19, 81

bird rehabilitation. *See* wildlife rehabilitation

bird songs: as communication, 2–5, 10, 81–82; as drumming ritual, 56–57; as gifts, 2–3, 5–6, 82, 85, 159–60; whisper songs, 81–82, 85

black bear habitat: conservation biology goals, 132–35; as contextually specific, 139–40; ecofeminist environmentalism on sustainability, 140–41, 144, 146; and entangled empathy, 125–26, 141–46; trade-offs for sustainability, 135–38

black bears: beechnut Honorable Harvest, 126–32, 141, 145–46; beech tree scarring by, 123–26, 144; communication and social behaviors, 126–27; ethical considerations, 131–32, 136–41, 143–46; food sources, 122–23, 127–31; habitat overview, 120–22; "nuisance" or "problem" behaviors, 115–16, 118–19

blowdown, 120–21

bobcats, 70–71

"body as knower," 3–4, 10

body-place collaboration, 3–4, 80–81

Boeing-Rocketdyne, 98–99, 100, 101

bomb cyclone, 83–84

boundaries, human-animal binary, 8, 10, 89–91

Boyle, Casey, 4, 23

*Braiding Sweetgrass* (Kimmerer), 47, 120

Bratta, Phil, 13

Bruns, Gerald L., 9

Burro Flats Painted Cave (ancient Chumash site), 98–99, 100–102

Byrne, David, 56

California Department of Fish and Wildlife (CDFW), 61, 63–70, 72–73, 86, 170n87, 173n47

California Department of Transportation, 96–97

California State Coastal Conservancy, 96–97

California Wildlife Conservation Board, 96

camera traps, 139, 178n92

Campus Point Beach (Santa Barbara), 61, 62, 70

Cascade-Siskiyou National Monument (CSNM), 48

cats (domesticated), 9, 40–41, 53, 168n16

cedar waxwings, 159–60

children: curiosity of, 149, 151–55, 159–60; and elemental relationships, 151–52; entangled empathy of, 149, 150–51, 155, 159–60. *See also* modeling and knowledge-sharing

Chumash people, 13, 14–16, 62, 68, 98–102, 163n53, 174n101

Clary-Lemon, Jennifer, 9, 52, 59

Clifford, James, 4

climate anxiety, 75–85; as contextual, 81–85; defined, 76–77; gift mindset for, 79–85; and narratives, 76–81; psychoanalytic approach to, 171n24; roots of, 77–78; and sense of place, 17–19, 21, 75–76; and solastalgia, 75–76, 79

Coal Oil Point Reserve (Santa Barbara), 68

Coca Test Stand Areas (Santa Susana Field Lab site), 99–100

Cohen, Jeffrey Jerome: on elemental relations, 24, 29, 36, 37, 45, 166n27; on narratives, 45; on nature, 7; on storied stone, 151, 154, 155

colonialism, 12–16, 52, 59, 77–78

Comeau, Jaclyn, 121, 130–31, 133, 139

communal generosity, 125–26, 144

communication, 2–3, 9. *See also* bird songs; entangled empathy; gift mindset; storytelling and narratives; *and specific types of languages*

community of sovereign beings, 9, 52, 94–95, 107

companion animals, 9, 40–41, 53

compassionate conservation: and ecofeminism, 141; and environmental meshworks, 131; on field data collection of black bears, 128; on habitat interchangeability, 138, 139–40; and human perception, 69; posthumanism comparison, 39; on rewilding projects, 129, 131; on sustainable energy projects, 136–37; on wildlife rehabilitation, 29, 30–35, 38–40, 42–43

connection and connectivity: of belonging, 80–81, 82; of ecosystems, 9, 125–26 (*see also* environmental meshworks); of entangled empathy, 32–33 (*see also* entangled empathy); as ethical obligation, 25 (*see also* connectivity projects; culture of reciprocity); gift of, 21, 26; and home, 10, 17–21, 23; Indigenous worldview on, 94–95; and sense of place, 3–4, 10; and Shifting Base-line Syndrome, 157–58

connectivity projects: background, 23, 25, 91; and culture of reciprocity, 89, 93–96, 104–5, 108–10, 174n109; examples of, 95–98, 105–8; paradox and promise of, 96–98; storytelling and narratives for, 95, 96–98, 101, 104–6, 108–10

conservation biology, 129

COVID-19 Bio-Logging Initiative, 112–13, 118

COVID-19 pandemic. *See* pandemic

coyotes, 20–21, 111–12

creation stories, 65, 102–4

Creswell, Tim, 3, 171n36

Cronon, William, 91

CSNM (Cascade-Siskiyou National Monument), 48

culture of gratitude, 29–30, 38, 49, 104–5. *See also* gift mindset

culture of reciprocity: Anthropause lessons on, 111–12, 116, 118–19; for black bears, 25–26, 123–26, 127, 143–46; connectivity projects as, 89, 93–96, 104–5, 108–10, 174n109; and entangled empathy, 58–61;

and environmental meshworks, 124–26, 131–35, 145; ethical responsibilities, 131–32, 143–44; and gift mindset, 6, 13, 16, 21, 23–26, 93, 108–10; and home, 58; Indigenous worldview on, 94–95; for mountain lions, 93; and wildlife rehabilitation, 29, 30

Davis, John, 122

Deerfield Wind Black Bear Study: about, 121–22, 133; on habitat connectivity, 132–35; for monitoring DWEP's impact, 139–40, 143; for monitoring Stark, 120–22, 127–32

Deerfield Wind Energy Project (DWEP): about, 122, 132–33; ethical considerations, 131–32, 136–41, 143–46; and habitat connectivity, 132–35, 143–44, 177n68; monitoring impact through bear study, 139–40, 143

deforestation, 76, 144

Delgado, Mikel, 168n28

Derrida, Jacques, 8–9

Devereux Lagoon (Slough) in Santa Barbara, 67–68

displacements. *See* fire displacements; urban ecologies

dolphins, 103

domesticated cats, 9, 40–41, 53, 168n16

drumming, 55, 56–57, 72–73, 170n83

dwelling place, 43–44. *See also* home

DWEP. *See* Deerfield Wind Energy Project

earthly gifts, natural resources as, 12, 18, 48, 57–58, 69, 134, 144

"earth others," 141–46, 166n27

Eastern jays, 81–82, 85

ecodistress, 79. *See also* climate anxiety

ecofeminism, 10, 136, 140–41, 144–46

ecology: as study of home, 19

elemental relationships: and children, 151–52; in environmental meshworks, 24, 29–30, 36–38, 44–45; posthuman perspective of, 43–44; in wildlife rehabilitation, 29–30, 34, 35–38, 43–45, 165–66n27

Elnu Abenaki Band of Ndakinna, 19–20, 133–34

Endangered Species Act (California), 170n87

entangled empathy: as anthropocentric mindset alternative, 6; of black bears and beech trees, 125–26, 141–46; of children, 149, 150–51, 155, 159–60; conservation approaches informed by, 87–90, 131; defined, 6, 9, 32–33, 54, 59–60, 74; and gift mindset, 2, 6, 12, 60, 159–60; Indigenous worldview on, 52, 59; and intervention conundrum, 40–42; language of animacy for, 54–57, 59–60, 72–74; modeling, 149, 159–60; for mountain lions (fire-lost), 51–54, 57, 72–73; for mountain lions (urban), 25, 88–90, 91–93, 109–10; wildlife rehabilitation informed by, 20, 32–33, 35–36, 37, 165–66n27

environmental melancholia, 79. *See also* climate anxiety

environmental meshworks: among black bears and beech trees, 125, 144; and culture of reciprocity, 124–26, 131–35, 145; defined, 9, 163n38; of "earth others," 142–43; ecofeminism on, 141; and field studies, 128; and fire displacements, 51–54; Indigenous worldview of, 9, 52, 141; of wildlife rehabilitation work, 24, 29–30, 36–38, 44–45

Environmental Protection Agency, 98–99

ethnography, body in place and, 3–4

feminist geography, 10, 19, 142–43, 161n3

Ferdandiño Tataviam Band of Mission Indians, 102

fire displacements: fire-lost, defined, 50, 168n16; megafires, 47–48, 50; Oregon mountain lion encounter, 24–25, 50–55, 57–59, 66–67, 71–73, 108, 168n17, 168–69n37; UCSB mountain lion sightings, 25, 60–71, 73–74; wildlife responses, 49–50

flight ways, 57, 58. *See also* language of animacy

fossils, 153–54, 159–60

fragmented habitats and lands, 86–110; connectivity projects' promise and paradox, 96–98 (*see also* connectivity projects); of Griffith Park mountain lion, 25, 86–96, 105, 109–10, 172n1, 172n5 (*see also* P-22); lost sites of belonging, 98–102; narratives on, 102–5, 106–8; place-making in, 90–96; public campaigns highlighting, 87–90, 91, 93, 99–100

Franceschi, Francesco, 11, 12, 14, 163n43

Franceschi Park (Santa Barbara), 11–16, 17, 20–22, 111–12, 163nn43–45

generational teaching. *See* modeling and knowledge-sharing

gift mindset: of abundance, 108–10, 125–26, 135, 158–59; and Anthropause, 118–19, 160; as anthropocentric mindset alternative, 5–6; background, 1–6, 12–16, 18; for climate anxiety, 79–85; and culture of gratitude, 29–30, 38, 49, 104–5; and entangled empathy, 2, 6, 12, 60, 159–60; for habitat sustainability and connection, 104–10, 134–35; for language of place, 13, 49; philosophical animism comparison, 143; and reciprocity, 6, 13, 16, 21, 23–26, 93, 108–10; for wildlife encounters, 51–54, 60, 63–67, 69, 72–74, 109

"given-new strategy" of place, 80, 171n29

Gjessing, Catherine, 138

grammar of animacy. *See* language of animacy

Grants Pass (Oregon), 48

great-horned owl, 156–58

Green Mountain National Forest (Vermont), 25, 120–24, 136–41, 143–46

Green Mountain Power, 133

Griffith Park (Los Angeles), 86–92, 109–10

Gruen, Lori (general): on anthropomorphism and projection, 40–42; on gift mindset, 18, 23; on language of animacy, 54, 59; and posthumanism, 8; on storied empathy, 146, 155; on wildlife encounters, 25

Gruen, Lori, on entangled empathy: and belonging, 54; definition, 6, 32–33, 74; of "earth others," 141–42; and elemental relationships, 35–36, 37, 165–66n27; of the encounter, 59–60; introduction of, 2; as source of hope, 131, 145; sympathy comparison, 32–33. *See also* entangled empathy

habitat sustainability, 120–46; bear habitat overview, 120–22; and bear-storied trees, 122–26, 144; connectivity projects for, 93–98, 104–10; conservation biology goals for, 132–35; conservation biology trade-offs, 135–38; as contextually specific, 139–40; ecofeminist environmentalism on, 140–41; entangled empathy and "earth others," 141–46; Honorable Harvest for, 126–32, 141, 145–46. *See also* fragmented habitats and lands

habituation, 42, 115–16, 118–19

Hammond, Forrest, 115, 121, 130, 139

Haraway, Donna, 9, 29, 77, 101

Harris, Leila, 161n3

Hawk, Byron, 56

Haworth Park (Bellevue, Nebraska), 82–84, 85

Hazen, Helen, 161n3

Heidegger, Martin, 43, 167n55

*Hidden Life of Trees, The* (Wohlleben), 125

highways: and wildlife crossings, 86–87, 88, 95–97, 105–6

H. J. Andrews Experimental Forest (Oregon), 18, 81

home: acclimatization effects, 11–12, 14 (*see also* human infrastructure and development); anxiety about climate change, 17–19, 21, 75–85 (*see also* climate anxiety); celebrating gift of, 1–6, 12–16, 18, 21, 23–26, 147–60 (*see also* culture of reciprocity; gift mindset; modeling and knowledge-sharing); connectivity to and from, 20–21, 25–26, 86–110, 120–46 (*see also* fragmented habitats and lands; habitat sustainability); definitions and contextualization of, 10, 16–26, 27–46, 54–55, 71–74, 167n55 (*see also* sense of place; storied places; storytelling and narratives; wildlife rehabilitation); language of, 3–6, 10, 12–16, 22–24 (*see also* language of animacy; language of place); in nature and with wildlife, 2, 6–9, 24–26, 47–74 (*see also* entangled empathy; environmental meshworks; fire displacements; Indigenous worldview; posthumanism); during pandemic, 22, 26, 111–19 (*see also* Anthropause animal behavior; pandemic)

home ranges: of black bears, 120–22, 127, 130–32, 135, 143–46; culture of reciprocity for sustainability of, 25–26, 123–26, 127, 143–46; fire's impact on, 48, 72; human infrastructure's impact on, 92, 111–12, 131–32, 135–40; of mountain lions, 48, 72, 87, 92

Honorable Harvest, 126–32, 141, 145–46

*How Music Works* (Byrne), 56

human infrastructure and development: acclimatization effects, 11–12, 14; Anthropause lessons for informing, 112–15; ethical considerations and obligations, 2, 17–19, 25–26, 52, 92–97; gift mindset for directing, 6, 12, 23, 60, 104–10; organized retreat from, 84; sustainable energy project paradox, 25–26 (*see also* sustainable energy projects)

Iberdrola, 133

Illinois geology, 152–53

Illinois trip. *See* modeling and knowledge-sharing

Indian pictographs, 100–101

Indigenous worldview: about, 9; on connectivity and reciprocity, 94–95; on conservation and restoration, 107; and ecofeminism, 141; of ecosystems, 52, 89; on entangled empathy, 52, 59; Honorable Harvest, 126–32, 141, 145–46; on human development, 133–34, 145; on language of animacy, 74; on people as youngest of all species, 65; and posthumanism, 9; utilitarianism comparison, 136–37

Ingold, Tim: on animic ontology, 36–37; on environmental meshworks, 9, 24, 29, 51, 163n38, 166n27; on home, 43–44, 167n55

injured birds. *See* wildlife rehabilitation

interconnections. *See* connection and connectivity; connectivity projects

internatural communication, 4–5, 51, 119, 134

intervention conundrum: of field studies, 129, 131–32; of wildlife rehabilitation, 29, 38–44

Jensen, Tim, 19

Jones, Lizzie, 158

Jordan, Chris, 33–35

junco, 28–29

Kalamazoo Nature Center (Michigan), 117

"Keep Me Wild" campaign, 72

Kennedy, George, 126

Kilham, Ben, 42, 122–23, 126–27

Kimmerer, Robin Wall: on connectivity and reciprocity, 93, 94–95, 104–5; on earthly gifts, 12, 18, 48, 57–58, 69, 144; on ecological restoration, 105, 107–8; entangled empathy modeling by, 159; gift mindset of, 2, 23, 24, 93, 125; on gratitude, 24, 29–30; on home through language of place, 49, 54, 69, 72, 74, 109, 110; on Honorable Harvest, 126; on human perception, 69; on Indigenous worldview, 9, 52, 65, 89, 94, 107, 134; on language of animacy, 5–6, 51–52, 53, 54, 59, 109; on mast fruiting, 124–26; and posthumanism, 8; on wildlife encounters, 25

Klondike Fire, 47–48, 50

knowledge sharing. *See* modeling and knowledge-sharing

Koziatek, Ryan, 117, 118

Krupp, Edwin, 100

Lagoon Island (California), 61–62

language of animacy: Anthropause lessons on, 112, 118; as anthropocentric mindset alternative, 5–6; anthropomorphization and projection comparison, 41; CDFW recommendations on, 63–67; for climate anxiety, 92–95; defined, 5–6, 51; drumming as, 55, 56–57, 72–73, 170n83; entangled empathy fostering with, 54–57, 59–60, 72–74; and environmental meshworks, 9; and gift mindset, 12; modeling of, 5–6, 23, 51–55, 59, 109, 160; openness to, 125, 149; philosophical animism comparison, 143

language of place: background, 12–16; defined, 3–6, 23–24; gift mindset for, 13, 49; home defined through, 49, 54, 69, 71–74, 109, 110; through languages of more-than-human kin, 4–5; for urban ecologies, 71–74

Lavanderia, 14

Lertzman, Renee, 79, 171n24

lesser goldfinches, 18–19

Liberty Canyon wildlife corridor (California): background, 25; fundraising for, 96–97; and Land relationships, 98–99, 101–2; narrative lens for contextualizing, 95, 96–98, 101, 104–5, 108–10; physical description, 95–96, 97–98; promise and paradox of, 96–98; as reciprocity, 93–94, 104–5, 108–10, 174n109

Limuw island (Santa Cruz Island), 102–3

Loder, Reed Elizabeth: on habitat interchangeability, 139; on sustainable energy projects, 136, 137–38, 140–41

Lorimer, Jamie: on connectivity and conservation, 93–94; on nature, 8; on wildlife's place in post-Natural world, 8, 90–91, 92

lost sites of belonging, 98–102

Lower Franceschi Park (Santa Barbara), 12–13, 17, 20–22

Massey, Doreen, 10

mast fruiting, 124–26, 141

McHugh, Susan, 22, 57

McKibben, Bill, 122

megafires, 47–48, 50

Midway Island (Hawaii), 33–35

millingstone (metate), 15–16

mockingbirds, 30–35, 40, 42–43, 44–45

modeling and knowledge-sharing, 147–60; background, 26, 147–49; creation stories, 102–4; of entangled empathy, 149, 159–60; of language of animacy, 5–6, 24, 51–55, 59, 109, 160; owl pellet example, 156–57; of reciprocal altruism, 146; and Shifting Base-line Syndrome, 157–58; of storied empathy, 146, 154–55; storied stones example, 149–54

"Montarioso" (Franceschi mansion), 11

more-than-human kin, defined, 2–3, 4–6, 161–62n3

mountain lions: and Endangered Species Act, 170n87; of Griffith Park, 25, 86–96, 105, 109–10, 172n1, 172n5 (*see also* P-22); Oregon homeowner's encounter with, 24–25, 50–55, 57–59, 66–67, 71–73, 108, 168n17, 168–69n37; UCSB sightings, 25, 60–71, 73–74

music and drumming, 55, 56–57, 72–73, 170n83

NASA (National Aeronautics and Space Administration), 99–100

National Park Service (NPS), 95–96

National Wildlife Federation, 87–88

National Wildlife Rehabilitators Association, 38

natural resources: as earthly gifts, 12, 18, 48, 57–58, 69, 134, 144

nature, at home in, 6–9

Ndakinna, 19–20, 133–34

nonverbal communication. *See* bird songs; drumming; language of animacy

off-site mitigation, 138

*oikos*, 17, 19, 71

Omaha (author's temporary residence), 80–85, 147

Oregon megafire, 47–48, 50

Oregon mountain lion encounter, 24–25, 50–55, 57–59, 66–67, 71–73, 108, 168n17, 168–69n37

Original Man, story of, 65

owl pellet, 156–57

P-12 (mountain lion), 96

P-22 (mountain lion): background, 25, 172n1; challenges faced by, 87, 172n5; entangled empathy for, 25, 88–90, 91–93, 109–10; fragmented habitat of, 25, 86–88, 93, 95, 97, 109; place-making by, 90–96, 105

P-36 (mountain lion), 96

P-37 (mountain lion), 96

P-65 (mountain lion), 95, 97

Packham, Chris, 158

palm cockatoo, 56–57

pandemic: as cultural moment, 1, 22; gift mindset on, 118–19, 160; and solastalgia, 75–76; travel affected by, 22, 26, 147–48; and wildlife, 111–19 (*see also* Anthropause animal behavior)

Parleys Summit wildlife crossing (Utah), 105–8

Pauly, Daniel, 158

pets. *See* companion animals

philosophical animism, 143

place-making. *See* body-place collaboration; language of place; sense of place; storied places

plastic: and albatrosses, 34–35; used in wildlife rehabilitation, 33, 34, 38, 165n22

Plec, Emily: on culture of reciprocity, 144; on internatural communication, 5, 51, 134; on solastalgia, 76

Plumwood, Val, 7, 141, 142–43, 166n27

posthumanism: on coexistence, 8–9, 90–91; compassionate conservation comparison, 39; on data collection and field monitoring, 131–32; defined, 8; on habitat connectivity, 25, 107–8, 144–45; and Indigenous worldview, 9, 52; and meshworks, 9; on nature and wildlife encounters, 8–9, 51–54, 65; on sustain-

able energy projects, 136–37; on urban habitats, 71–74; on wildlife rehabilitation, 39–40, 42–44

Potawatomi people, 5–6

Powell, Malea, 13

power of unity among trees, 124–25

Pratt, Beth: on connectivity and conservation, 21, 91; on human adaptation, 118; on Liberty Canyon wildlife corridor, 97, 101–2; on public empathy for P-22, 87–88, 89, 109; on wildlife's place in post-Natural world, 90, 91

predator-satiation hypothesis, 124–25

"Presence and Absence in the Watershed" (Plec), 76

projections. *See* anthropomorphization

Rainbow Bridge story, 102–4, 163n53, 174n101

Readsboro turbines (Vermont), 132–33

reciprocity. *See* culture of reciprocity

relocation of wildlife, 173n47

renewable energy. *See* sustainable energy projects

*Rethinking Maps* (Harris & Hazen), 161n3

rewilding projects, 129, 131, 135

Rice, Jenny, 4, 23

Riley, Seth, 96

*Rising: Dispatches from the New American Shore* (Rush), 18

Ritvo, Harriet, 11–12

Romani, John, 100

Rose, Deborah Bird, 143

Rush, Elizabeth: on climate change, 18, 76, 79, 84; on empathetic practice, 73; on home, 81; on internatural communication, 4

salamanders, 94–95

Salazar, Alan, 102–4, 163n53, 174n101

Santa Barbara Airport, 68

Santa Barbara foothills: and Chumash, 13–16, 102–4; and climate anxiety, 79–81; Franceschi Park, 11–16, 17, 20–22, 111–12; hikes through, 1–12, 16–22, 111–12; UCSB mountain lion sightings, 25, 60–71, 73–74

Santa Barbara Museum of Natural History, 15

Santa Cruz Island (Santa Barbara County), 102–3

Santa Monica Mountains, 88, 95–97, 99

Santa Monica Mountains Fund, 88

Santa Susana Field Lab, 98–99, 100, 101

Santa Ynez Band of Chumash Indians, 99–102

#SaveLACougars campaign, 87–90, 91, 93

Save Open Space (SOS), 99–100

Save People Save Wildlife, 106

scat, 20

Schaller, Shannon, 117, 118

Searsburg turbines (Vermont), 132–33

Seegert, Natasha, 20, 21, 41, 54

selfies with P-22 likeness, 88–89

sense of place: through body in a place, 3–4, 23; for climate change and anxiety, 17–19, 21, 75–76; defined, 10; through feminist geography, 10, 19, 142–43; through gratitude and curiosity, 58, 80–81, 171n29; home defined through, 17; as knowledge of species and landscape, 17; through song birds, 3, 4–5, 10; through storytelling, 19–20

Shifting Base-line Syndrome (SBS), 157–58

Simi Hills habitat, 95, 97

Simpson, Leanne Betasamosake, 77

"slow-blinking," 53–54, 72, 168n28

solastalgia, 75–76, 79

song birds. See bird songs

sovereign beings, community of, 9, 52, 94–95, 107

space, gift of, 66, 69, 72, 109

Spell of the Sensuous, The (Abram), 161n3

Stark (black bear): ethical considerations for, 131–32, 137, 139, 143–46; monitoring of, 120–22, 127–32

Stevens, Clark, 96, 97–98

stone (storied), 15–16, 149–55

storied empathy, 146, 154–55

storied places: of black bears, 120, 123–26, 144–45; connectivity projects as, 95, 96–98, 101, 104–5, 108–10; defined, 21–22; and "earth others," 142–43; of Indigenous people, 11–12, 98–99, 101–4, 134; of mountain lions (fire-lost), 57; of mountain lions (urban), 92, 105; sharing with future generations, 151–52, 160; and stone, 15–16, 149–55

storied stone, 15–16, 149–55

storytelling and narratives: through body in a place, 23; and climate anxiety, 76–81; connection and connectivity through, 19–20; for connectivity projects, 95, 96–98, 101, 104–5, 108–10; for conservation campaigns, 91–92, 102–4, 109–10; of fragmented habitats and lands, 102–5, 106–8; as part of environment meshworks, 44–46; for reconciling dissonance, 13–16; storied empathy, 146; in wildlife rehabilitation, 44–45. See also modeling and knowledge-sharing

sustainable energy projects: background, 25–26, 122; and environmental meshworks, 131–32; ethical considerations, 131–32, 136–41, 143–46; and habitat connectivity, 132–35, 143–44

Sweet, Samuel, 69

Sylvan Park (Santa Barbara), 10

Taddei, David, 115, 116, 117

Talopop, 99

Tataviam people, 102

Taylor Creek Fire, 47–48, 50

technoscience, 34–35, 38, 101. See also sustainable energy projects

Thomas Fire, 47, 62, 168n16

Thunberg, Greta, 78

Tiptip (Lagoon Island), 61–62

traditional ecological knowledge, 104, 110

transcorporeality, 7, 33–34, 37

trees, collective action of, 124–25

turtle doves, 158

Turtle Island story of Original Man, 65

Uexküll, Jakob von, 37, 163n38

Uksholo, 68

Umwelt theory, 37, 163n38, 166n33

University of California Natural Reserve System, 68

University of California Santa Barbara (UCSB) mountain lion sightings, 25, 60–71, 73–74

urban conservation, 90–96

urban ecologies: during Anthropause, 112, 113–15, 117–18; for bobcats, 70–71; community messaging on dangers in, 62–69, 72; as fragmented habitats, 86–89, 93, 95, 97, 109; language of place for, 71–74; and matter of perception, 60–62, 69–71; place-making in, 90–96, 105; UCSB mountain lion sightings, 25, 60–71, 73–74. *See also* connectivity projects

Urban Wildlife Week, 88

US Fish and Wildlife Service, 50

US Forest Service, 121

Utah Department of Transportation (UDOT), 106

Utah Division of Wildlife Resources, 106

utilitarianism, 136–38

Van Dooren, Thom, 10, 21–22, 57, 92, 105

Van Susteren, Lise, 79

Vermonters for a Clean Environment, 133, 137

Vermont Fish and Wildlife Department (VFWD): on Anthropause animal behavior, 115–16; black bear study by, 120–22, 127–35, 139–40, 143 (*see also* Deerfield Wind Black Bear Study); on critical black bear habitat, 123, 138, 145; on habitat interchangeability, 139–40

Vermont Public Radio, 121, 127–28, 129

Vermont Public Service Board, 133

*Visualizing Posthuman Conservation in the Age of the Anthropocene* (Propen), 33, 35, 56

Walker, Melody, 19–20, 133–34, 137, 145

web of life, 37. *See also* environmental meshworks

Weiss, Joseph, 77

wildfires. *See* fire displacements

wildlife and wilderness, defined, 7–9

wildlife corridors. *See* connectivity projects

wildlife rehabilitation, 27–46; as altruistic, 42; compassionate conservatism on, 29, 30–35, 38–40, 42–43; in culture of gratitude, 24; and elemental relationships, 24, 29, 30, 34, 36, 43–44; and entangled empathy, 20, 32–33, 35–36, 37; environmental meshworks of, 24, 29–30, 36–38, 44–46; ethical considerations, 38–44; goal of, 38–39; home and shelter artifacts of, 28, 29, 30, 34, 36, 37–38, 43–44, 165n22; intervention conundrum of, 29, 38–44; narratives and storytelling in, 44–45; posthumanism on, 39–40, 42–44; reflections on, 27–28, 30

Wohlleben, Peter, 125

Woolsey Fire, 99

Wright, Sarah: on belonging, 5, 14–15, 30, 37; on home, 19, 34